On the Backroad
to Heaven

CENTER BOOKS IN ANABAPTIST STUDIES

George F. Thompson, *series founder and director*
Donald B. Kraybill, *consulting editor*

Published in cooperation with the Center for American Places,
Santa Fe, New Mexico, and Harrisonburg, Virginia

On the Backroad
to Heaven

Old Order Hutterites,
Mennonites, Amish, and Brethren

Donald B. Kraybill

Carl F. Bowman

The Johns Hopkins University Press
Baltimore & London

© 2001 The Johns Hopkins University Press
All rights reserved. Published 2001
Printed in the United States of America on acid-free paper
2 4 6 8 9 7 5 3 1

The Johns Hopkins University Press
2715 North Charles Street
Baltimore, Maryland 21218-4363
www.press.jhu.edu

Library of Congress Cataloging-in-Publication Data

Kraybill, Donald B.
On the backroad to heaven : Old Order Hutterites, Mennonites, Amish, and Brethren /
Donald B. Kraybill, Carl F. Bowman.
p.   cm. — (Center books in Anabaptist studies)
Includes bibliographical references and index.
ISBN 0-8018-6565-4 (alk. paper)
1. Hutterite Brethren.   2. Old Order Mennonites.   3. Amish.
4. Old German Baptist Brethren.   I. Bowman, Carl F.   II. Title.   III. Series.
BX8129.H8 K73 2001
00-010406

A catalog record for this book is available from the British Library.

Figures were prepared by Linda L. Eberly.

For Amos B. Hoover and Fred W. Benedict,

wise interpreters of

Old Order ways

Contents

Preface   ix
Acknowledgments   xv

CHAPTER ONE: The Old Road to Heaven   1

CHAPTER TWO: The Hutterites   20

CHAPTER THREE: The Mennonites   60

CHAPTER FOUR: The Amish   101

CHAPTER FIVE: The Brethren   137

CHAPTER SIX: Common Convictions   179

CHAPTER SEVEN: Four Roads to Heaven   213

CHAPTER EIGHT: Preserving a Pilgrim People   236

CHAPTER NINE: Ironies of a Postmodern Journey   258

Notes   281
Selected References   309
Index   323

Preface

In the summer of 1998, television crews from around the world converged on Lancaster, Pennsylvania, to cover the story of two young men arrested for selling cocaine. On another day, in another place, the story would hardly have been newsworthy. But this was not an ordinary day. The accused were Amish lads who had been selling drugs for the Pagan Motorcycle Gang. What a sensational story—barefoot Amish boys trafficking in cocaine with the Pagans! The world was mesmerized with a story that married the most unlikely of partners in the sale of sin. The major media networks, both national and international, joined in a feeding frenzy.[1] Even *Time* and the *New Yorker* magazines featured this sensational tale of two exceptional groups entangled in a surprising mixture of virtue and vice.[2]

The Pagans and the Amish are two of many exceptional groups in American society. This book tells the story of four such groups—the Old Order Hutterites, Mennonites, Amish, and Brethren. For the most part, these Old Order Anabaptist groups reside on the margins of American life. Americans they are, but rather unconventional ones. Mostly unnoticed except for occasional news features in the media, they live quietly on the edge of the larger social landscape.

In his book *American Exceptionalism* (1996), Seymour Martin Lipset argues that America is an exceptional nation in many ways—not better or superior, but simply different from other modern nations. We are at once the best and the worst—an irony that Lipset calls a double-edged sword. American society, according to Lipset, exhibits some of the following virtues. We are the most individualistic, the most rights-oriented, the most optimistic, the most religious, the most voluntaristic, and so on. At the heart of American exceptionalism lies a profound commitment to the individual—to individual rights and liberty—an idea that helped to propel the American Revolution and that later became inscribed in the Bill of Rights.

The American emphasis on freedom and liberty, however, has led to another kind of exceptionalism as well. The United States has very high rates of imprisonment, divorce, single-parent families, drug use, homelessness, and litigation. This double-edged sword underscores the best and the worst of American exceptionalism.

Lipset was describing the broad contours of mass culture, but despite its seductive power, some distinctive cultural islands remain amidst the mainstream. In many ways the four Old Order groups in this study are exceptions to American exceptionalism. Apart from the Hutterites, all of the groups immigrated to the New World prior to the American Revolution and largely remained outsiders in the centuries that followed.

They are exceptions to the American experience in several ways. First, they question individualism and its package of rights and freedoms. For these tradition-oriented groups, the primary social unit is not the individual but a redemptive church community. Instead of individual rights and personal achievement, they talk about obedience, self-denial, and the authority of the church. In this most fundamental way, they are outsiders.

Second, members of Old Order communities question the importance of citizenship; they do not hold the nation-state central, support political movements, hold political office, or fight in the wars of the nation. In lieu of civic participation and political engagement, they emphasize the importance of collective responsibility within their redemptive communities. Old Orders prefer to care for themselves rather than lean on government programs of welfare, social security, and other subsidies, which they sometimes call "handouts."

Third, for the most part, these are preindustrial, production-based societies that have not joined the world of consumer consumption. Although some members stray into shopping malls, the overwhelming ethic in these communities is production in the service of the community, not conspicuous consumption for leisure and personal pleasure.

Finally, in a rather audacious challenge to the larger cultural system, they question the value of formal education even beyond the eighth grade. These Old Order communities are not convinced that science and technology provide solutions that will build community and bring happiness. In all of these ways, the Old Order societies described in this book lie outside the social mainstream.

But if they lie outside what are generally considered the positive aspects of American exceptionalism, they avoid its negative aspects as well. Compared to national norms, the rates of drug abuse, divorce, incarceration, homelessness, welfare dependency, and unemployment are remarkably low and often negligible within the ranks of these traditional communities. There are occasional episodes of alcohol abuse and sexual misconduct, but all things considered, what these communities have lost in individual freedoms they have gained in community solidarity and well-being. Unlike many Americans, who, according to Robert Putnam, increasingly go bowling alone, Old Orders, if they bowled at all, would certainly do it together.[3]

In a word, they are exceptions to both dimensions of American exceptionalism. In the words of one Hutterite farmer, "We have created our own little country." It is quite a different country, hidden for the most part among the backroads of American society. But it is nevertheless an intriguing country that enhances the diversity of the larger society in colorful ways.

We have selected four of some fifty different Anabaptist groups in the United States for the purposes of our study. Anabaptists trace their heritage back to the Radical Reformation of 1525 in Switzerland and South Germany that emerged in the wake of the Protestant Reformation. A variety of Hutterite, Mennonite, Amish, and Brethren groups have been spawned by the Anabaptist movement. Worldwide membership in Anabaptist-affiliated groups numbers slightly over a million.[4] In the United States more than four dozen different groups with Anabaptist connections claim about 500,000 members.[5] The four groups in this study are in the traditionalist wing of the Anabaptist spectrum and hence are known as Old Orders. They preserve older forms of religious ritual and reject many aspects of mainstream culture that have been adopted by other Anabaptist groups, which operate colleges, use modern technology, and pursue professional occupations. Thus in many ways the Old Orders are an exception inside the Anabaptist fold as well as within the nation.

As sociologists, we have a particular interest in how Old Order groups are able to create and sustain viable communities in the contemporary

context. The majority of Anabaptist groups have accepted higher education, adopted high technology, and absorbed many of the values of mass
culture. How do Old Orders, we wonder, develop strategies that enable
them not only to survive but indeed to thrive as exceptions to the exception? We have selected four Old Order groups that have been established
for more than a century and that have a sizeable base of members. Each
group is also part of a broader stream of Anabaptist life—Hutterite, Mennonite, Amish, and Brethren.

Although the groups share a common religious heritage and at first
glance appear similar, they are also remarkably different. The Hutterites
are truly communal—living without checkbooks, credit cards, wills, or
private telephones. By contrast, the Mennonites, Amish, and Brethren accept private property. The Brethren drive cars and own computers, two
practices that the Mennonites and Amish reject. The four groups use different strategies to create and sustain their Old Order identity. The Hutterites are geographically segregated from the larger society, whereas the
Brethren relate more closely with it. In many ways the Amish and Mennonites are more alike in how they interact with the outside world. We
explore how each group constructs and reproduces a symbolic universe
that confers meaning on their religious journey.

The primary contribution of our book lies in its comparative approach,
which enables us to tease out the various ways these groups shape and
perpetuate their identities. We devote an introductory chapter to each of
the groups, but these are not thick ethnographies based on extended fieldwork. Considerable research and a substantial body of scholarly literature already exists on the Amish and Hutterites. Less work has been done
on the Old Order Mennonites and Brethren, and thus our chapters on
these two groups offer a more original analysis. The unique contribution
of our work, however, flows from our comparative analysis.

Several key questions undergird our investigation: How is it that at
the beginning of the twenty-first century these traditional communities
have not vanished, but indeed are flourishing? What strategies have enabled them to preserve their cultural identity in the midst of the powerful forces of mass society? They are all survivors, but each group has developed its own strategy for survival. Although each group has created
its "own little country," they are all tied to the larger society in various
ways but especially through trade and commerce. Despite their tilt
toward tradition, they are undergoing considerable change. Old Order

societies continually renegotiate the lines of distinction between their ethnic enclave and the outside world. In recent years they have worried that the use of cell phones, computers, and cars might compromise their religious values and lead to the demise of their community. To what extent can they use technology without disrupting the solidarity of their community? How does each group mark the boundaries between virtue and vice both within their group and between themselves and the larger world? Beyond merely tracing the cultural borders, we are interested in how the lines are continually renegotiated in the face of internal and external pressures.

Moreover, these groups raise fundamental questions about the nature of human societies—particularly about the interplay between the individual and the larger collectivity. As we noted above, these communities break the standard contours of the social landscape. Their distinctiveness makes them interesting, but they are more than simply interesting. In many ways they represent a protest against progress, a protest against many of the forces that have shaped the contemporary world. Their collective life and patterns of living constitute an argument about the essential ingredients of a wholesome society—a society that cultivates human well-being. Thus they are not only interesting but also instructive if they provide some insights into the sources of human satisfaction and happiness. Our venture into these Old Order communities raises critical questions about our own society as well. Pondering their ways prods us to ask new questions about our own culture and the nature of contemporary society.

Our analytic approach follows the tradition of cultural analysis. We are interested in how groups construct meaning through symbolic objects and behaviors and how ritualized experiences transmit deep understandings about a group's social organization and worldview. We have not imposed a central analytical concept on our interpretations but have tried as much as possible to allow the groups to tell their own stories.

The plan of the book is fairly straightforward. Following an introductory overview, we devote a chapter to each of the groups—Hutterites (Chapter 2), Mennonites (Chapter 3), Amish (Chapter 4), and Brethren (Chapter 5). Then in Chapter 6 we explore the common convictions that undergird the worldview of all four groups, the shared commitments that order their lives. Differences become the focus of Chapter 7 as we trace some of the key distinctives of each group and ask how these communities differ. In Chapter 8 we show how each group constructs and sustains its own distinctive identity as a pilgrim people. Finally, in Chapter 9, we reflect on some of the ironies surrounding traditional communities in a postmodern world and consider some of the challenges they may face in this new setting. Headed for heaven, they have taken a backroad well off the main boulevard, but how will they fare as they intersect with information highways filled with e-commerce billboards?

Finally, a note about our stylistic use of several words. We occasionally use the word *English,* as the Amish do, to refer to English-speaking outsiders or non-Amish in general. *Worldling* is a word used by the Brethren in a similar fashion to designate people of the larger world around them. Sometimes we use the label *moderns* to refer to people who have adopted the outlook, values, and behavior of contemporary society. And, yes, a word about *modernity.* We realize that this is a rather slippery and elastic word that carries many meanings. We use it in two ways. At times we use the word *modernity* loosely in a broad sweep to capture the sentiments, values, and perspectives of the contemporary world. We also, especially in Chapter 9, use *modernity* in a more technical sense to refer to the social arrangements and intellectual understandings that were produced by that period of history known as the Enlightenment. Our two usages of the word *modernity* should be clear in their context.

Acknowledgments

This book was incubating for many years; consequently, our debts of gratitude are numerous. We are especially indebted to dozens of Old Order members who opened their hearts and homes to us at every turn. Their gracious hospitality and patience with our endless questions is a tribute to the goodness that we often found in these communities. In addition to the many anonymous informants who shared graciously of their time, we want to express particular thanks to several Old Order historians who were especially helpful: Isaac Horst, Allen Hoover, Fred Benedict, Glen Landes, and the venerable dean of Old Order Mennonite studies, Amos B. Hoover. In the endnotes we thank numerous people who helped with particular chapters, but several deserve special recognition for their role as research assistants in various phases of the project: Florence Horning aided us with the Mennonite research, and Orlando Goering gathered data for us on Hutterite population changes. Both of them contributed substantially to the quality and depth of our work.

A number of our colleagues read earlier drafts of the manuscript and offered invaluable comments and suggestions that have substantially improved the accuracy and interpretation of our text. In particular we wish to thank David Decker Sr., Marlin Jeschke, Gertrude Huntington, and Robert Rhodes for critiquing the Hutterite chapter; and Levi Frey, Amos B. Hoover, Allen Hoover, James P. Hurd, and John F. Peters for helpful feedback on the Mennonite chapter. The comments of David Weaver-Zercher aided us in clarifying the argument of Chapter 9. Donald F. Durnbaugh, Conrad Kanagy, Steven M. Nolt, Stephen Scott, Richard Stevick, and an anonymous reviewer provided useful comments and corrections on the entire manuscript. These generous colleagues have contributed their time and suggestions in ways that have enhanced the quality and accuracy of the text.

We have enjoyed excellent institutional support as well as administrative and clerical assistance at various stages of the project. At the Young Center of Elizabethtown College, Brenda Spiker provided word processing for early versions of the manuscript, and Gretchen Wenger provided editorial assistance and began the process of indexing. At Messiah College, Krista Malick did much of the word processing in the later versions of the text, developed a style sheet, and completed the indexing. Joan Malick provided oversight and assistance with many phases of the project. We are grateful to be surrounded and blessed by helpful, courteous, and efficient colleagues who have aided us in ways that have helped to make this an enjoyable project.

Linda Eberly designed the graphics that grace these pages. We are especially grateful to Mr. Ron Bell, director of photography at the *Roanoke (Virginia) Times* for graciously providing photographs of the Old German Baptist Brethren. Most importantly, we thank George F. Thompson, president of the Center for American Places, for his unwavering interest and support of our project during the years of its evolution.

Finally, we celebrate our partnership and friendship that began years ago in a classroom at Elizabethtown College and that has continued to flourish over the years with the aid of early morning coffee.

On the Backroad
to Heaven

CHAPTER ONE

The Old Road
to Heaven

Why must we shun the pleasant path that worldlings love so well?
—Brethren hymn

OLD ORDER ROOTS

The four groups in our study—Hutterites, Mennonites, Amish, and Brethren—trace their lineage to the Anabaptists of sixteenth-century Europe. The Anabaptist movement emerged in southern Germany and Switzerland in the wake of the Protestant Reformation in 1517. The first Anabaptists were young radicals who were chafing at the pace of the Reformation. They wanted religious reforms to move faster and to break more sharply with established Catholic patterns. In 1525 in Zurich, Switzerland, impatient students of the Protestant pastor Ulrich Zwingli baptized each other as adults. This defiant act laid the foundation for an independent church, free of state control, and issued a bold challenge to Catholic, Protestant, and civil authorities alike.

Members of the new "free" church were called Anabaptists (rebaptizers) because they insisted on rebaptizing adults who had already been baptized as infants in the Catholic Church. Adult baptism was a capital offense in sixteenth-century Europe because it threatened the marriage

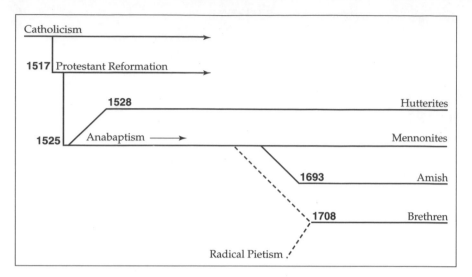

FIGURE 1.1 European Roots of the Hutterites, Mennonites, Amish, and Brethren

of civil and religious authority that had developed over the centuries. Infant baptism conferred membership into both Catholic and Protestant churches. It also granted automatic citizenship, which gave civil authorities the power to tax and conscript. So the question at stake was not merely the age of baptism, but a much deeper issue of authority in church/state relations. Where did ultimate authority rest? The Anabaptists placed the authority of the Scriptures above civil edicts. They turned their backs on traditional Catholic teaching, evolving Protestant doctrine, and the laws of the Zurich city council. The young upstarts chose to follow their own interpretation of Scripture and the literal words of Jesus recorded in the New Testament.[1]

Known as radical reformers, many Anabaptists paid dearly for tearing asunder the church-state fabric that had been woven together over the centuries. Thousands of Anabaptists were tortured and killed by religious and civil authorities—burned at the stake, drowned in lakes and rivers, starved in prisons, and beheaded by the sword. The harsh persecution fanned the fires of protest as the movement spread into northern Germany and the lowland countries around Holland. Many Anabaptists fled for safety into remote areas where they took up farming and tried to avoid detection. Memories of the persecution linger in the minds of

Hutterite youth wear the distinctive clothing of their colony. *Source:* Mary Koga

A Mennonite mother and daughter cut sweet corn. *Source:* Carl Hiebert

many Anabaptists even today and temper their relations with the larger society.

Dozens of contemporary Anabaptist groups, including the four in this book, trace their roots to the Anabaptist movement of the sixteenth century. Anabaptists migrated to North America in the seventeenth, eighteenth, and nineteenth centuries in search of religious freedom, political stability, and fertile soil. Today their descendants, scattered around the world in many cultures, embody a wide variety of religious practices. Although many Anabaptist groups have blended into modern culture, the Old Order communities have actively resisted acculturation. Old Order identities formed in the late 1800s as some Anabaptist groups struggled with a variety of social changes spawned by industrialization.[2] The four Old Order groups profiled here share a common theological heritage, but each, of course, has its own particular story.

Four Pilgrim Groups

The Hutterites. The Hutterites take their name from an early Anabaptist leader, Jacob Hutter. They branched off from the Anabaptist movement in 1528, three years after its beginning, and communal property soon became their distinctive trademark. Bitter persecution often forced the Hutterites to migrate in search of tolerable conditions. They sojourned in Moravia, Austria, Transylvania, Romania, and Russia, and then came to the United States in the 1870s. No longer found in Europe today, they live in some 425 agricultural colonies, each averaging about 90 members, in the Dakotas, Minnesota, Montana, and the Canadian provinces of Manitoba, Saskatchewan, and Alberta.

The Hutterites continue to embody many of their traditional practices and beliefs. Religious services are held each evening before a common meal. Sermons on Sunday are often read from sixteenth-century texts. Despite their traditional worldview, the colonists readily use the latest computerized equipment to operate large farms on thousands of acres. Families live in private apartments but eat in the colony dining room. Children attend a school on the colony that is typically supervised by a local public school. Private property, wills, personal credit cards, résumés, and televisions are unheard of among these communal people.

The Mennonites. Many Anabaptist groups eventually became known as Mennonites through the influence of Menno Simons, a Dutch Anabaptist leader in the mid-1500s. A few Mennonites arrived in the New World as early as 1683, but most of the Swiss-South German immigrants came in the eighteenth century. With a warm welcome from William Penn, Pennsylvania became a favorite haven for Mennonites and other persecuted religious minorities. Eventually the Mennonites fanned southward into Maryland and Virginia as well as westward to Ohio, Indiana, Illinois, and beyond. The Old Order Mennonites emerged as a separate group in the late 1800s when some more progressive Mennonite groups began adopting new innovations. Although many Mennonite groups have merged into American culture, the Old Order communities maintain many traditional Mennonite practices.

The Old Order Mennonites own private homes and farms in rural areas where they live among non-Mennonite neighbors. Many of their homes have electricity and telephones. Although they use horse and carriages for transportation, steel-wheeled tractors are permitted for field work. They meet for worship on Sunday in austere meetinghouses without carpeting, electricity, or indoor plumbing. Mennonite men do not

Winter time at an Amish homestead. *Source:* Keith Baum

A Brethren family reads a biblical text. This exercise, called "taking the text" is done before meals in many homes. *Source: Roanoke Times*

wear beards, but the plain clothing of both men and women sets them apart from the larger society.

The Amish. The Amish also trace their lineage to the Anabaptist movement of 1525. They were part of the Swiss stream of Anabaptism until 1693 when they formed their own group under the leadership of Jakob Ammann, a Swiss Anabaptist leader who moved to the Alsace region of present-day France. The Amish soon became a conservative group within the Anabaptist family. Although they share common roots, the Amish and Mennonites branched into separate bodies in 1693 before they migrated to the New World. Some Amish arrived in Penn's Woods (Pennsylvania) in the mid-1700s, and others came in the 1800s. They often settled near Mennonite and Brethren communities. The "Old Order" label developed in Amish communities after the Civil War when some progressive Amish adopted new practices and eventually merged with Mennonite groups. Those who resisted the changes became known as the Old Orders. Today the Old Order Amish reside in some twenty-five states, mostly east of the Mississippi, and in the Canadian province of Ontario.

Unlike the Mennonites, the Amish meet to worship in their homes every other Sunday. Telephones, television, and electricity are missing from their homes. The Amish use horse-and-buggy transportation for local travel and often rent vans with local drivers for longer trips or business. In recent years some Amish have developed profitable small businesses and are no longer farming. Children typically attend a one-room Amish school through eighth grade and then join the family work force.

The Brethren. Strictly speaking, the Brethren are not an organic offshoot of sixteenth-century Anabaptism, but they are still directly linked to the Anabaptist story. Influenced by both Pietism and Anabaptism, the Brethren formed in 1708 in central Germany. Although they were grounded in Radical Pietism, they embraced most of the doctrines of the Anabaptists with whom they often associated—adult baptism, the separation of church and state, pacifism, and church discipline. Alexander Mack Sr. is recognized as the leader of the first Brethren, who were also known for many years as Dunkers or German Baptist Brethren.

The first Brethren baptisms in Germany's Eder River signaled the rejection of the religious individualism that had marked Radical Pietism, which had sparked their spiritual awakening. While Brethren sought to keep the Pietist interest in a deep, almost mystical spirituality, they exchanged individualistic views of the religious life for understandings of community discernment, discipline, and correction that were much more typical of their Anabaptist neighbors. In fact, with the exception of an insistence upon immersion baptism, which eventually earned them the name "Dunkers," Brethren became barely distinguishable from the Mennonites, at least to outsiders.

The Brethren migrated to Pennsylvania after 1719 and eventually fanned out to Maryland, Virginia, Ohio, Indiana, and westward. During the 1860s and 70s, the Brethren were torn by controversies involving church discipline, plain dress, revivalism, higher education, and various departures from the "ancient order" of the Brethren. Subsequently, the German Baptist Brethren experienced a three-way division in the early 1880s, and the Old Order group adopted the name *Old* German Baptist Brethren to distinguish itself from the other two groups. A variety of perceived accommodations to modern culture caused the Old German Baptist Brethren to withdraw from the larger fellowship in 1881, in an effort to preserve "the faith once delivered to the saints." The more progressive branches eventually evolved into two denominations, the Church of the Brethren and the Brethren Church, which have since spawned other groups such as the Dunkard Brethren and the Fellowship of Grace Brethren Churches. Many of these groups now share little in common with the Old German Baptist Brethren, who have carried the banner of Brethren conservatism for more than a century. Old German Baptist Brethren are presently organized into some fifty congregations in fifteen different states.

In many ways the Old German Baptists interact more closely with the larger society than the other groups. They drive cars and have telephones and electricity in their homes. Television and video, however, are not permitted. Many Brethren children attend public schools. It is not unusual for Brethren to own a business or to work in a non-Brethren business. Traditional dress helps to set them apart from the larger society. The wor-

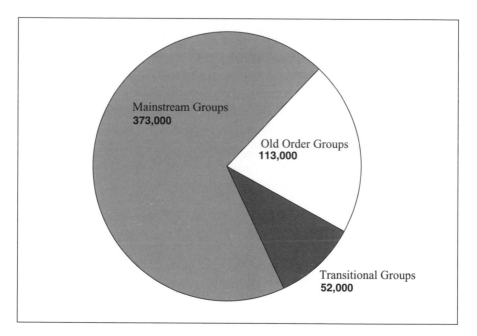

FIGURE 1.2 Estimated Adult Membership of Anabaptist-Related Groups in the United States

Note: Anabaptist-related groups include those affiliated with various Hutterite, Mennonite, Amish, Brethren-in-Christ, and Brethren bodies.

Sources: Mennonite Directory (2000), *Mennonite Church Information* (2000), *Church of the Brethren Yearbook* (2000), and various Old Order directories and informants.

ship services and ritual practices of the Old German Baptist Brethren follow ancient forms.

Each of these Old Order communities has blazed a pilgrim's path on the margins of contemporary society; each has chosen a backroad, so to speak, on their journey to heaven. Any group that charts a different course to the pearly gates will stir curiosity as well as face misunderstanding. Ignorance, lack of contact, and caricatures in the media sometimes blur public understandings of peculiar groups like these. The following section explores some of the myths that enshroud Old Order communities.

MYTHS AND REALITIES

Social Antiques. A prominent stereotype portrays Old Order people as relics of the colonial era—cooking over open fires, dipping water buckets into wells, making candles from beeswax, and spinning wool from their own sheep. These communities, according to some myths, are immune to change because they live today as their ancestors did centuries before. Social antiques of a sort, they are viewed as pristine specimens of early American life. By turning to them, we can supposedly learn how our ancestors lived before the rise of factories and modern technology.

This image of Old Order life suggests that these communities have been insulated from the vibrations of industrialization. They do indeed stress separation from the world as a religious doctrine, but they are not cultural fossils from another era. To the contrary, they are constantly changing. While trying to remain separate from the larger society, they continually adopt new products, change their ways, and shift their cultural fences. Old Orders do value tradition—a few still milk their cows by hand, and many preserve vegetables from their gardens—but they are hardly social heirlooms from earlier times.

Shunning technology. A related distortion portrays Old Orders as shunning modern technology. Media images of horse-drawn carriages on busy highways symbolize a radical rejection of twentieth-century technology. Many Old Order groups do drive horse-drawn carriages, and all of them ban certain types of technology, but none of them categorically boycott it. These are not modern day Luddites. In fact, all four groups use some state-of-the-art technology. The Hutterites plant and harvest their

Roller blades are popular in some Amish settlements. *Source:* Keith Baum

crops on vast prairie fields with gigantic modern tractors. The Mennonites routinely use telephones and tractors. Some Amish dairy farmers use automatic milkers and artificial insemination. The Brethren own microwaves and drive cars, though usually modest ones with darker colors.

The four groups employ technology selectively, albeit somewhat cautiously. They are dubious of technologies that might contaminate their values or disrupt the solidarity of their communities. All the groups, for example, forbid the ownership of television, which of course would open channels to the larger culture. On the use of motor vehicles, the groups vary. Individual Hutterites do not own cars, but the colonies operate trucks and vans for community purposes. The Brethren drive cars on a regular basis. The Amish and Mennonites forbid driving motor vehicles, but they do hire "taxi" service when their destination exceeds the practical limitations of horse and buggy travel.

Ignorant and Backward. A television series featuring an Amish family showed a young Amish woman who was startled by the light inside a refrigerator in a neighbor's home. Such scenes suggest that Old Orders are backward, uninformed, and naive. Moreover, the taboo on high school by some of the groups may imply that they are ignorant. Some outsiders are appalled to learn that many Old Order teachers have not been educated beyond the eighth grade. These teachers are not certified, nor are their schools accredited by professional organizations. Rooted in rural areas, denied high school diplomas, restricted in travel, shielded from television, and lacking the refinement of the arts, Old Order members may, at first blush, appear culturally disabled. In conversation with outsiders, they might ask questions like, "What language do they speak in France?" or "Where exactly *is* the World Wide Web?" Such questions may suggest that they are shackled by provincialism. Moreover, the uniformity of Old Order life conjures up images of mindless, robotic behavior.

A Mennonite harvests wheat with a self-propelled combine. *Source:* Keith Baum

While it is true that Old Order people do not have résumés or academic diplomas, and are not acquainted with the graces of middle-class manners, it is unfair to call them ignorant. Without television they may miss the latest political scandal, but they have ample wisdom in the depths of their communal reservoir. From delivering babies to burying the dead, they live their lives with little need of self-help manuals. The Hutterites ably manage productive farming operations with hundreds of animals on thousands of acres. Amish and Brethren entrepreneurs whose annual sales top a million dollars may not hold MBAs, but they understand how to market products. The bounty of handcrafted items flowing from all of these groups bespeaks the elegance of simplicity and the beauty of homespun ways. Members of Old Order groups may appear to dress alike, but they are not pressed from a cultural mold that pares off individual expression and artistic creativity.

Stern Puritans. Outsiders who observe these communities may think that members are filled with piety and offer prayers at every turn. Sensational cases of shunning, publicized in the media, imply that leaders castigate wayward members in a callous fashion.[3] Excommunication and the shunning practiced by some of the groups may feel harsh to modern folks who cherish moral tolerance.

Amidst their religious devotion, however, there is ample humor, laughter, and levity in these communities. Although members may display a sense of quiet reserve, they also enjoy the pleasure of good fellowship at weddings and Sunday evening singings, and the thrill of exciting volleyball and softball games. Frequent visiting, often mingled with work, is a special source of delight. Quilting parties and work frolics blend work and play in the spirit of community. Many Old Order people enjoy hunting, fishing, hiking, skating, and other outdoor sports.

These are, indeed, religious groups; but like any human community, the measure of devotion and sincerity varies from person to person. These groups have high religious ideals, but they are not perfect. Greed, gossip, envy, deceit, and revenge sometimes lift their ugly faces. And there are occasional cases of alcohol abuse, sexual abuse, and domestic violence as well. Despite their outward cloak of righteousness, these people are people.

Declining and Dying. Living on the fringe of American society, Old Order groups are oftentimes viewed as social relics fading into oblivion. Groups who have the audacity to spurn the virtues of modernity, to buck

A Brethren couple enjoys a moment of humor. *Source: Roanoke Times*

the fads and fashions, to call higher education irrelevant, and to turn their backs on some forms of technology will likely die, we suppose, in a matter of time. They might be interesting and different, but they surely will not endure. In due time, like other deviants, they too will succumb to modernity and bury their traditions in the graveyard of cultural castoffs.

Such doomsayers may be surprised to learn that many Old Order groups are not merely surviving but are indeed thriving.[4] A few schismatic Old Order groups have failed, but many are growing. In fact, some are doubling almost every generation. Large families and strong retention rates have produced the growth rather than missionary efforts to convert outsiders. The four communities surveyed in this book pose an intriguing question: How is it that those who shun modern ways are able to not only survive but also flourish in the midst of contemporary society?

THE OLD ROAD TO HEAVEN   13

Hutterites use modern equipment to till large farms. *Source:* John Wipf

Uniform and Identical. A myth of similarity also masks the diversity of Old Order life. Media photographs often focus on the uniform attire worn by members of these groups. A few public symbols—black hats, beards, head coverings, and buggies—quickly become the earmarks of Old Order life in the public consciousness. These distinctive symbols create an impression of uniformity across the groups. The myth of similarity suggests that members of these groups are cultural clones—and not only clones, but unreflective and thoughtless ones as well.

There are certainly many areas of common agreement and practice among these groups—commonalities that we explore in Chapter 6. But despite their common concerns, these groups are not cultural facsimiles. Many differences exist within and between them as well. Some Hutterites have telephones in their homes, and others do not. Most Amish homes have indoor bathrooms, but some do not. And although most Brethren have not attended college, a few have advanced degrees. The differences within each group are often complicated and hidden to the outside eye.

The differences are even more pronounced between the groups. The Hutterites use CB radios, but the Brethren have prohibited them. The

Amish forbid the ownership of private cars, but the Brethren drive them all over the country. The Mennonites use tractors in their fields alongside their Amish neighbors, who farm with horses. Mennonites, Amish, and Brethren practice footwashing and exchange a "holy kiss" in their religious rituals, but the Hutterites do not. And surely the greatest difference is the Hutterite practice of communal living.

Real differences thread their way within and between these communities. Nevertheless, many common themes and practices imprint a distinctive ethos on Old Order life. What is the essence of Old Order life? How does their worldview differ from the assumptions and perspectives of mainstream American culture?

OLD AND ORDERLY

Old Order Anabaptist groups have a distinctive view of the nature of moral authority. For them, such authority emerges from *traditional practice,* rests on *collective wisdom,* and covers a *broad scope* of behavior. Not surprisingly, oldness and orderliness are highly valued. This unique understanding of moral authority is the defining feature that sets these communities apart from the larger culture.[5]

Old Order communities look to the past for their moral compass. Ancient sources of authority are prized above contemporary ones. Traditional practice and the wisdom of the past carry more influence than scientific argumentation. Looking back for moral authority is a major departure from the contemporary quest to find moral guidance in human reflection, critical thinking, and scientific understanding. As self-conscious people of preservation, Old Orders look to the past more than they look to the future.

Moral authority is grounded for them in their collective understandings that are often called *Ordnung*—a German word that roughly translates into 'rules and discipline.' These rules for living, which developed over the generations, provide a blueprint for an orderly way of life. For Old Order people, moral authority is found, not in individual experience, but in the counsel of the church. The community, not the individual, is the chief agent of ethical discernment; communal wisdom supersedes individual experience and personal opinion. Moreover, the church holds uncontested authority to discern a wide spectrum of moral issues.

Amish and Mennonite teens compete in a game of cornerball during a farm auction. Amish boys are the target; Mennonite boys are throwing. *Source:* Dennis Hughes

The moral order of Old Order life covers a broad scope of behavior. It encompasses not only religious ritual but also dress, technology, family life, economic practice, leisure, and many other issues. This is partly so because with little specialization, Old Order communities are preindustrial in many ways. They typically rest on an agrarian base, an extended kinship system, a geographical community, and ample face-to-face interaction. The Old Order world is a religious one, and moral authority stretches over it like a sacred canopy. Unlike highly specialized societies, the total package of Old Order life is bound together by a common moral order.

Grounding moral authority in traditional practice and communal discernment and granting it broad application produces several social consequences. These expressions of Old Order practice reflect their contrarian notions of moral authority.

First, Old Orders are countercultural groups because they challenge contemporary notions of moral authority. By rejecting human intellect, individual experience, and rational thinking as sources of ethical authority, Old Order groups are oppositional groups even *within* their own religious traditions. As countercultural communities, Old Orders challenge the Enlightenment project and all the notions of science and progress that have flowed from it.

Second, their view of moral authority leads Old Orders to cherish traditional religious ritual because it blends both oldness and orderliness together. Ritual points to the past and also articulates the structure of communal authority. Religious ritual recalls the wisdom of the past and legitimates the authority structure of the community. As it recalls and reenacts the moral order, ritual also reproduces it in the minds of the young. Because ritual links *old* and *order* together in powerful ways, Old Order groups self-consciously devote great efforts to preserve it. Ritual, in many ways, publicly articulates a community's identity and self-understanding of its moral order. Indeed, many Old Order groups formed precisely because they wanted to preserve traditional rituals that were under siege. Moreover, ritual is typically the last distinctive to fall when an Old Order group finds itself following more contemporary moral authorities.

Finally, because their moral order rests on tradition and collective wisdom, Old Orders carefully screen changes that might erode the solidarity of their community or their assumptions of moral authority. Many of their technological restrictions protect members from moral contamination and help to preserve the cohesiveness of their communities. Old Order communities do accept change—indeed, much change—but they are most likely to accept changes that coincide with their moral order and that add to, rather than replace, traditional practices. These are cultural conservationists who cherish the beauty of traditional ways but who also accept technological advancements that fit within their moral order and social structure.

Old Orderliness is obviously a matter of degree. It goes without saying that all human groups, even the most future-oriented ones, uphold some traditions and have collective standards. Some Old Order groups are more Old Order than others. Groups such as the Hutterites do not use the Old Order label, but they certainly fit our definition. On the other hand, some groups that wear the label are losing their sense of Old Or-

An Amish funeral procession on a backroad to heaven. *Source:* Keith Baum

derliness. We are reluctant to draw sharp lines of demarcation but prefer to see Old Orderliness across a spectrum. Key markers of an Old Order identity include the preservation of traditional ritual, the use of a special dialect for worship, plain clothing, selective use of technology, and the downplaying of personal experience and individual choice. These religious marks, as well as others, help to fortify an Old Order identity.

THE OLD ORDER ARGUMENT

Every human group makes an implicit argument about its meaning and purpose by the way it lives. The propositions may not be written down or even verbalized, but the patterns of a community do, in many ways, constitute its argument about the essence and meaning of life. What is the argument that flows from Old Order communities? What assumptions guide their journey on the backroad to heaven? Old Order notions about the good life turn upside down, in many ways, some of the taken-for-granted assumptions of contemporary life. Old Order pilgrims contend that:

The individual is not the primary reality.
Communal goals transcend personal ones.
The past is as important as the future.
Tradition is valued over change.
Preservation overshadows progress.
Newer, bigger, and faster are not necessarily better.
Personal sacrifice is esteemed over pleasure.
Local involvement outweighs national acclaim.
Work is more satisfying than consumption.
Obedience to authority brings order and unity.
Spiritual salvation comes via the grace of community.
Friends are more important than status, fame, or wealth.
Yielding to community brings meaning, identity, and belonging.
Maintaining the unity of community is the supreme value.

These affirmations confirm that members of Old Order communities are, indeed, pilgrims and strangers in our land. They have experienced much change, but for the most part, their core values have withstood the relentless press of so-called progress.

There is, of course, much slippage from such lofty ideals. Pride, envy, jealousy, and greed sometimes fracture community harmony. Spats in family and church sometimes splinter the peace of congregational life. Alcohol abuse and sexual abuse sometimes infect the hidden corners of these communities. But despite these faults, the argument of Old Order communities is simply this: Those who seek happiness, fulfillment, and well-being will most likely find it if they are willing to yield to the collective wisdom of a faithful congregation. Those who surrender to the precepts of Providence embedded in the wisdom of community will receive the blessings of meaning, identity, and belonging. That, at least, is the assumption of the pilgrims on the backroad to heaven who have shunned "the pleasant path that worldlings love so well."

CHAPTER TWO

The Hutterites

We are brought into true submission—in the spiritual Ark of Noah . . .
—Hutterite elder

LIVING IN THE ARK OF THE LORD

The Hutterite story began in 1528 in Moravia when a small band of Anabaptists began sharing possessions in common. Named for Jakob Hutter, one of their leaders, the group experienced tumultuous persecution, migration, and strife. After some three hundred and fifty years of turbulence, nearly twelve hundred Hutterites sought better fortunes in the New World in the 1870s. They settled in the Dakota Territory where some four hundred of them founded three colonies based on a communal economy.[1] The majority of the immigrants, known as *Prairieleut, or* "Prairie people," abandoned communal living and gradually joined various Mennonite groups.[2] The minority that continued communal living elected to follow the voice of traditional authority. They represented the "Old Order" of things in Hutterite life even though they never used that specific label.

The communal Hutterites branched into three tribes: *Schmiedleut, Dariusleut,* and *Lehrerleut—leut* meaning "people." Each group was named for its respective leader. Michael Waldner's people became known as the *Schmiedleut,* the "blacksmith's people." The followers of Darius

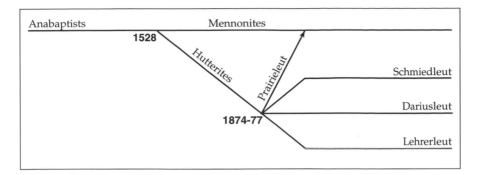

Anabaptists   Mennonites

1528

Hutterites   *Prairieleut*

Schmiedleut

Dariusleut

1874-77

Lehrerleut

FIGURE 2.1 Formation of Hutterite Groups in North America

Walter were dubbed the *Dariusleut*. Another leader, Jacob Wipf, was a *lehrer* (teacher), so his people were called the "teacher's people" or *Lehrerleut*. Although the three branches of Hutterites—Schmiedleut, Dariusleut, and Lehrerleut—share many common beliefs, they have separate leaders and function as independent groups. Members of the three groups rarely intermarry. Although there is much diversity within each group, the Lehrerleut tend to be the most traditional. The Schmiedleut are the most progressive in their use of technology and interaction with the outside world. Two different affiliations emerged within the Schmiedleut in the 1990s in a somewhat contentious division.[3]

The Hutterites are fast becoming diverse in their approach to community living, their use of technology, and their interaction with the outside world. There are many variations in dress and practice within and between the different *leuts,* making generalizations difficult and hazardous. One Hutterite described the differences this way: "The Lehrerleut are one kind of Hutterite, the Darius another, the Schmiedleut another—yet all three groups share a basic grounding and a raft of common traditions and influences." To an outsider everything may look the same, but beneath the surface, "there is a great deal of variety and many different trends are underway, even among the more conservative colonies."[4] At the risk of sweeping important differences aside, the description that follows profiles some of the more common patterns of Hutterite life.

The oldest communal group in North America, the Hutterites have enjoyed remarkable growth in the twentieth century. The three immigrant colonies of the 1870s have multiplied to more than four hundred and

TABLE 2.1 HUTTERITE COLONIES BY AFFILIATION AND LOCATION

	Affiliation			
	Dariusleut	*Lehrerleut*	*Schmiedleut*	*Total*
UNITED States				
Minnesota	-	-	6	6
Montana	14	32	-	46
North Dakota	-	-	6	6
South Dakota	-	-	52	52
Washington	6	-	-	6
Total				116
CANADA				
Alberta	84	62	-	146
British Columbia	1		-	1
Saskatchewan	29	28	-	57
Manitoba	-	-	105	105
Total				309
TOTAL	133	122	169	424

Source: *Hutterite Telephone and Address Book* (2000).

twenty-five colonies with about ninety members each. They are found in five states and in four Canadian provinces. About one fourth live in the United States—primarily in South Dakota and Montana. The rest reside in Canada, with the largest concentrations in Alberta, Manitoba, and Saskatchewan, as shown in Table 2.1.

Unlike other groups profiled in this book, the Hutterites live in agricultural colonies that are segregated from the larger society.[5] Many of the colonies farm thousands of acres that seem to stretch forever beneath generous prairie skies. Colony buildings, clustered like a small village, are often invisible from major roads. Although outside consultants and suppliers visit on a regular basis, each colony is physically cloistered from the outside world. The sizable farming operations are, of course, linked to the economy of the region, but residential segregation shields colonists from daily interaction with outsiders. Nearby colonies often help each other with special projects that require extra labor and join together for weddings and funerals, but the world of the local colony is *the* world of the typical Hutterite. In the words of one Hutterite, "We have our own country." Without television and other mass media, life revolves around the cares of a hundred kindred souls.

Although the number of persons living in a colony may range from 50 to 150, it typically hovers around 90. Every fifteen to twenty years, depending on local conditions, colonies divide as they outgrow their facilities. The colony lives as an extended family, eating meals together in a common dining hall and sharing laundry facilities as well. Each family has an apartment that includes a coffee area, living room, bathroom, and bedrooms. Three or four apartments adjoin each other in long barrack-like houses that encircle the dining facilities and church building in the hub of the colony. The typical family has five or six children. They normally attend school through eighth grade and are usually baptized into the Hutterite faith at 18 to 25 years of age.

Hutterites sometimes compare their colony to Noah's ark, which provided a haven for the chosen in Old Testament times.[6] This striking image captures their sense of self-sufficiency and separation from the larger world. Religious convictions guide their journey as they navigate heavenward through surging seas of sin. A biblical literalism, handed down over the ages, shapes their social life and religious outlook. Church services are held before each evening meal as well as on Sunday morning.

Family apartment units on a Hutterite colony. *Source:* Jan Gleysteen

Language, dress, gender roles, religious ritual, child rearing, and common property all reflect the weight of four-and-a-half centuries of tradition.

The Hutterites speak an Austrian dialect called *Hutterisch* as well as English, which they learn in school. They also study an archaic form of High German that is typically used in sermons. Their dialect is peppered with many words from the countries of their European sojourn.[7] The dialect enables them to converse directly, as it were, with their religious ancestors, who are much closer to them in spirit than their English neighbors, who speak the idiom of an unregenerate world. Language thus helps to mark the boundaries between sacred and secular, pious and profane.

Although they reject worldly values, Hutterites have no scruples about tapping worldly technology to boost farm productivity. Colonies vary in their mix of agricultural enterprises, but a typical colony might have 100 cows, 1,000 hogs, and 50,000 turkeys and might farm 5,000 to 10,000 acres of land. Colony-owned trucks and vans haul supplies, products, and people. Huge tractors pull a full array of modern equipment across the vast stretches of colony land. Large trailer trucks haul grain and feed to nearby mills.

Computers track management records and control equipment for various farming operations.[8] Each colony has sizable shops that specialize in woodworking, plumbing, electrical, and mechanical support. New buildings are constructed, equipped, and repaired by colony members themselves. Except for dishwashers, colony kitchens are fully automated with electric ovens, mixers, and freezers. Although tradition dictates many religious and social norms, modern technology is widely embraced for farming and household operations.

Hutterite life is balanced on a tripod of socioreligious values: sharing goods in a community of faith, surrendering self-will for communal harmony, and separating from an evil world. The three themes of sharing, surrendering, and separating—reiterated in many different ways—undergird the worldview and moral order of Hutterite life.

SHARING GOODS

The abolition of private property is the hallmark of Hutterite culture, distinguishing them from other Old Order groups. Private property, in Hutterite eyes, symbolizes greed and vanity and leads to many other expressions of evil. Indeed, an early Hutterite writer called private property a "murderous" and "noxious weed," and charged that greed "is one of the worst sins . . . that belongs together with fornication and all other impurity."[9] Peter Riedemann, an early Hutterite leader, taught that "God from the beginning ordained naught private for man, but wanted all things to be common. . . . Therefore whosoever will cleave to Christ and follow him must forsake . . . created things and property."[10]

Sharing material goods is seen as the highest and most obedient form of Christian love. In the words of a Hutterite writer, "Christ taught that the greatest commandment is to love God above everything else and your neighbor as yourself. In order to fulfill this highest command of love, we pattern our life according to the first apostolic church of Acts."[11] Living in community is motivated by the example of the early church as described in Acts 2:44–45: "And all that believed were together and had all things in common; and sold their possessions and goods and parted them to all men as every man had need."

Individual Hutterites are provided for equally, and apart from a few personal things—clothes, knickknacks, dishes, books—they have no real property. Everyone works without pay. Some colonies provide a monthly allowance of $2 to $10 for personal effects, but others do not. Allowances are sometimes accumulated several months to buy a special treasure, such as a pair of binoculars. In some colonies parents receive $20 for each child to buy Christmas gifts. Individuals receive no paycheck, use no credit cards, pay no medical bills, prepare no wills, and have no worries about retirement. At baptism, members relinquish any claim to colony property. Those who abandon colony life may take only the clothes they are wearing and a few personal items when they make their exit to the larger world.

The colony, organized as a legal corporation, buys and sells products, often in large quantities, on the public market and with other colonies. The corporation pays taxes and owns title to the land and equipment. Colonies are somewhat self-sufficient, with their own gardens, orchards, poultry and cattle, as well as shoemakers, tailors, and electricians. Nevertheless, many supplies and much equipment must be purchased from outside distributors. Bartering sometimes occurs within colonies, between colonies, and between colonists and outsiders. Bartered items might include furniture, toys, vegetables, clothing, and antiques. Other colonies forbid bartering because it encourages personal gain and runs counter to traditional Hutterite teaching.

Colonists use automated equipment to clean and prepare chickens for freezing. *Source:* Ivan Glick

Individuals receive an allotment of clothing about once a year from the colony manager. In some colonies women have their own sewing machines. A family may have a few personal knickknacks as well as some furniture, but the larger household items are owned by the colony. Community of goods, taught by the Hutterites long before Karl Marx was born, is not easy to preserve in a world that considers private property an inalienable human right. Indeed, "Life in community is a daily battle," says one Hutterite writer—a battle against selfishness and jealousy.[12]

Although the Hutterites fear evil in the outside world, they must struggle daily with the greed that surfaces within. Just because possessions must be left at the colony's door does not mean the ark remains free from contamination. A Hutterite leader noted already in 1650: "Men hang on to property like caterpillars to a cabbage leaf." The same elder charged that Christians who cling to possessions, are like "moles and foxes that undermine the communal plantation."[13] The lure of property has continued over the generations. Despite persistent teaching, colony leaders must be on the lookout for "caterpillars" and "moles" in their midst who are tempted to trade colony property for a personal treasure—

a camera, a radio, or even a *Playboy* magazine. Contraband of one sort or another can be found in the hidden crevices of most colonies.

SURRENDERING SELF

Community of goods can only be achieved as individuals surrender their selfish interests for communal goals. Mainstream youth are taught to think for themselves, to make up their own minds, to get ahead, and to make a name for themselves. To the Hutterite, such thinking leads to a bloated self-image that fosters idolatry and spoils spiritual harmony with God and with others. True worship and genuine community can only be experienced as self-will is broken and fully surrendered to God and community. The full surrender of the self—giving it up to a higher cause—is what the Hutterites call *Gelassenheit*. Here the enemy is not low self-esteem, but selfishness.

Writing to fellow Christians in 1565, a Hutterite elder said, we must "unburden ourselves of our pernicious self-will . . . which belongs in Hell." He continued with a favorite Hutterite image. Like a grain of wheat or a single grape, "each individual must give himself up, must die to himself if he wants to follow Christ on His way." As the grain is crushed to make flour and the grape is smashed for wine, so "our own will undergoes the same for the sake of community." He concluded by arguing that "no grape can stay as it is . . . grapes or kernels that remain whole are only fit for pigs or the manure heap. They are far from being bread and wine . . . the stubbornness of self-will must be broken and we must be willing to suffer and to die."[14] The image of crushing grapes in a wine-press is present in the Lord's Supper sermon, as well as in many other Hutterite writings. In sermons and elsewhere, members are often admonished to offer themselves as grains of wheat to be crushed into the bread of Christ's body, the church.

Such crushing of self-will sounds harsh to moderns who cherish unfettered individualism. But to Hutterite thinking, shedding self-interest is the only way to enjoy the fruits of communal life—fruits described by one writer as "permanent well-being, . . . enduring joy and genuine happiness."[15] Moderns living outside the communal ark must assert themselves and chart their own course to survive in a competitive society. For Hutterites, however, the survival skills of modern life threaten the very foundation of an orderly community. Thus arrogance, pride, and self-will must be eradicated not only in childhood but throughout the entirety of life.

The surrender of the self is a religious sacrifice that the Hutterites achieve through socialization, surveillance, and sanctions. Children are indoctrinated into Hutterite ways by being completely immersed in colony life. Adults are under constant surveillance because their life for all practical purposes is restricted to colony environs. In the words of one preacher, "It is good to live in community, for here there are always one hundred eyes watching you."[16] When informal means of social control fail, deviants face formal sanctions—strappings sometimes in the case of children, public confessions for adults, and excommunication for the recalcitrant.[17]

Children learn the ways of surrender at an early age. When they first run a comb through their hair or strike back at a playmate, they have stepped across the threshold of innocence and are old enough for a reprimand.[18] At about three years of age they enter the *Klein Schul*, a nursery school of sorts, where they quickly learn to respect the authority of the colony and the adults who care for them. "Community of goods starts in kindergarten," said one Hutterite elder. Children are taught cooperative behavior and learn that toys are community property to be shared by all. Disobedient children may be corrected with a ruler, a leather strap, or a willow switch. At the age of six, children begin to attend German school for several hours on weekdays and on Saturday. The German teacher carries the responsibility to teach German as well as basic moral and religious values. In all of these settings, and also in their work, children learn the virtues of obedience, the ballast that keeps the ark afloat.

A Hutterite writer once noted that two obstacles block the path to Christian community—"self-will" and "worldly possessions." In many respects the Hutterite system is designed to convert self-will to sweet surrender and selfishness to joyful sharing. "All believers must be led to joyful submissiveness. It is in this submission that we break with the Devil and our self-will. . . . Nobody belongs to himself." The call to surrender brings a yieldedness—a surrender of self for the welfare of the community. But the surrender of self extends beyond a mystical purging of vanity; it translates into daily sharing of material goods. By blending together personal surrender and communal sharing, sinful humans are able to enter the ark of the Lord.[19]

A Hutterite mother and child. *Source:* Jan Gleysteen

Separating from an Evil World

The Hutterite ark has floated in turbulent seas ever since its launch in Europe. The large Hutterian history book, the *Chronicle,* lists some 2,173 martyrs who "laid down their lives for the Master and the Church."[20] The stories of martyrdom, recorded in German, live on in Hutterite memory today. Anecdotes, sermons, and publications reiterate the stories of suffering that even today shape the Hutterian view of the world.

A Hutterite booklet that presents their beliefs to the larger public says, "We repeat that the Hutterite Church was like the first church, under the cross, and a persecuted Church as Christ had prophesied." The writer then cites the martyr accounts from the *Chronicle:*

Some were gruesomely tortured on the rack, were torn apart and died. Some were burned alive to ashes and powder as heretics. Some were toasted on beams and tortured with red-hot irons. Many were penned up in buildings and set to fire. Some were hanged on trees. Some were killed with the sword and chopped to pieces. Many had gags put into their mouths with tongues torn or cut out, so they could not testify to their faith, and were so led to the stake or scaffold . . . Many were cast into the water and drowned. Others were cast into prisons and dungeons, where they lay amongst rats and vermin till they died. There was no torture or manner of death too cruel. In spite of all that, they remained steadfast and faithful with joy and great fortitude, singing and praying in the face of death, praising the Lord that he had made them worthy to die for his sake. Nothing could move them from their faith and love of Jesus Christ, our Lord.[21]

The stinging persecution chiseled a deep and lasting suspicion of the world into the Hutterite mind. The call to separation from the world is buttressed with religious language and biblical teaching. Hutterite writers note that "the world hated" Jesus and that the Scriptures say "the whole world lieth in wickedness."[22] Suffering became the mark of true Christian discipleship, a sure sign that one was walking in the footsteps of the Savior. The image of the ark also underscored the lines of separation, for as one Hutterite preacher said, "You are either in the ark or out of it."[23]

The Hutterite belief that their ark was floating in troubled waters was confirmed when World War I exploded in 1917.[24] The three immigrant colonies of 1877 had already multiplied to seventeen, but Hutterite well-being suddenly stalled in the face of war. As German-speaking pacifists, Hutterite youth faced harassment for refusing to wear military uniforms and to bear arms. Joseph and Michael Hofer, along with two other Hutterite youth, were sentenced to thirty-seven years in prison for refusing to don military uniforms and accept active duty. Severely mistreated in the infamous prison at Alcatraz, they were later transferred to Fort Leavenworth, Kansas, where Joseph and Michael died from mistreatment and malnutrition.

This incident and other anti-German sentiments inflamed by the patriotic fervor of war spurred Hutterite leaders to close their colonies and head for Canada. Within one year, fifteen colonies were established across the border. The rapid exodus to Canada in 1918 left only one surviving colony in South Dakota. Some years later, as the fires of patriotism waned, many of the old colony sites in South Dakota were repossessed by new colonies—giving the Hutterites a permanent base in both countries by midcentury.

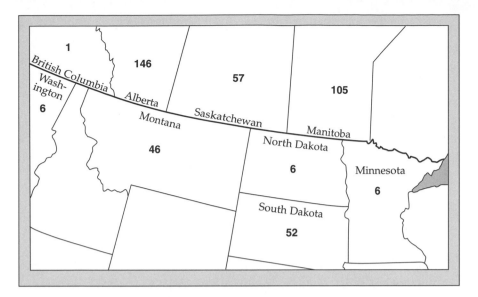

FIGURE 2.2 Distribution of Hutterite Colonies in North America
Source: Hutterite Telephone and Address Book (2000).

Hutterite conflicts with civil authorities in the twentieth century have flared up over land use, taxes, education, military service, and social security.[25] The many clashes with government authorities were complicated by differences in U.S. and Canadian policies and the many layers of legislation—federal, state, provincial, and local. The discord was fueled by the rapid growth of Hutterite colonies as well as by the encroaching fingers of the welfare state in both Canada and the United States.

When new colonies form, they frequently disturb the social life of rural communities. Several colonies in the same area, each with 8,000 acres of land, can dramatically affect land prices, school systems, and local consumer markets. Thus, Hutterites often face protests from citizen groups and business organizations when they prepare to plant new colonies. In some cases the antagonism has escalated into arson or vandalism.[26] Canadian provinces have tried to limit the number of acres a colony may own as well as the proximity of colonies to each other. Saskatchewan, for example, restricts colonies to 10,000 acres of land and a distance of thirty-five miles apart.[27] A variety of similar arrangements have been worked out with different civil authorities at various levels to regulate and monitor the expansion of colonies.

Government attempts to expand public education have also pricked Hutterite convictions. Believing that the education of their offspring is essential to preserving their way of life, Hutterites have refused to bus their children to consolidated schools filled with secular ideas, teachers, and peers. The typical compromise places a small public school on each colony.[28] The public school system provides a non-Hutterite teacher and supervises the curriculum in a one-room school on colony facilities. It is a workable arrangement for both parties. Public officials can select teachers and monitor curriculum. The Hutterites are happy because their children remain on the colony and are not exposed to worldly peers. Moreover, colony elders can monitor the school and urge the teacher to respect Hutterite values. Hutterites also operate their own German school, which often meets in the same classroom for an hour or so each day. The German school imparts distinctive Hutterite values and beliefs to the young.

In recent years, Hutterite pacifists have enjoyed easier times because both the United States and Canada exempt conscientious objectors from military service. Economic arrangements, however, have been more difficult. Government policies are based on assumptions of private property, personal income, and individual home ownership—all of which create problems for a communal group. After many rounds of legal conflicts, the Hutterites agreed to pay a "deemed income tax." This is estimated by dividing colony income by the number of adults, taking appropriate deductions, and then paying an average tax for each member. The colonies refuse, however, to participate in Social Security or the Canadian Pension Plan, which they consider unnecessary for a group that cares for the welfare and retirement of its own members. Both American and Canadian governments have exempted the Hutterites from these social welfare programs. They do, however, pay income, school, real estate, and sales taxes like other citizens.[29]

Political and economic separation does not insure that members will remain insulated from the world, however. The Hutterite strategy for separation is rather simple: establish colonies in isolated rural areas beyond the reach of urban vice. By controlling the use of vehicles and monitoring who enters and leaves the colony, the Hutterites are able to regulate interaction with outsiders. Members traveling outside a colony are often accompanied by another member, providing a mobile system of social control. The relative isolation of many colonies makes it difficult to walk to town or to interact privately with outsiders. Non-Hutterites of-

ten visit colonies to conduct business, and some Hutterite leaders participate in agricultural organizations. Some colonies are involved in social
service projects in their local communities. A colony in Minnesota sends
volunteers to assist in a homeless shelter. All things considered, though,
contact with outsiders is limited. Interaction with the English school
teacher is the most significant outside contact of Hutterite children.

Separation from the world is also maintained with taboos on television, radio, and other forms of mass media. "TV brings destruction," said
a German teacher, "and Hollywood is the sewer pipe of the world." Despite the traditional taboos, some progressive colonies have televisions in
their schools to watch educational videos and satellite classroom broad-
casts. One colony rented a tractor for several months with a radio in its
cab. The colony manager urged drivers not to listen to it, but he admit-
ted that some likely did when they were out in the fields alone. When the
colony eventually purchased the tractor, the radio was torn out. Radios,
however, are becoming more prevalent in some colonies. Some colonists
may read farm magazines or newspapers, but the average member does
not read *Time* or *Newsweek* on a regular basis. Worldly entertainment
outside the colony is forbidden.

By regulating exposure to outside media, the colony limits contact
with outsiders and filters contaminating influences, hoping to keep the
ark secure and the world at bay. Easy exposure to ungodly values, Hutterites believe, would undermine their entire way of life. They do tap the
services of outside professionals—veterinarians, medical doctors, dentists, lawyers, bankers, and accountants. Most babies, for example, are
born in hospitals. Nevertheless, in all of these contacts, Hutterites are
mindful that the ark of their salvation floats upon a sea of wickedness that
could quickly pull them down.

PIETY IN THE VESTIBULE OF HEAVEN

Hutterites sometimes describe their colony as a vestibule of heaven.
"When you are in it," one member said, "you're still not in heaven, you
still must suffer."[30] How does piety look in the vestibule of heaven? It is
orderly, regimented, and highly resistant to change. Despite migration,
technological change, and the proliferation of new colonies, Hutterite religious practices are remarkably well preserved. A ritualized program of

A Hutterite minister displays his hat outside his apartment. *Source:* Ivan Glick

indoctrination, regimentation, and compliance ensures constancy and impedes change. The minister carries unquestioned authority over all aspects of colony life. Selected by lot according to biblical precedent, he oversees the spiritual and social welfare of the colony. Other colony leaders report to the minister, who speaks with the weighty voice of Hutterite tradition. Mindful of the long-term consequences of this appointment, colonies ordain their leader after several years of probation. In some colonies an assistant minister may be selected to help an aging one. In addition to his religious duties, a minister participates in the daily flow of work as needed—driving tractors, milking cows, or helping to plant and harvest crops. Although other leaders have frequent contact with outsiders, the minister is the primary keeper of external relations.

Although not formally trained, the minister is the ever-visible symbol of religious presence and authority. When he walks from his apartment to the church building each evening, other members quickly follow to participate in the half-hour service that he leads. He is the first to enter, the last to leave the meetinghouse, and the only one who stands or speaks during services. The minister presides over Sunday morning services as well as baptisms, marriages, funerals, and communion each spring. If the minister and his assistant are away from the colony, religious services are canceled. The minister also supervises the punishment of backsliders. Symbolic of his revered status, the minister and his assistant eat alone in his apartment rather than in the communal hall.

A minister shoulders the burden of transmitting Hutterite faith and preserving its ancient forms. His responsibility is so heavy that "no one wants to do his job," said one member. Ministers typically have a repertoire of several hundred sermons that are highly treasured and carefully copied. In both the evening and Sunday services, he reads a sermon written in Europe centuries ago and passed across the generations.[31] The use of these ancient sermons preserves Hutterite tradition, prevents individual interpretation, and limits the minister's freedom. Hutterites believe that their sermons embody the truth so well that new interpretations of Scripture would only introduce error.

Ancient truths are passed on to the youth in the German school as well as in Sunday afternoon classes, where students are quizzed on the content of the morning sermon. The German teacher, who sometimes also serves as minister, is largely responsible for the moral and religious education of the young. Learning occurs largely through memorization and repetition. German scripts and Bible verses are copied. Individual study and interpretation of Scripture is discouraged.

In preparation for baptism, candidates study a series of questions and answers. One question asks, "Do you desire thus to consecrate, give, and sacrifice yourself with soul and body and all your possessions to the Lord in Heaven, and to be obedient unto Christ and his Church?" In the Hutterite view, religious faith is not something to be studied or examined; it is something to be accepted. Unlike forms of religious education that encourage independent thought and critical thinking, Hutterite training involves indoctrination. Freethinkers would wreak havoc in these tightly ordered communities.

Religious services follow traditional patterns day after day. The ancient format, duplicated in memory, varies little from colony to colony. A typical evening service begins with ten minutes of singing followed by a fifteen-minute sermon and a five-minute prayer. The congregation kneels forward in prayer with folded hands. The folded hands also accompany the memorized prayers that are offered before and after every meal and snack. The ritualized prayers, repeated throughout the day and across the week, are a continual reminder of the sacred canopy that stretches over community life. Hutterites find security, meaning, and blessing in the daily recital of religious ritual.

Beyond collective ritual, other markers also distinguish the vestibule of heaven. Distinctive garb, though varied among Hutterite groups, publicly declares their identity when members shop in nearby towns. Hutterite teaching warns members of the temptations that abound in the outside world. Fearful that worldly pleasures will lead to wickedness, the church has proscribed many forms and venues of vice—dancing, theater, card parties, pool rooms, smoking, movies, television, radio, bathing resorts, festivals, concerts, and banquets—each of which might erode the foundation of the vestibule of heaven.[32]

Some children once found a visitor to their colony smoking behind a barn. When asked by an elder what they were doing, the children sheepishly replied, "watching this man sin." Although tobacco is forbidden, alcohol is not. Each colony has its own wine cellar, and visitors are freely offered a choice of home-brewed dandelion, rhubarb, or grape wine. In one colony workers enjoy a wine "lifter" during a midmorning break from killing chickens. Commercial beer is consumed in some of the colonies. One colony celebrates the end of the seeding season with beer and barbecued steak and the end of harvest days with beer, whiskey, and roast duck. Although colonists are urged to use alcohol with moderation, it sometimes is abused. Colony leaders try to prevent alcoholism and occasionally send abusers to seek help from Alcoholics Anonymous.

Although the vestibule of heaven excludes worldly entertainment, it places few restrictions on technology apart from taboos on the camera, car, radio, and television. In some colonies radios, cameras, and musical instruments are becoming more common, although this is certainly not the case with the more traditional ones. Unlike the Amish, Hutterites use the latest technology in all their farming and domestic operations. Computers, fax machines, copy machines, intercoms, hearing aids, CB radios, portable phones, and other state-of-the-art devices are widely used. One colony has some twenty CB radios on its trucks and tractors. This encourages continual chatter and banter throughout the day. Farm managers track feed and grain prices on personal computers. Pesticides, insecticides, and chemical fertilizers are commonly used. Artificial insemination and superovulation are used in some colonies to increase the production of dairy herds.

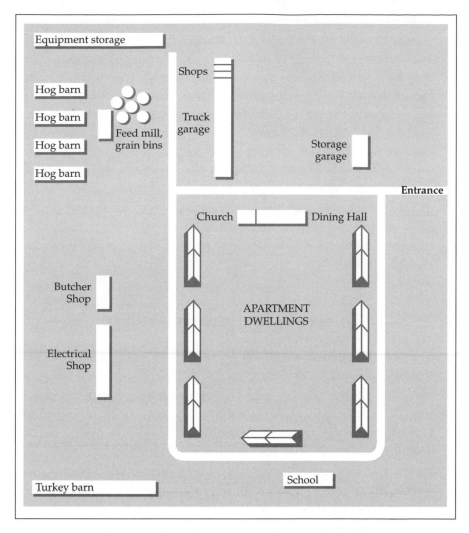

FIGURE 2.3 Spatial Arrangement of a Hutterite Colony in Manitoba, Canada
Note: Diagram not drawn to scale.

One colony installed a $225,000 computer-controlled feeding system that mixes each cow's feed according to her production. Another colony built a completely computerized swine operation that houses 1,000 sows. Modern farm equipment enables one person to seed more than 400 acres a day with a large tractor and seeder that cost nearly $200,000. Although the spiritual realm is highly regimented and traditional, the material realm pulses forward through twentieth-century airwaves and fiberoptic cables.

More than other Old Order groups, the Hutterites compartmentalize change by building a cultural wall between religious and economic life. While they reject virtually any change in the realm of religious ritual, they freely embrace technological change and innovation in economic affairs. Rational thought is banned in religion, but the fruits of science and logic are welcomed in agricultural production. Indeed, "Nothing is too modern if it benefits the colony," said one member.[33] In the words of a German teacher, "We can't turn our backs to technology. We must censor it and take the best of it." Thus new forms of technology are easily embraced when they enhance the economic productivity and well-being of the entire colony, but items that pamper personal comfort are less likely to find approval. Some colonies, for example, began using thermostats in the farrowing houses of their sows before installing them in their own homes.[34]

SOCIAL ROLES ABOARD THE ARK

The regimentation of religious life is also reflected in social roles. One colony manager describes his colony as "a hive of bees where everyone has a job." Role expectations revolve around status, age, and gender. In terms of status, the minister holds the highest position of authority. Subordinate to the minister is the manager or "colony boss," who oversees the business operation of the colony. The minister and manager work closely together, usually meeting each morning, and conferring frequently throughout the day. Other key positions include the field boss, who assigns and supervises farm work; the German teacher; and an assistant minister, if there is one.

Adult men are assigned to specific areas of responsibility—cowman, beekeeper, shoemaker, plumber, goose man, and so on. Each of them is the "boss" of their respective area. Although some jobs are seasonal, most are long-term, if not for a lifetime. Occasional rotations occur, depending on personal skills and the needs of the colony. Major roles for women include head cook, gardener, and head of the kindergarten. In one colony the key leadership roles were distributed in the pattern of seniority shown in Table 2.2.

The ladder of authority in each colony has five rungs: (1) the minister(s), (2) the council, (3) married men, (4) all baptized members, and

TABLE 2.2 PATTERNS OF SENIORITY BY GENDER

Males	Females
Minister	Head cook
Assistant minister	Gardener
German teacher	Kindergarten teacher
Business manager "colony boss"	Children's dining room
Farm manager "field boss"	Dairy assistant
Dairyman	Rotating jobs
Electrician	
Chickenman	
Hogman	
Carpenter	

Source: Adapted from the listing of occupational roles in the Forest River Colony as presented by Waldner (1990: 28).

(5) unbaptized children. The minister(s), manager, and field boss serve as an informal leadership committee that meets each morning to plan the day's events. A council of five to seven men serves as an executive committee for the colony's social, economic, and religious affairs. This leadership body includes the minister, the manager, and the farm boss, as well as two or three older men, including the German teacher. The council discusses issues and brings proposals to the church business meeting, where baptized men make the final decision.

The Hutterite Church includes all baptized members but men serve in leadership roles. Women do not participate in policy discussions, do not vote, and are not eligible for leadership roles. Men always recite the prayers at meals and in public settings. Even in the spiritual preparation for communion, men stand and voice their fitness in a public meeting, while women reveal their readiness for communion to their husbands at home.

Gender roles are highly prescribed along traditional lines.[35] Women work in child care, gardening, food preparation, cleaning, and clothing. They are elected to their positions by the men, however. A few women have permanent positions, but most do domestic jobs that rotate on a weekly basis. The head cook is responsible to plan menus and oversee daily meal preparation, but the colony manager must approve her requests. At marriage, a young bride leaves her own colony to join her husband's, which likely includes several of his brothers and their wives. This patrilocal pattern of marriage, as well as traditional role expectations, places women outside the formal circle of power. There are, of course, many informal ways in which women exert influence, but in official roles they are always subservient to men.

Beyond status and gender, age also regulates expectations. The young child enters kindergarten at about age 3. From 5 to 15 years of age, children attend German school for an hour or so each day. The young people eat in a separate dining room until age 15, which marks their passage toward adulthood. At this age boys and girls begin eating with adults, end their formal schooling, and receive major work assignments in the colony.

Baptism and marriage signify additional steps in the ladder to adulthood. Baptism normally occurs between ages 18 and 25. Marriage takes place in the early to middle twenties, after baptism. Older adults move into retirement in their late forties. They continue to assist with community work, but the bulk of heavy toil falls on the shoulders of the young.

Behavior in Hutterite colonies is carefully organized around status, gender, and age. Each category has its own ladder of authority—religious over secular, ordained over laity, male over female, elderly over youth, baptized over unbaptized, married over single, and so forth. Moreover, as one member noted, "Anyone can punish someone else on a lower level." An older minister, topping all the categories, carries considerable influence in colony affairs, whereas young women influence little more than their offspring.

These social distinctions are reaffirmed and sacralized every day in religious services. The seating pattern for worship enshrines gender, age, and status distinctions in God's eternal order. The council members, all men, sit on a bench at the front of the austere room, facing the congregation. Women file in on the right side of the small chapel and men on the left. The youngest sit on the front benches and the oldest in the rear. Although specific seats are not formally assigned, everyone has a particular place defined by their gender, age, and status. If someone misses a service, his or her seat remains empty. The small group of elders facing the congregation keep a watchful eye over members during the service and file out behind them as they leave. Members file in and out of the meeting according to their rank—younger ones enter first and leave last.

The oldest woman follows the youngest boy out the door. The orderly pattern assures each person a clearly defined niche within the system and pronounces a daily blessing upon the structure of authority.

Acceptance of one's place and willingness to obey one's superiors oils the flow of social life. Such tightly defined roles appear restrictive and oppressive to outsiders. However, when these tidy roles are accepted as disbursements from the hand of Providence, they enhance social harmony especially when dozens of persons live in close proximity.

Socialization and Schooling

The orderliness of Hutterite culture also undergirds the stages of child rearing, each of which is separated by a standard rite of passage. Passing from one stage to another, children learn not only Hutterite virtues but also the patterns of authority. One of the remarkable features of Hutterite socialization is the widely shared responsibility for child rearing. Unlike modern life, where the burden of socialization falls on the shoulders of parents, all colonists are responsible for training, correcting, and disciplining children.

The process of socialization begins with the nuclear family. Hutterite songs, prayers, and other routines define the child's world from birth. Even before their first birthday, children will clasp their hands in prayer when food comes their way. The small child feels the warmth of the colony by sitting on many laps and basking in the attention of others.[36]

At the age of 3, children move to the second stage when they enter the *Klein-Schul,* or nursery. Here they come under the direct supervision and care of the colony. At this tender stage of development, they leave the care of their family and learn the basic mandates of Hutterite life: obey, surrender, share, and cooperate. In the nursery the child receives less personal attention than before. No longer protected by innocence, nursery children now become accountable for their behavior.

Two important transitions take place at age 6 as children reach the third stage of socialization. First, they eat in the children's dining hall, separate from the adults. Segregated by sex in their seating, they learn Hutterite lore related to manners, prayers, gender roles, and authority. An even more important benchmark for 6-year-olds is their entry into both the German and the English school. In the dining room and the Ger-

A kindergarten (*Klein-Schul*) teacher and her pupils. *Source:* Jan Gleysteen

man school, they are under the strict supervision of colony adults who guide their moral development.

The German school indoctrinates the young into Hutterite history, beliefs, and values. "The eternal salvation of our children is at stake," writes a minister in describing the purpose of the school.[37] The German school is typically held in the English school house on the colony. The children meet for an hour or so before and after the English school as well as for a half day on Saturday. The German teacher is a married man who carries the solemn responsibility of implanting the ways of righteousness in the minds of the young. In one Canadian colony, the German teacher takes the picture of the British queen off the wall at the beginning of the German school and then replaces it at the end. This symbolic act transforms the room into sacred space for the German lessons.[38] The German school is the greenhouse of faith, the place where Hutterite beliefs and habits become deeply rooted in the minds of the young.

Hostetler and Huntington describe the activities of the German school: "During this time they practice writing German script, read German, recite their memory verses from Hutterite hymns, the Book of Psalms, the New Testament or a Hutterite history book. The German teacher admonishes them about their beliefs and even more about their behavior."[39] The traditional emphasis on rote memorization is declining in the more progressive colonies. The German teacher disciplines students for misbehavior in the classroom as well as outside. Boys caught trapping wild animals or playing with a radio outside the classroom may receive a strapping from the German teacher who, like a surrogate parent, cares for their spiritual welfare. However, the stern teacher who reminds children of their duties with a smack of his ruler will shift roles at home and playfully crawl on the floor with his grandchildren.

After an hour of German school in the morning, an English teacher appears in the same classroom.[40] This non-Hutterite teacher, hired by the local school district, instructs young colonists through the ninth grade. The children now suddenly turn from sixteenth-century Hutterite hymns to the language and ideas of the modern world, but with certain restrictions. For younger children, this is their first exposure to English. Although school children are under the tutelage of a non-Hutterite teacher, they nevertheless remain on the colony, near the watchful eye of elders and away from the corrosive influence of secular peers.

Trained in a secular college and accountable to the public school system, the English teacher follows a standard curriculum but tries to respect the concerns of the minister and the German teacher. One English teacher explained that when she teaches science, she tries "to be careful about topics like evolution and reproduction and doesn't use novels that have stories in them about girls getting pregnant." This particular teacher also leaves "the witches out of Halloween" and checks with the colony minister about questionable characters in holiday plays. In this particular colony, the minister does not object to Christmas plays so long as they retell the biblical story, and he also permits Halloween decorations in the school.

One Canadian public school district has twelve colonies within its jurisdiction. At the urging of a Hutterite advisory council, the district literally tears from the textbooks pages covering AIDS, reproduction, and sexual development. Hutterite elders do not want their youth exposed to these topics. Students are not permitted to read novels that discuss rape, violence, or drugs. Yet the same school that tightly monitors morality uses teleconferencing and computers to teach mechanics to upper-level students. Even the younger children learn how to conduct experiments in the English school. Thus, the same school that introduces Hutterite minds to the scientific, calculating worldview also cooperates with Hutterian elders by sidestepping sensitive areas like human reproduction. But the scientific views of the English school may be spreading, for one German teacher confesses that his pupils, "don't believe the stork story anymore."[41]

The German teacher speaks with the voice of unquestioned moral authority as he supervises the spiritual well-being of the youth. He is the primary agent of religious socialization and carries the burden for rooting the colony's tradition in the minds of the young. Thus, it is not surprising that young Hutterites meet with the German teacher on the eve of their fifteenth birthday as they prepare to step into adulthood. When fifteen-year-olds "graduate" from the German school, they recite their morning and evening prayers without supervision and receive a catechism book to prepare for baptism. Religious instruction continues in the Sunday school that meets on Sunday afternoons. Although the younger children also attend, the Sunday school is slanted toward teenagers who have finished German school but are not yet baptized. Children and youth recite Bible verses as well as the stories they heard in the morning sermon.

The fifteen-year threshold is also marked by other significant changes. The young people now enter the adult dining room and sit with their respective sexes. Fifteen-year-olds are given a wooden chest, a dresser, or a desk with a lock. This becomes their only private space for storing personal belongings. Along with this rite of passage, youth are often given custody of a particular tool related to their work—a hammer, a paint brush, a rake. Young boys are assigned to an apprenticeship with an adult, perhaps the electrician, the dairyman, or the goose boss. By the time they are seventeen, both sexes are given major work assignments. The transition years between age 15 and baptism are sometimes called the foolish years, for although they know the boundaries of the moral order, young people can experiment with evil more freely at that time than they can after baptism.

Baptism marks the official entry into the vestibule of heaven. Because baptism is the most important act of commitment, it is, for all practical purposes, the point of no return in Hutterite life. Baptismal candidates pledge to surrender all their belongings to the colony and take nothing with them if they leave. Young adults, typically between 18 and 25 years of age, prepare for baptism by memorizing a catechism and joining an in-

A newly married bride and groom. *Source:* Mary Koga

struction class for several weeks on Sunday afternoons. The sacred service of baptism occurs once a year, usually on the Sunday before Easter, or on the Sunday of Pentecost.

Marriage is the final port on the journey to adulthood. Courtship may stretch over several years and is often carried on by correspondence because of distance and infrequent contact between colonies. Young people typically marry someone from another colony. They learn to know each other through work projects and other social events that colonies do together. Marriages are not arranged, but a young man must request permission of his parents, of his colony via the preacher, of the elders of the bride's colony, and finally of the parents of the bride—all of whom could potentially veto the plans. Thus the family and the church play a major role in sanctioning a marriage. After an engagement ceremony and celebration in the bride's colony, the wedding takes place on a Sunday morning in the groom's colony. Sometimes several couples are married in the same service.

Marriage is the culmination of the long process of socialization. The husband is now able to participate in the decision-making body of the church, and the wife joins the female subculture in her new husband's colony. Socialization beyond marriage is reinforced by daily religious services as well as by strong expectations to be good role models for the next generation.

SOCIAL TIES AND INTERACTION

Unaffected by broader standards of tact and decorum, face-to-face interaction in Hutterite culture is very direct. With a boldness that may seem brusque to outsiders, the colony manager speaks pointedly to other members: "You do this," "You clean up here," "Don't sit there," "You take the broom, over here." They are not insulted by his straightforward style. A minister giving directions by phone to an outsider in another state says, "You write this down with a pencil." The social finesse of middle-class manners is uncommon in this culture that prizes blunt, straightforward directives.

Paying little attention to acquaintance rituals, Hutterites immediately confront visitors with pointed questions that would be considered forward in other cultural settings: Why are you here? Where did you come from? What is your job? Are you married? Instead of offering to take a visitor's coat, a Hutterite host may say, "Put it on that table" or, more often, may say nothing. Visitors who pass the screening are invited to the minister's or manager's apartment and offered a variety of homemade wines as a sign of hospitality.[42]

The brusque style is not intended to insult or belittle, but merely reflects the values of suspicion, honesty, and efficiency that have not been smothered by the superficial graces of middle-class culture. The austerity of communication also underscores the orderly authority in Hutterite life. There is little room for ambiguity, hesitation, or uncertainty here; every word has a purpose and place in the grammar of face-to-face interaction.

There are other distinctives in Hutterite patterns of interaction as well. Hostetler and Huntington note that staunch male and female subcultures serve an important role within the colony.[43] Since strong family allegiance can undermine colony solidarity, one or two strong families can skew colony decision making. Successful colonies always find ways to keep the power of nuclear families in check. Vigorous gender subcultures help to dissolve the potential threat of the nuclear family. Membership in a gender subculture also dilutes the influence of individual households, which in turn helps to equalize power relations within the colony as a whole.

Husbands and wives may feel more loyalty to their gender subculture and to the colony as a whole than to their immediate families. Since men regulate production and control the formal power of the colony, women sometimes complain that they are overwhelmed with work. And for their part, men sometimes blame colony problems on the women. Said one preacher, "Our colony troubles would amount to very little if it were not for the women."[44] The first question a group of women asked a visitor touring their dining area was, "Do the men in your church make the women wash the dishes?" In this particular colony the manager had declared, "We'll never have an automatic dishwasher here as long as I'm boss." Such decisions are typically made by several people in leadership roles. The tensions between gender subcultures may ultimately serve the well-being of the total colony by limiting the power of extended families. Such gender-based divisions, however, are not egalitarian but rest on the power of patriarchy.

The nuclear family may be neutralized by gender subcultures, but extended kinship ties among Hutterians run thick. Since new brides take up residence in their husbands' colonies, it is not unusual to have only two surnames, or in some cases only one, in a colony. Table 2.3 shows the distribution of names across the three groups of Hutterites based on the surnames of ministers and managers.[45] Among the Schmiedleut, 70 percent of some three hundred leaders had four surnames—Hofer, Waldner, Wipf, and Wollman.

Indeed, only ten surnames account for 90 percent of the more than eight hundred leaders among all the Hutterite groups. Based on the survey of leaders, Hofer and Waldner are the most popular names, with 25 and 18 percent respectively as shown in Table 2.3. Without active mission efforts and with few outsiders embracing Hutterite ways, European names continue to dominate. Many colonies consist of a dozen or fewer nuclear families. If four sons are married and take up residence in a colony, it would not be unusual for their children to have some twenty first cousins living in the same colony.

Hutterite colonies have many children and few elderly. Indeed, 42 percent of the colonists are under 15 years of age and only 3 percent are 65

TABLE 2.3 DISTRIBUTION OF SURNAMES OF HUTTERITE LEADERS
BY AFFILIATION

Name	Affiliation			
	Dariusleut	Lehrerleut	Schmiedleut	Total
Hofer	32	16	26	25
Waldner (Weldner)	4	19	28	18
Wipf (Wiph)	3	19	9	10
Stahl	17	0	4	7
Wurz (Wurtz)	10	9	3	7
Kleinsasser	0	14	5	6
Tschetter	15	0	2	6
Maendel (Mandel)	0	6	7	4
Walter	11	0	0	4
Entz	0	13	0	3
Six other names	8	4	16	10
Total	100%	100%	100%	100%
N	(269)	(222)	(322)	(814)

Source: *Hutterite Telephone and Address Book* (2000). This directory lists the minister and secretary of each colony.

years and older, compared to 24 and 17 percent, respectively, among rural South Dakota whites. Moreover, 61 percent of the population in a Hutterite colony is under 25 years of age.[46] With its social structure tilted toward the young, Hutterite society focuses on schooling and education rather than on geriatric services and pensions. The few elderly do receive consistent and compassionate care from their extended family and other colonists.

GROWTH AND EXPANSION

The Hutterites have enjoyed remarkable growth in the twentieth century. As shown in Figure 2.4, the three immigrant colonies of the 1870s had mushroomed to 425 colonies by the dawn of the twenty-first century.[47] In the decade of the 1980s, sixty-eight new colonies were established, about seven per year. The steady growth has been produced by a high birth rate and very little attrition. Very few non-Hutterites join the colonies.[48] Hutterites do not engage in mission efforts, and leaders rec-

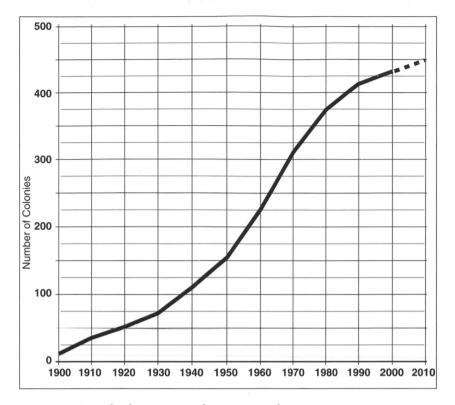

FIGURE 2.4 Growth of Hutterite Colonies in North America, 1900–2010
Source: J. Hostetler (1997) and *Hutterite Telephone and Address Book* (2000).

ognize that it is easier to become a Hutterite by birth than by assimilation.[49] In the words of one minister, "Because pride is such a difficult
thing to overcome, it seems to work much better if you are born in a
colony."

In the first half of the twentieth century, the Hutterites averaged ten
completed children per family and were cited as one of the fastest growing human groups. In recent decades, however, Hutterite birth rates have
been dropping. In a study of sixteen colonies in South Dakota in the early
1990s, Orlando Goering found a completed family size of eight children
for women over 45 years of age. This represents a drop of two children
per family from midcentury rates. However, the average family size
among younger women, from all evidence, appears to be shrinking even
further: to five or six children. Schmiedleut colony leaders uniformly re-

TABLE 2.4 CRUDE BIRTH RATE AND FERTILITY RATIO FOR SELECTED HUTTERITE COLONIES AND THE SOUTH DAKOTA RURAL WHITE POPULATION, 1950–1990

Year	Birth Rate per 1,000		Fertility Ratio	
	Hutterite	South Dakota	Hutterite	South Dakota
1950	45.9	23.4	96.3	61.9
1970	43.0	14.7	95.5	45.0
1990	35.2	12.1	71.0	38.7

Source: Demographic records of 18 Schmiedleut colonies in South Dakota and U.S. Census data. Gathered and tabulated by Orlando Goering for the authors.

port "five or six" when asked the average number of children per family. As Table 2.4 shows, the birth rate per 1,000 persons has dropped from forty-six in 1950 to thirty-five in 1992.

Although the Hutterite birth rate dropped 23 percent from 1950 to 1990, it is nevertheless three times higher than the rural South Dakota rate of twelve births per 1,000. A variety of explanations have been offered for the tumbling birth rates despite a formal taboo on birth control. Some analysts have argued that the widespread use of technology by colonies has diminished their need for human labor. Difficulties finding land for spawning new colonies may also play a factor. Hutterites are increasingly using modern medical care, and most children are born in hospitals, thus increasing exposure to counsel from healthcare professionals. Colony leaders appear willing to listen when professional physicians advise women to limit family size for "health reasons." One minister, explaining why he accepts a physician's advice to limit families, said, "I don't want to override a specialist."

Family size is limited by a number of means. Some women may be getting married later and waiting longer to have children. Women sometimes request notes from physicians when they want to stop bearing children. Older women are permitted to have hysterectomies or tubal ligations. Some physicians are also prescribing birth control pills and dispensing condoms.[50] The elastic phrase "health concerns" is widely accepted by colony elders as sufficient reason for limiting family size. In the words of one Hutterite mother, "We don't believe in birth control, but when the doctor says 'that's enough,' or if we shouldn't have more for health reasons, we have to do something." The availability of birth control technology and the negative attitude of healthcare professionals toward large families have combined to reduce family size among a people who ostensibly oppose family planning.[51]

The shrinking size of Hutterite families has wide-ranging consequences for their population growth, the age at which colonies divide, and their internal division of labor. The declining birth rate has increased the time until a colony can spawn its first daughter colony. At midcentury the branching out happened, on the average, about every fifteen years. In recent decades the interval has expanded to twenty years. Over the generations, the Hutterites have found the optimum colony size to be about a hundred persons. When a mature colony approaches that limit, plans are laid to spawn a daughter colony over several years. The actual division may wait until the colony reaches 130 to 150 persons, thus assuring that both the mother and daughter units will have adequate resources to function independently. Since several million dollars will be needed to purchase land and equipment for the new colony, the mother unit begins saving years in advance. Even though the new location may be as far as a hundred miles away, members of the mother colony will help to construct the new buildings.

The procedures for dividing a colony vary somewhat from colony to colony. At the time of the move, leaders divide equipment and supplies between the two colonies. Leaders sort families into two lists that roughly balance age groups and skills. In some colonies the two groups draw lots to determine which group will need to move. In some Lehrerleut colonies, both groups pack their belongings before the lots are drawn. Typically, however, lots are cast prior to packing. Among the Schmiedleut, casting lots is rarely used.

Establishing a new colony is a dramatic moment in colony life. Families who have lived closely together for many years are suddenly pulled apart. Depending on the fate of the lot, some persons may have to move three or four times in their lifetime. Unlike modern notions of mobility, however, the decision to move is not an individual choice.

EXCLUSION AND DEFECTION

Discipline practices vary considerably from colony to colony. Several levels of punishment are typically used to reinforce the moral code of Hutterite life. Members charged with a minor transgression—owning a hidden radio, for example—may be asked to make a public confession during worship or to stand throughout the sermon as a sign of humiliation. "It makes you feel like a dumb pig," noted one member.[52] For more serious breaches of conduct, offenders may face up to two weeks of exclusion and shunning. An exclusion of several days may be used for offenses such as smoking dope, abusing alcohol, or owning a gun.[53] More flagrant offenses—stealing and selling communal property, visiting massage parlors, or engaging in adultery—may trigger a lengthy exclusion or expulsion if the deviant does not repent. The Hutterites believe that a transgressor in exclusion is "in the hands and under the power of the devil" and that the person "must struggle and pray to be released." Some colonies have no established time frames for exclusion. The process of discipline is flexible and seeks through love and compassion to bring the wayward person back into fellowship.

The patterns of shunning vary among and within the leut. In one colony the shunning takes four forms. In some way, these are rituals of shaming designed to encourage repentance and restoration into the community.[54] The offender sits on a chair in the hallway entrance to the meetinghouse. Excluded from worship, the person must face other members as they enter and leave the daily services. Second, transgressors eat alone in the basement of the dining hall. Third, sometimes they are assigned to jobs that isolate them from other members. Traditionally, some Hutterites believed that if someone died while under the ban they would go to hell. Thus, some colonies assigned excluded members to safe jobs where they are not vulnerable to injury and death. For example, a shunned person might not be asked to build a chimney or climb to the top of a roof but might be assigned less dangerous work, such as pulling nails from old lumber. Finally, excluded members in some colonies sleep in the kindergarten building to learn to become "humble like a child."

The various aspects of shunning, which vary from colony to colony, emphasize humility, shame, separation, and repentance. Hutterites compare exclusion to the practice of the Old Testament Israelites who controlled the "outbreak of a disease like leprosy" by keeping the infected ones outside the city wall. The wall of exclusion helps to remind members of the moral code that separates the righteous from evil and serves to drive the sinner to repentance. In the words of one Hutterite, "Discipline should be viewed as a blessing to those who are in it, for it allows them an opportunity for repentance and to set matters right with God and the church."

At the end of exclusion, those who express remorse are reinstated into the community in a ritual similar to baptism. Explained one Hutterite, "It's just like baptism with the same questions, but no water." Conversely, the unrepentant are expelled from the colony and are not welcome in others. They are, however, able to return to their home colony upon confession of their sin. Shunning normally occurs within a colony, but in the case of a division between colonies, the different factions may also exclude each other's members.[55]

Defections from Hutterite colonies typically occur in the late teenage years or among adult married couples. Although defections do occur, they are likely under 5 percent, on the average, of the younger population. It is not uncommon for unmarried boys to run away and explore the outside world before baptism. Leaving the colony with little more than the clothes on their backs, they find outside employment for several months or a year. Some are lost forever, but the majority of runaways return to the colony, confess their errors, and are baptized into the faith.[56] In recent years some colonies have required an AIDS test before accepting a prodigal back. Some colonies develop a reputation for having an unusually large number of defectors. Others have reputations for unusual difficulties with alcoholism or sexual abuse, which sometimes also contributes to defection.[57]

Some persons also abandon colony life in adulthood—a much more serious defection, since they have been baptized into the Hutterite faith. Some observers report an increase in the number who are leaving as adults in recent years. One colony manager said that a neighbor colony had a "chicken boss who was smoking and going to massage parlors and running with women. He was married and had children, and so the minister wouldn't let him go away alone." He eventually left the colony "to try the world, but may come back if he repents." Pentecostal groups that stress spiritual freedom, emotional experience, and a "born again" faith occasionally entice colonists away from the rote rituals and somber spirituality of Hutterite life. One scholar noted that those who leave as adults for religious reasons rarely return, but those who leave as youth for worldly reasons—to explore the world—often come home.[58] Some colonies make an effort to follow dropouts and bring them back.

The costs of departure are high. While the degree of shunning varies from colony to colony, those who leave are banned and typically not permitted to meet family members who remain with the colony. Some colonies may, with the permission of the minister, permit excluded persons to visit their family, depending on the merits of the case. The severity of shunning hinges to some extent on the attitudes of the deviant. With few economic and social resources, they are forced to start life anew. Deserters cite a variety of reasons for abandoning colony life—disillusionment with leadership, abuse of power, harshness of discipline, controlled behavior, and a theological accent on works rather than grace. Charged one defector, "They are living on tradition, they are not based on the Lord. . . . You do not have to wear those clothes. The Lord looks on the heart. It does not matter if your hair is parted in the middle." Another added, "They say we broke our covenant when we left the colony and are going straight to hell. But I didn't break my covenant with God, and that's what's important. I feel sorry for the colony people. They are sincere but wrong." Not surprisingly, adult dropouts are rather harsh in their judgment of colony life.[59]

A widow and mother of ten who left the security of colony life said, "I was born into the protective cocoon of the Hutterite world. . . . I had food to eat when I was hungry, clothes to wear, and a roof over my head. However, everything in life has a price tag, and the price tag for this abundance is called *Gelassenheit*—total submission and absolute obedience to the rules that govern the Hutterite world." Describing her experience outside she concluded, "I was ill-prepared to survive in this strange and alien world . . . but I have found purpose and meaning in life beyond just producing a house full of children that will be required to produce another house full of children *ad infinitum*."[60]

Defectors face the harsh reality of surviving in an alien culture built on assertive individualism and financial independence—a culture that is foreign to Hutterite ways. Thus, it is not surprising that some defectors join the same church on the outside and find ways to support each other as they cope with the strain of adjustment and survival beyond colony life.

The Hutterites are the oldest and most successful communal group in North America. They challenge modern understandings of the good life, especially contemporary assumptions about individual achievement, choice, freedom, mobility, equality, opportunity, property, pleasure, higher education, and intellectual curiosity. Convinced that these are not prerequisites for happiness, they argue that the good life is anchored in the virtues of self-denial, suffering, sharing, patience, obedience and conformity.

How are new generations of Hutterites persuaded to accept this radical argument? How have these unconventional people been able to sidestep the forces of history so successfully? The recipe for their prosperity is found in a unique blend of at least eight cultural and social ingredients.

Ideological Monopoly. The Hutterites have constructed a dualistic worldview that leaves little room for uncertainty. Theirs is a world of bipolar opposites: God and man, eternal and temporal, carnal and spiritual, righteous and wicked, right and wrong, men and women, colony and world. Hutterite social organization transmits this worldview and, more importantly, maintains a monopoly over it. They have created what sociologists call a tight plausibility structure. That is, colony life eliminates competing worldviews by restricting interaction with outsiders who might erode the plausibility of Hutterite beliefs. Leaders also denigrate the influence of worldly ideas by defining the outside world as a den of wickedness and ungodliness, "a city of vanity." By maintaining a tight monopoly over their own world, Hutterites have been able to preserve their cherished way of life. Their social organization and behavioral patterns are designed to reinforce and preserve the ideological monopoly that is essential to their survival.

Comprehensive Socialization. One of the ways in which Hutterites maintain an ideological monopoly is by immersing their young in a comprehensive program of socialization that continues throughout adulthood. The task of raising and training children is taken very seriously. Except for the English school, child care and instruction is withheld from outsiders and even, to a great extent, from Hutterite parents themselves. Television, day-care centers, summer camps, and far-away schools are all absent. All the vehicles of ethnic socialization—nursery, German school, Sunday school, and baptismal instruction—place the preservation of the faith on the shoulders of the colony, particularly on the German teacher. Even the public school, located on colony property, falls under the scrutiny of Hutterite elders. Explicit social roles and public rites of passage clarify for each person who they are and what is expected of them at every turn. If success can be measured by low rates of attrition, this system of indoctrination, so repulsive to modern thinking, does successfully transmit Hutterian ways across the generations.

Social and Economic Dependence. Communal membership makes Hutterites dependent on the colony for their social and financial survival. Without economic resources or training in financial affairs, it is difficult for persons to abandon the ark. Those who do must start life anew without financial help. Hutterite patterns of education and residential segregation also create social dependence. Those who leave the colony carry few of the social skills necessary to function in the outside world. Their entire support system—family, friends, and history—remains within the colony. Some, of course, do leave and are able to find outside work with the practical skills they have learned. But the social, emotional, and familial strings that tie members to the colony make it difficult to break away. Such social and economic dependency grants the colony enormous power over individuals.

Social Control. All societies must find ways to control the behavior of their members in order to prevent anarchy. Socialization is the most powerful form of social control, but the residential segregation of Hutterite life adds even more controls. Colony life provides continuous surveillance of behavior and shelters individuals from outside influence. Departures and aberrations are easily detected and reported. Severe limits on private space, personal time, and private belongings channel behavior within the normative goals of corporate life. When informal controls break down, Hutterites readily punish children and shame adults to produce desirable behaviors. If necessary, members are shunned for a short time within the colony and eventually excommunicated if they persist in deviance. In all of these ways, social controls funnel individual behavior into desirable patterns that bolster the common life.

Regulating Outside Interaction. Hutterite colonies carefully monitor social interaction with outsiders. The residential segregation of the colonies effectively insulates members from the larger world. Traditional taboos on automobiles, radios, televisions, and personal telephones also shield them from contaminating influences. The practice of endogamy prevents members from marrying anyone outside the ark of the Lord. And by regulating who may travel into nearby towns, colonies also limit access to the world beyond. These means of regulating interaction with the larger society preserve Hutterite identity, underscore the lines of separation, and buffer them from alien cultural influences.

Limiting Colony Size. The Hutterites are astute social engineers. By limiting colony size, they are able to maximize social control without a centralized administrative structure. Over the years Hutterite elders have learned that colonies under 50 or over 150 people are plagued with a multitude of problems. These difficulties are avoided by branching out when a colony exceeds 150 souls. The optimal size of one hundred enhances the dignity of the individual, enables informal controls, and minimizes bureaucratic structures. Each colony enjoys considerable self-autonomy, and leaders have a sense of local self-determination. Moreover, in small colonies individuals feel close to the seat of power even though they may not sit on it, which may compensate a bit for the rigorous control of personal behavior.

Selective Change. A part of Hutterite success flows from their acceptance of new technologies that bolster their economic well-being. They readily adopt technology that boosts productivity, while filtering out changes that threaten communal commitments.[61] Innovation in the religious realm is carefully restricted. By maintaining a sharp dichotomy between technological and religious change, Hutterites have enjoyed the products of a worldly society without drinking from its philosophical spring. By carefully monitoring change, they have managed to enhance their economic well-being without jeopardizing their separatist souls.

Religious Legitimation. Hutterite life is ensconced in a web of religious meanings. The calls to surrender goods, to deny self, and to separate from the world are all framed in religious language, reminding members that they are part of a divine project. Religious understandings enshrine their everyday activities and thus powerfully legitimate well-preserved patterns of social life. The call to obedience uttered by the elder echoes the voice of God. Breaking colony rules is tantamount to sinning against heaven and if not confessed will lead to eternal damnation. These deep religious convictions undergird the entire social system of these pilgrims on the backroad to heaven.

The Hutterites have created a remarkable social experiment that has endured for several centuries. In their eyes, however, communalism is not an interesting social experiment but a sincere attempt to obey Christian teachings that point to eternal life. They believe that their earthly efforts create a foretaste of life eternal—the vestibule of heaven, as they call it. Outsiders may scoff at such notions and argue that, when measured by contemporary standards of happiness, colony life looks more like the anteroom of hell.

In Hutterite society the individual is permitted little self-expression through dress, music, art, and dance. There is little room in this community for intellectual curiosity, sincere doubt, or ambiguity. Individuals may be exhorted to strive for heaven, but they are not encouraged to reach for the stars. Rather, they are admonished to obey their elders. Private time and personal rights, so cherished in the larger culture, disappear in Hutterite life. There is no private property, no personal bank account, no private meal, no personal phone to the outside world, little private space, and precious little personal time in colony life.

All the trappings of individualism—personal rights, belongings, and prerogatives—that are so precious to children of the Enlightenment are stripped from the individual in Hutterite life. In traditional tribal fashion, the community lifts the burden of choice from the shoulders of the individual. There are no worries about career goals, vacation plans, lifestyle options, fads, or fashions here, where the community cares for all. Choice, that symbol of freedom that tops the list of modern virtues, is feared and restricted here. Orderliness and control are the Hutterite values that lead to eternal life.

The community reigns supreme over the individual. In caste-like fashion, occupational roles are assigned to individuals by the men of this patriarchal society. The community determines work schedules, allots clothing, assigns apartments, allocates wine, vetoes marriages, requires attendance at church, shames the deviant, and excommunicates the wayward. Based on their interpretation of Scripture and tradition, the community determines what is virtue and vice, what is pious and evil, even in the realm of personal behavior. And in this patriarchal society, "community" means that male leaders are the ones who determine the rules and speak on behalf of heaven.

Religion is the great legitimater that empowers community life. Indeed, without religious imperatives Hutterite life would surely falter. But moderns might wonder if communal success is only possible with divine aid and worry that the Hutterite experience exemplifies religion in the service of oppression. If religious indoctrination is used to stifle the human spirit, suffocate individuality and thwart freedom of choice this may be closer to the anteroom of hell than the vestibule of heaven.

The Hutterites may violate modern understandings of the ingredients of happiness, but despite their unorthodox ways they have created stable communities that provide an uncommon measure of meaning, identity, and belonging for members. All know who they are, to whom they belong, and why they were born. There is no unemployment here, and indeed people gladly work without thought of a paycheck. There is joy and laughter here, some occasional humor, and of course no worry about retirement or financial security.

This may not be heaven on earth, but it is hardly a road that leads to hell. The growing list of maladies so common to postindustrial societies is rather short here—alienation, homelessness, drug addiction, divorce, domestic abuse, depression, and loneliness. Private property is abolished; but everyone is fed, clothed, and housed with more than ample means. Children are disciplined, but they are very welcomed and loved. Private space is nil, and a hundred eyes are watching, but loneliness is unheard of on this backroad to heaven. The Hutterites have maintained medieval-like villages, insulated from the outside world, that have enabled them to bypass many of the ills of modern life on their heavenward journey. Their experiment involves radical commitments that have, nevertheless, endured over the centuries—commitments that challenge contemporary assumptions about the best road to the pearly gates.

CHAPTER THREE

The Mennonites

Salvation is a gradual project.
—Mennonite farmer

GUARDIANS OF THE HERITAGE

Mennonites trace their roots to the Anabaptists of sixteenth-century Europe. They take their name from a prominent church leader, Menno Simons, who converted from Catholicism to Anabaptism in 1536. Swiss and South-German Mennonites settled in Pennsylvania throughout the eighteenth century and soon became known as outstanding farmers. They gradually moved westward and southward with the frontier, settling in Maryland, Virginia, Ohio, Indiana, Illinois, and other states as well as in Ontario, Canada.[1] Mennonites with Dutch-Russian roots, coming in later waves of immigration, settled in the Great Plains, the Far West, and Canada.

Some forty different Mennonite groups organized in more than two thousand congregations reside in North America today. The groups that have assimilated into mainstream society operate colleges, use modern technology, participate in professional occupations, and dress in contemporary styles. The more traditional, or Old Order Mennonites, reject higher education, restrict the use of technology, and embrace a rural, separatist lifestyle. Old Order Mennonites can be sorted into two major types—those who drive automobiles and those who do not. Those who use horse-and-buggy transportation, sometimes called "team Mennonites" have formed numerous small groups. This chapter focuses on three prominent groups of "team" Mennonites who affiliate together and are organized into three church bodies known as the Groffdale, Virginia, and Ontario (Canada) Conferences.[2]

The Old Orders emerged within the Mennonite fold between 1872 and 1913.[3] After the Civil War, tradition-minded Mennonites began resisting some innovations that were creeping into the church. Those who clung to traditional ways eventually were called Old Orders. Viewed as cultural relics by more progressive Mennonites, the Old Orders see themselves as preservers of the faith. Indeed, they view their progressive Mennonite cousins as wayward liberals. The Old Orders claim less than 10 percent of the U.S. Mennonite membership, which includes an assortment of both mainstream and conservative Mennonite groups.

The Old Order movement budded in the 1860s when conservative-minded members criticized innovations in Mennonite churches near Elkhart, Indiana.[4] A formal separation occurred in Indiana and Ohio in 1872. The resistance gradually spread to Ontario, Canada, in 1889; to Lancaster, Pennsylvania, in 1893; and to Harrisonburg, Virginia, by 1901.[5] Leaders in various states who were guarding the older traditions exchanged letters and visited sympathetic congregations. Although never formally organized, the Old Order movement was well entrenched by the turn of the century. What were the social forces that propelled this movement of renewal and resistance?

After the Civil War, industrialization began transforming American society from farm to factory. The progressive mindset that drove industry brought changes into the life of the church as well. Some Mennonite leaders began borrowing practices from other Protestant churches. Those with a more conservative bent, soon to be known as Old Orders, protested the acceptance of Sunday school, evening services, revival meetings, the use of English in worship, the foreign missions movement, higher education, and other aspects of American culture that were beginning to influence Mennonite life. For Old Orders the sources of spiritual renewal were found in new affirmations of older ways, not in innovative practices from the outside. More than mere reactionaries, they sought to renew the church by reclaiming and revitalizing the precious patterns of the past.

A Mennonite farmer explained the emergence of the Old Order movement this way: "The Old Orders stayed put and held onto the old things, while the progressives went after new things. The more Old Order you are," he said, "the more you think of yourself as sticking to the old ways. You're on the bottom rung of the ladder. The others are moving up."

The Old Order movement can be seen as an alternative renewal movement that reaffirmed the value of traditional understandings in the face of social change.[6] Now a century old, the Old Order movement continues to guard many historic traditions, while many more progressive Mennonites absorb the values of contemporary culture. Today, some "upper-rung" Mennonite groups permit divorce, military service, the ordination of women, homosexual members, and other cultural practices that Old Orders consider sin by biblical standards. Although they share a common theological heritage, Old Order and mainstream Mennonites live very different lives today.

OLD ORDER OBJECTIONS

Since arriving in the New World, Mennonites of Swiss and German descent have spoken a dialect known as Pennsylvania German or "Pennsylvania Dutch." It separated Mennonites from non-German groups and came to symbolize their meek and lowly way of life. English was the currency of the larger society—a world of power, prestige, and politics. Unlike their lowly dialect, English was a high and sophisticated language that could open the doors to the dominant society. As Mennonites of all stripes interacted more with outsiders in the mid-nineteenth century, they naturally began speaking more English. With more and more youth learning English in public schools, progressive church leaders began conducting worship services in the language of the rising generation. Conservatives, on the other hand, protested. They didn't want the foreign language of a worldly society intruding into the very heart of sacred ritual.

Protestant-style Sunday schools caused even greater consternation among tradition-minded Mennonites. Progressive Mennonite leaders welcomed the Sunday school as a much-needed vehicle of Christian education. But to cautious sectarians, Sunday schools were carelessly borrowed from worldly churches that did not espouse the twin pillars of Mennonite faith—nonresistance and nonconformity. Many Sunday schools were also "union" ventures, conducted jointly by several denominations. Separatists to the core, the conservers shied away from such ecumenical projects. Moreover, conservatives feared that the Sunday schools would undercut the role of the family in religious education. The Scriptures, in their eyes, were very clear that *parents* should train their children in the fear of the Lord.

On a deeper level, the Sunday schools represented a specialized and rationalized approach—an industrial model of religious education. Now religious faith would become a cognitive exercise—something to study, memorize, and debate. Mennonites had always emphasized the *practice* of faith, not the study of abstract doctrines. Besides, the Sunday school teachers, who typically taught their classes in English, often displayed a self-confident spirit that eclipsed the habits of Mennonite humility. Sunday school, conservatives argued, would instill pride in young people. Indeed, its proponents often expressed "bold, self-assured attitudes" that hardly reflected a meek and quiet spirit.[7] Moreover, some women taught Sunday School, thus signaling a change in gender roles. In all of these ways, Sunday schools threatened the time-tested patterns of the past that had successfully preserved the faith by simply immersing children in the waters of community life.

Both carriages and bicycles are used to travel to Sunday services at Mennonite meetinghouses. *Source:* Dennis Hughes

Conservatives also objected to holding Protestant-style evening services. These emotion-filled meetings were often called "protracted meetings" because they stretched over a two-week period of time. These meetings featured visiting and sometimes flamboyant evangelists who emphasized personal experience and stirred emotions. Protracted meetings challenged the entrenched patterns of authority as well as some long-held understandings of salvation. Revival meetings reflected the values of an incipient individualism that, conservatives worried, would in time erode the communal foundations of Mennonite faith and life.

Many Mennonite meetinghouses in the nineteenth century did not have an elevated pulpit—a Protestant symbol that raised leaders above their fellow members. To remain on equal footing, Mennonite preachers stood behind a small table. In the Lichty congregation near Lancaster, Pennsylvania, some progressive members built a small platform in their meetinghouse in 1889 to raise the pulpit several inches off the floor. Other members, annoyed by the innovation, tore it out under the cover of darkness. Although few conflicts enjoyed so much intrigue, the incident shows the intensity of feeling that fueled the Old Order movement in one settlement in the late 1800s.[8]

In all of these squabbles, tradition-minded Mennonites were not quarreling with basic Mennonite beliefs or doctrines, nor were they simply resisting a tide of innovation that might sweep them into the mainstream. Rather, they were trying to preserve and renew what they considered to be the core of Mennonite faith. Beneath the rhetoric of public debate was a clash of different moral orders. Old Order sentiments ran against the progressive embrace of individualism, rationalization, and specialization that accompanied the rising tide of industrialization. Old Orders feared that all of these changes would, in time, erode the spiritual and social foundations of their redemptive community.

The introduction of English, Sunday schools, and revival meetings each in their own way embodied a confident individualism that mocked the lowly ways of humility. Bucking trends that they feared would pull them into a whirlpool of worldliness, Old Order Mennonites clutched the anchor of tradition, while large numbers of other Mennonites drifted toward the Protestant mainstream. By the dawn of the twentieth century, the Old Order movement was well entrenched in some regions of the larger Mennonite church.

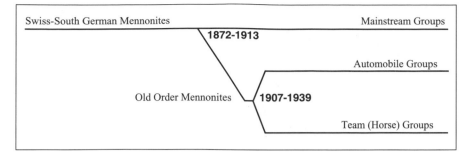

FIGURE 3.1 Formation of Old Order Mennonite Groups in North America

The Team Mennonites

Despite Old Order commitments to conservative ways, new forms of technology stirred controversy in their communities in the early decades of the twentieth century. Heated discussions erupted over the use of electricity and telephones because some members considered them unneeded connections to the outside world. The use of automobiles was another controversial issue. Debates over one or more of these issues led to divisions within Old Order communities in Indiana in 1907, Pennsylvania in 1927, and Ontario in 1939. In each case the more progressive group eventually began to buy cars, and the more traditional group continued to travel by horse and buggy.[9] In Pennsylvania, the automobile group initially insisted that vehicles and their chrome bumpers be painted black to symbolize the separation of the church from the world. Often called "blackbumpers," these car-driving Old Order Mennonites tolerated other forms of technology and eventually accepted English into their worship services as well.[10]

Preserving older habits, the conservatives within Old Order communities continued using horses or "teams" to pull their buggies. They soon became known as the "team" or "horse-and-buggy" Mennonites.[11] The distinction between automobile and team groups gradually crystallized in various settlements, resulting in two streams of Old Order Mennonites by mid-twentieth century. The team Mennonites, profiled in this chapter, are thus double conservatives—having affirmed traditional ways first in the 1890s when other Mennonites were acculturating and then again in the 1920s and 1930s when some Old Orders began driving

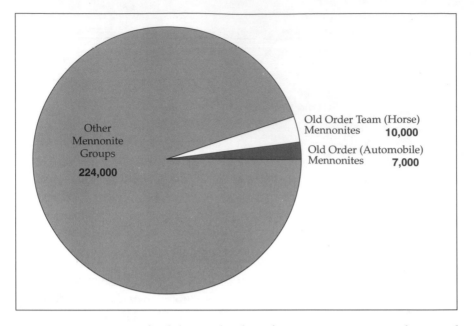

Other
Mennonite
Groups
224,000

Old Order Team (Horse)
Mennonites   **10,000**

Old Order (Automobile)
Mennonites   **7,000**

FIGURE 3.2 Estimated Adult Membership of Mennonite Groups in the United States
Note: Estimates of Old Order team and automobile membership include Canada.
Sources: Mennonite Directory (2000), *Mennonite Church Information* (2000), N. Hostetter (1997), and various Old Order directories and informants.

automobiles. From their perspective, team Mennonites are the oldest of the Old Order, genuine guardians of the heritage, because they have staunchly resisted the forces of change on several occasions.

Unlike the Hutterites, Mennonites own private property. They live on farms and in villages interspersed with English neighbors. Most Mennonites are farmers, though in recent years some have established small shops and industries. Like the Amish, Old Order Mennonites use Pennsylvania German in worship and speak it in everyday conversation in all their settlements except in Virginia.[12] Church services are held in austere meetinghouses that typically lack electricity, plumbing, indoor toilets, modern heating, and air conditioning.

Team Mennonites, unlike the Amish, use tractors in their fields. Most lay members have telephones and electricity in their homes. Mennonites operate one-room parochial schools for their children and generally consider high school unnecessary. They wear plain clothing, although it is less distinctive than that of the Amish. Small plaids, patterns, and figures are acceptable in dresses and shirts, but jewelry of any type is taboo. Women wear a devotional head covering, a cape, and an apron and use a shawl instead of a coat. Mennonite men, unlike their Hutterite, Amish, and Brethren counterparts, do not wear beards and thus are not as easily recognized as "plain" people.

Counting adults and children, the team Mennonites number about 24,000 in North America. Sizable families and a strong rate of retention have enabled them to enjoy steady growth in the twentieth century. More than 70 percent of them live in Pennsylvania and Ontario, but they also reside in nine other states as shown in Table 3.1. New settlements— established in Kentucky (1975), Missouri (1970), New York (1971), Ohio (1973), and Wisconsin (1973)—are rapidly spreading their numbers beyond the traditional strongholds of Pennsylvania, Virginia, and Ontario. Based on the growth of families in the Groffdale Conference between 1987 and 1997, one scholar estimates that their population will double about every sixteen years.[13] Their own internal growth, as well as the cost and scarcity of good farm land in eastern Pennsylvania, has encouraged

TABLE 3.1 ESTIMATED TEAM MENNONITE
POPULATION (ADULTS AND CHILDREN)
BY STATE AND PROVINCE

Pennsylvania	9,650
Ontario	6,900
New York	1,800
Virginia	1,550
Missouri	1,000
Ohio	800
Wisconsin	800
Indiana	700
Kentucky	400
Iowa	300
Michigan	100
Total	24,000

Source: Directory (1997), Directory (1993), and informants in each of the settlements. The estimated population of children and adults includes the Groffdale Conference, Virginia Conference, and Ontario Conference, as well as several independent team groups that are not affiliated with a larger conference.

many families to move to other states. Over a thirty-year period (1968–1998) about 45 percent of the families in one Pennsylvania church district moved to other states.[14] One member in Lancaster County's mother settlement noted that "almost every family has children who moved to other areas: there is a lot of excitement about moving."

ORGANIZATION AND AUTHORITY

Old Order Mennonite church life is loosely organized on three levels: *settlement, congregation,* and *conference.* A settlement is simply the geographical area where members live in proximity. Members of different Mennonite affiliations sometimes live in the same settlement. The congregation is the basic social and religious unit beyond the extended family. Congregations with a common *Ordnung* participate in the same conference, which is an organizational unit held together by a biannual meeting of ordained leaders. Apart from the Scriptures, the conference body, consisting of all ordained leaders, is the highest source of moral authority. The conference body regulates the *Ordnung,* which applies to all congregations. Church life also intersects closely with large extended families that form the foundation of Mennonite society.

Most team Mennonites belong to one of three conferences: Groffdale, Virginia, or Ontario in Canada. The largest conference, Groffdale, is based in Lancaster County, Pennsylvania. Deriving its name from an old congregation, the Groffdale Conference has congregations in Pennsylvania as well as in eight other states. The three major conferences (Groffdale, Ontario, and Virginia) cooperate in general ways and permit each other's ministers to preach in their services. Although sharing similar beliefs, the conferences diverge on some practices. Ontario, for instance, prohibits closed carriages but permits rubber tires on tractors, small pulpits in meeting houses, and long ties for young men.[15] The Groffdale Conference permits closed carriages but prohibits standard rubber tires on tractors, ties on men, and pulpits in meetinghouses.

Despite these and other differences, all three groups share an Old Order worldview. As shown in Table 3.2, the three conferences have about fifty-seven meetinghouses, and nearly one hundred and forty ordained officials. An assortment of small independent team groups do not affiliate with any of the three larger conferences.[16]

Conference Affiliation	Meetinghouses	Bishops	Ministers	Deacons	Estimated Population
Groffdale	41	11	58	31	14,000
Ontario	15	3	16	15	6,900
Virginia	3	1	4	2	1,000
Independent	-	-	-	-	2,100
Totals	59	15	78	48	24,000

Source: Groffdale Conference Calendar of Meetings 1999, Kalender der Mennoniten-Germeinden in Ontario 1993, Hurd (1999:26, 39), and informants in each settlement.
Note: Population estimates include children and adult members. Apart from estimates by Scott (1996), little statistical information is available on the small, independent team groups.

Mennonites have large families organized along traditional lines. In the Groffdale Conference, families average between eight and nine children. Indeed, about 10 percent of the families have twelve or more children. Slightly over 50 percent of the community is under 18 years of age.[17] Single parent households, typical in the larger society, are unknown among the Mennonites, where nearly 90 percent of the households are traditional family units. The remaining ones consist of widowers, widows, and unmarried women.[18] Large families and a robust rate of retention feed the growth of the community.

Beyond the extended family, the local congregation forms the basic unit of Mennonite life. In addition to Sunday morning services, frequent visiting provides the social glue of community life. "The congregation is the social center, the focal point," said a Mennonite farmer. Horse-and-buggy transportation keeps social life tethered around the local congregation. Mennonites typically participate in the congregation closest to their home, but congregations do not have precise geographical boundaries like those of the Amish. Said one member, "There's no rule against it, but it's frowned upon if you drive past another meetinghouse." About two-thirds of the Groffdale congregations gather for worship every Sunday. Some congregations continue the older practice of meeting every other Sunday. In a few cases, meetinghouses are shared with Old Order automobile groups every other Sunday.

Members frequently worship with other congregations and spend

Mennonite men erect a new barn. Extended family and community networks spring into action in response to community needs. *Source:* Keith Baum

Sunday afternoon fellowshipping with friends and relatives. Ontario congregations typically follow the older pattern of holding services every other Sunday. Using a traditional hosting system, Ontario families prepare extra food on the Sunday that services are held at their meeting-house. Visitors from other congregations enjoy "dinner" in the homes of friends following the worship service. "The only disadvantage," confessed one member, "is that we have to feed so many people and sometimes it takes two sittings." Sunday afternoon visiting is an important ritual that strengthens the web of community. Frequent visiting weaves together relationships in the congregation, neighborhood, extended family, and larger ethnic community. Families sometimes rent buses or vans to visit distant settlements for weddings, funerals, and special church meetings. The fabric of Old Order life is reinforced by the rituals of visitation.

Team Mennonites do not have their own church newsletter or magazine. Many, however, read *Die Botschaft* (The Message), a weekly newspaper circulated widely in both Amish and Mennonite communities.

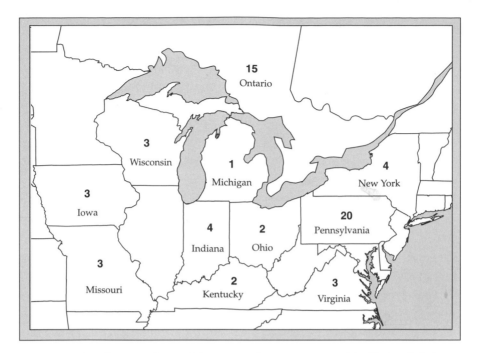

FIGURE 3.3 Distribution of Team Mennonite Congregations in North America
Source: Groffdale Conference Calendar of Meetings (1999).

Despite the German title, the text is in English. Correspondents from settlements across the country inform readers of the weather, harvests, visitors, church affairs, social gatherings, and other tidbits of news from their local area. Old Order Mennonites also read and contribute essays to three magazines produced by Pathway Publishers, an Amish press located in Ontario, Canada. These media are important means of building community awareness and solidarity across many Old Order settlements.

Mennonite leadership is organized around three roles: bishop, minister, and deacon. A bishop typically oversees the ministers and deacons of several congregations. As the senior official, a bishop presides over baptisms, weddings, confessions, communions, and excommunications. He also instructs the baptismal candidates, interprets the *Ordnung,* and guides the overall welfare of the community. The senior bishop, ordained the longest, serves as chairman of the conference and thus exercises considerable influence over the social and religious life of the community.

Ministers are responsible for preaching in Sunday services as well as

TABLE 3.3 SOCIAL RESTRICTIONS OF THE GROFFDALE CONFERENCE

Forbidden: Test of Membership		
Buying lottery tickets	Large worldly picnics	Political meetings
Electioneering	Life insurance	Secret societies
Hiring lawyers	Manufacturing weapons	Serving on jury for murder case
Horse racing	Military service	Surprise birthday parties
Labor unions	Police duty	Theater

Strongly Discouraged: Not Test of Membership		
Alcoholic drinks	Fortune tellers	Pornographic books
Amusement places	Games of chance	Quack doctors
Bowling alleys	Golf courses	Shows
Buying on Sunday	Hunting trips	Skating rinks
Card games	Movies	Tobacco
Coed swimming	Pleasure places	Worldly music
Festivals	Pleasure trips	Yoga
Fishing trips	Pool rooms	

Source: The Ordnung of the Groffdale Mennonite Conference. The restrictions vary somewhat in Virginia, Indiana, and Ontario.

for leadership in congregational and community life. They typically preach from a chapter in the Bible rather than on a topical theme as is common in other denominations. Deacons aid the work of ministry by reading Scripture during worship. They also assist at baptism and help to serve the bread and wine at communion. Like their Amish counterparts, deacons also collect material aid when members are afflicted by medical emergencies or natural disasters. Moreover, they help the bishop to enforce the Ordnung of the conference by visiting wayward members.

Ordained leaders do not receive any formal pay but may receive occasional gifts of food or other gestures of good will. Without formal theological training, they serve the congregation throughout their active lives. Viewed as servants of the congregation, they are charged with maintaining its spiritual welfare and preventing any wayward drift into the world.

Old Order Mennonite society has no bureaucratic organizations. There are no corporate headquarters, paid officials, or annual conventions—not even retirement homes, publishing houses, mission boards, colleges, or seminaries. One-room schools, organized by local parents, are the only formal type of organization. On this level, Mennonite society stands far apart from the complicated structures and large-scale organizations that dominate American society.

Even mutual aid in time of fire, flood, or other emergency is handled in an informal fashion. An informal mutual aid committee organizes assistance, but in the moment of need everyone "pitches in" to help clean up rubble or rebuild a home. Reluctant to depend on commercial insurance to bail them out of disasters, they turn to fellow believers for aid and support. Mennonites believe that their "confidence should be in the Lord." Members are urged to trust in God and in the resources of their community.

A Fence around the Sheep

Although the rules and discipline of the church, known as the *Ordnung,* are transmitted through example and discussion, a written version is available to the leaders of the Groffdale Conference.[19] They read it to the congregation twice a year at the preparatory service before their biannual communion services. "The members will correct us," said one bishop, "if we miss anything in it."

An embodiment of the moral order, the *Ordnung* serves a variety of functions: it (1) anchors the church to its heritage, (2) confesses its Christian faith, (3) marks the boundaries of the community, (4) affirms the authority of church leaders, (5) articulates basic Mennonite values (6) regulates the use of technology, (7) expresses the essence of Mennonite identity, and (8) promotes order and unity across the church. It also defines the role of bishops, ministers, and deacons, as well as the threefold responsibilities of lay members: "to be obedient to the word of God . . . , to keep the rules and ordinances of the church, and to support the ministers of the congregation." In short, the *Ordnung* is a guide for daily living, specifying both the pathways and the prohibitions of Mennonite life.

A Mennonite historian compares the *Ordnung* to a fence around the sheepfold as described in the New Testament Gospel of John. In his words, "There is a fence around the sheepfold; not to deprive the sheep of better pasture; but to shelter them from marauding wolves. The door to the fold is always open to the sheep, so they can enter and leave at will, to seek pasture. The wolves and thieves cannot enter by the door, but may try to enter by climbing the fence. How foolish it would be for the sheep to try to tear down the fence."[20] The *Ordnung,* in Mennonite eyes, provides guidelines that form a fence around the fold of faith.

To use another image, the *Ordnung* also serves as a means of keeping order in the household of God. It is the broom, so to speak, of the ordained officials. As stewards of the household of God, Mennonite leaders sometimes talk of "keeping house"—keeping order in the church. In the words of the *Ordnung,* "We want to add nothing nor subtract anything from the Gospel but simply keep house with the whole Gospel of Jesus Christ and with the evangelical counsel of the church."[21] The *Ordnung* includes taboos and expected behaviors, but it acknowledges that "external ceremonies alone cannot save anyone." True faith involves being "born anew of water and the spirit." Ordained leaders, interpret and enforce the *Ordnung.* Although this collective understanding is endorsed by the entire conference, individual bishops can exercise some influence in its application.

One member explained that there are really five levels of moral conduct in Mennonite life. On the first level are acceptable behaviors—the hundreds of things that people are permitted to do without question—eat ice cream cones, wear shoes, play softball, kiss their spouse, and read the daily newspaper.

The second step consists of mild taboos that Mennonites simply take for granted but rarely discuss. Riding in hot air balloons, wearing wristwatches, neckties, or bikinis, using nail polish or cosmetics of any type—these are simply understood as off limits for upright members of the community. Someone who engages in these behaviors will of course stir commotion in the community.

Third-order things are "testified against" by the church but are not a test of membership. There, of course, are some variations in prohibited behaviors from settlement to settlement. Borderline activities include owning stylish furniture, attending festivals, going on pleasure trips, or receiving social security payments. In the words of one bishop, "Good members just don't do these things," yet they are not strictly taboo. These talked-about and frowned-upon activities also include, among other things, purchasing goods on Sunday, drinking alcohol, attending festivals, playing golf, and listening to worldly music. From time to time members may be tempted to indulge in these and other activities, shown in Table 3.3, and thus the church needs to "testify against them." Someone who

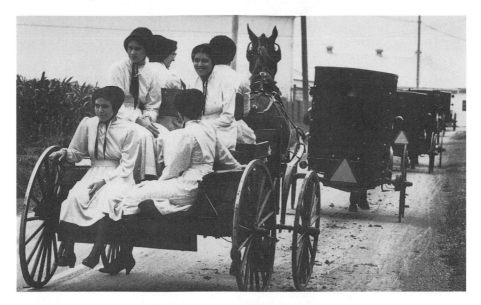

Six Mennonite women on their way to a youth gathering. The *Ordnung* governs dress styles as well as transportation. *Source:* Keith Baum

engages in them may be admonished to stop but will not likely be expelled from the church. Some may persist with a habit such as smoking without risking expulsion from the church.

Forbidden behaviors, on the other hand, include the ownership of automobiles, computers, and televisions and entrance into the military. Those who cross these lines face excommunication if they fail to confess their behavior and change their ways. These fourth-order things, strictly forbidden by the *Ordnung,* are a test of membership. Someone who enters military service, races horses, or joins a labor union will, if not repentant, be excommunicated from the church. Some behaviors, once forbidden in earlier days, are difficult to remove from the *Ordnung.* "Large worldly picnics," technically forbidden, are "pretty much a joke" said one member. "We have a lot of large picnic gatherings, and no one says much about it."

The fifth and final moral level includes things that, according to Mennonite belief, are forbidden by biblical teaching—drunkenness, fornication, divorce, and swearing oaths. Because these are "already covered by Scripture," the church sees no need to speak of them in the *Ordnung.* The

Ordnung specifically addresses levels three and four—"testified against" and "forbidden"—and by implication any activity clearly forbidden by biblical teaching as well.

Ordained leaders are expected to model higher ideals of behavior than others in the community. Thus, borderline behaviors that are discouraged for lay members are forbidden for ordained officials. Ministers in the Groffdale Conference, for example, may not farm tobacco. In the 1940s and 50s, some lay members began installing electricity in their homes despite the frown of the church. Ministers, however, were not permitted to use electricity in their homes until the mid-1990s. Standards of dress are also stiffer for ministers and their wives. Ordained men, for example, are expected to wear a special overcoat in the winter.

The lines drawn by the *Ordnung* symbolically separate the church from the world. Mennonite leaders admit that "not everything is evil about the things forbidden." In the words of the *Ordnung*, "If we owned all these worldly things, we would not be separate from the world and its worldly symbols. So we believe it is pleasing to God, that we do not have these things and do not set our hearts on them, but rather believe in the Lord Jesus Christ."

In the final analysis, the *Ordnung* represents the sacred authority of the church over the individual. The various applications of the *Ordnung* may at times appear to be inconsistent and confusing. And indeed, interpretations of it by church leaders may vary, because the detail of practice does not always matter. What does matter is the individual's attitude toward the authority of the church and his or her willingness to obey it.

A Plain and Humble Life

Unlike modern culture that values personal achievement and acclaim, Mennonite life lifts up the virtue of humility. "God resisteth the proud and giveth grace to the humble," leaders frequently note, citing James 4:6. In the *Ordnung*, members are admonished "not to think after high things, but rather to keep ourselves lowly, and live in humility as pilgrims and strangers in this world." They are called to humble themselves in the sight of the Lord and urged not to boast or do things that call attention to themselves and mock the virtue of meekness. Pleas for humility and simplicity call members to self-denial and obedience. The *Ordnung* reads,

"Let us be plain and humble in our homes, clothing, carriages, and everything we own." Mennonite leaders are even reluctant to count individual members, preferring instead to count households and congregations. The values of Mennonite culture accent communal patterns that contrast with the individualism of modern life that trumpets self-acclaim.

Jewelry and makeup of every sort are taboo. Even wristwatches are forbidden, because they are "objects of pride and decoration." Women are urged to keep their pocket watches "under their capes" and not use them "for adornment." Cameras are forbidden, and members are not to pose for photographs. Mennonites discourage personal photographs and portraits because they highlight the individual and encourage pride. Photographs are sometimes compared to "graven images" that are prohibited by the second commandment in Exodus 20:4. Colorful decorations on buggies, carriages, and harnesses are also discouraged, along with "stylish" furniture. "You don't have to have a car to have pride," remarked one bishop. Pride expresses itself in any splashy display of clothing as well as in speech and posture.

Musical instruments are forbidden in homes and, of course, in worship services. The *Ordnung* is very specific in identifying pianos, organs, violins, and guitars. These instruments are not only symbols of worldly culture but also tools of self-expression that might cultivate pride if individuals show off their musical skills. Accordions, although not strictly off-limits, are "counseled against" and frowned upon in youth singings and gatherings. Mouth organs, small and unpretentious, are acceptable.

Commercialized entertainment is considered a self-gratifying activity that leads to mischief, worldliness, and sin. Thus, members are counseled to "stay away" from amusements—shows, movies, festivals, card games, pool rooms, golf courses, bowling alleys, "and all worldly music and pleasure places." The taboo list includes horse races, pleasure trips, fishing and hunting excursions, and beach trips, as well as attendance at professional sporting events.[22] Such amusements are considered a waste of time that encourages self-indulgence and intermingling with the world in ways that might lead to sloth and pride.

Coupled with pleas to live a plain and humble life are admonitions to obey the *Ordnung* of the church and its ordained leaders. Indeed, the *Ordnung* accents the virtues of repentance, penitence, and confession. Those who refuse advice, who remain stubborn and disobedient, will eventually be excommunicated. The emphasis on humility and obedience underscores the primacy of the community over the individual, steering members away from worldly behavior and harnessing their energies for the collective good.

The *Ordnung* gives explicit guidance for attire. The wearing of worldly styles, Mennonites believe, betrays a heart attuned to the world. Common dress marks the boundaries of the community; it preaches a continuous sermon about identity, belonging, and separation. Those who wear the garb forgo their right to self-expression and signal compliance with the moral order. Members who scorn dress regulations evince, in Mennonite eyes, a proud and unrepentant heart.[23]

After they are married, men are expected to wear dark, plain suits for worship services; colored or "two-tone" suits are not permitted. The following items are also taboo for men: belts, neckties, cowboy clothing, caps with bills, colored hats, colored coats, and any stylish clothing or shoes. Men do not wear beards, and the *Ordnung* advises them not to go shirtless, wear long hair or sideburns, or grow a mustache. Baseball players may not wear uniforms, but small game and deer hunters may wear orange colored safety jackets. Front bill caps and neckties, never worn by Groffdale men, are widely worn by Ontario Mennonites.

Women are expected to wear a cape and apron over their dresses. They also wear a head covering large enough to cover their ears, with strings that tie under the chin. Their hair is not to be cut or worn loosely, but rather is pulled tightly into a bun under the head covering. The following items are taboo: short dresses, slacks, formfitting dresses, and sheer or large print fabrics. Unlike the Amish, Mennonites permit clothing with small print designs. Large, bold, or brightly colored prints in shirts and dresses are not acceptable. Moreover, women may not wear collars, lace, or wide cuffs on their dresses, or other new styles of clothing. Plain bonnets and shawls are worn for worship. The *Ordnung* also admonishes parents not to "adorn their children."[24]

There are always some members who chaff at the requirements, so church leaders continually need to remind their flock to stay away from the stylish dress that leads to pride and worldliness. But despite occasional streaks of pride, Mennonite attire appears plain and simple beside the designer fashions in shopping malls.

Mennonite writer Isaac Horst calls his people "separate and peculiar" in a booklet by that title. Their basic theological beliefs are described in eighteen articles of faith drawn up in 1632 by Mennonites in Dordrecht, Holland.[25] The so-called Dordrecht Confession of Faith, also used by the Amish, contains Orthodox Christian beliefs as well as those unique to Mennonites. Nonconformity, also known as "separation from the world," is a pervasive theme in Mennonite life. The "world" in the Mennonite mind means the norms, values, and institutions of the broader society. Grounded in a variety of biblical texts that call the church to separate itself from evil, the principle of separation from the world regulates external social relations, filters the influence of the broader culture, and nurtures a distinctive Mennonite identity. This Anabaptist version of a two-kingdom theology emphasizes the separation of the church from the larger society and serves as a map for Mennonites on the backroad to heaven.

"Our desire," writes one Mennonite historian, "is to be a chosen generation, a royal priesthood, a holy nation, a peculiar people, a glorious church without spot or wrinkle."[26] Old Order leaders sometimes describe themselves as pilgrims and strangers who are merely passing through the present world in search of an abiding heavenly city.

As noted above, Mennonites forbid participation in public fairs, national celebrations, civic clubs, organized sports, and political campaigns. Membership in lodges, secret societies, and labor unions is also taboo. In the Groffdale *Ordnung*, young people are encouraged to spend their leisure time "among themselves, not in worldly places or in town, as the world, buying soft drinks, ice cream, and such things on the Lord's day." Ontario Mennonites explicitly forbid members from serving as board members on councils, public organizations, and corporations. While the conviction to be a separate people persists, its practical application is updated and revised to accommodate changing social conditions.

Separation from the world, however, does not prohibit contact with outsiders. A study of Ontario Mennonite men found that 76 percent had a "good" friendship with someone outside the Mennonite faith. Moreover, 60 percent had helped repair or rebuild a neighbor's barn, and over 50 percent had exchanged labor with their non-Mennonite neighbors.[27] The level of interaction with outsiders would likely be lower in some other communities.

Among Ontario Mennonites, lightning rods are forbidden because they might obstruct the will of divine providence. Life insurance is off-limits because it places a monetary value on human life and betrays a lack of trust in God and the church to assist in time of need. The Groffdale *Ordnung* discourages "buying and selling as a daily business." Members are permitted to sell the products they produce but not to work as merchants who only buy and sell for profit. Betting, gambling, playing the lottery, and indulging in other "games of chance" are forbidden as well as going to fortune tellers.

Separation from the world also entails a separation of church and state. Mennonites cite various scriptures to buttress the line between righteousness and worldly citizenship. To remain on the side of righteousness, church members refrain from holding public office and participating in political campaigns. Ontario Mennonites forbid voting, and the Groffdale Conference strongly discourages it. Government subsidies are generally refused because Mennonites believe the church should care for its own and not rely on the state. Mennonites have been exempted from Social Security in the United States and from the Canadian Pension Plan. Church members, according to Mennonite teaching, are responsible to care for the material needs of one another.

By the same logic, leaders counsel against receiving welfare payments, food stamps, unemployment and disability payments, and workers' compensation for job injuries. And yet separation from civil authority does not imply disdain or belligerence. On the contrary, Mennonites pay their taxes and seek to honor and pray for government leaders. But praying is different from voting—Mennonites are urged to refrain from direct political participation. Said one member, "We do what the government demands as long as it doesn't go against our nonresistant way of life."

Mennonites seek to practice the literal words of Jesus to "love enemies" and "resist not evil," as well as the Apostle Paul's admonition to overcome evil with love rather than vengeance. They have sometimes called themselves a "defenseless people."[28] Practicing nonresistance, Mennonites, in the words of the *Ordnung*, try to "live the Sermon on the Mount . . . , do no evil to anyone, do not go to war, or do noncombatant service, or police duty," nor help manufacture "war weapons or train for war." Parents are counseled not to buy guns or military type toys for their children.

As conscientious objectors, Mennonites refuse induction into the military. Fortunately, both the United States and Canada have historically provided alternative options for conscientious objectors. Beyond a boycott of military service, nonresistance is a broad principle that applies to all aspects of domestic, social, and business life. Hence, Mennonites refuse to engage in litigation to protest violations of their rights or to file legal charges against others who have trespassed or wronged them in some way. The *Ordnung* specifically forbids hiring "lawyers to defend ourselves in a court trial."

Serving on a jury for a murder case is taboo in the Groffdale Conference because it might lead to the death penalty. All voting and jury duty are prohibited by Ontario Conference, and the coercive tactics of labor unions place them off limits as well. The Mennonite avoidance of politics is tied to their belief in nonresistance. To hold public office not only places one on a worldly pedestal, it also means participating in a system that will ultimately resort to violence, litigation, and other means of coercion to protect its interests. For all of these reasons, political participation, especially office holding, is viewed as inconsistent with the peaceful and meek ways of Jesus.

FITTING IN WITH MENNONITE WAYS

Because they do not actively seek outside converts, the Mennonite future rests on the recruitment of their young. From an early age, Mennonite children are molded in the ways of humility by parents and community members who emphasize obedience and respect for authority. Parents set specific guidelines for behavior, support private schools, and forbid access to mass media. Spankings or strappings are added occasionally because parents believe that the Bible teaches them to train children in the path of obedience.

While many evangelical groups emphasize dramatic personal conversion, Mennonites have a different view. "Salvation is a gradual project," said one member. "We start earlier and work on it longer. It's not so much what's up here," he said pointing to his head, "it's more a matter of fitting in with our ways. I don't think there is a Mennonite who could tell you the day and time they were saved. Even at baptism some may not be completely saved, but baptism helps to point them in the right direction."[29]

Rather than calling for dramatic, emotion-filled turning points, which one member dubbed "flash conversions," Mennonites believe that salvation occurs quietly as young people gradually fit into the ways of their people. A younger member insisted, however, that, "there does come a time, a moment at the crossroad when a person is born again, but we don't play it up because we fight against pietism." In the Mennonite view, salvation is found within the church, the redemptive community, as individuals find a peaceful relationship with God and their fellow believers.

Proper training funnels their offspring toward salvation and membership in the life of the church.[30] Indeed, in one church district in Pennsylvania, 95 percent of nearly two hundred children joined the church.[31] The "gradual project" appears to be largely successful, because across all the settlements about 80 percent or more of the children join the church. The exact number fluctuates from community to community, but all things considered, about four out of five young people join the church of their birthright.[32]

Children grow up in the thicket of a large family where it is not uncommon to have a hundred first cousins. In the Groffdale Conference, 44 percent of the families carry three surnames: Martin, Zimmerman, and Hoover. Ethnicity runs even thicker in Ontario, where 61 percent of the families hold three names: Martin, Weber, and Brubacher.[33] Deprived of television, day care, and most commercial toys, children learn farm and household chores at an early age. They enjoy homespun play, simple toys, the companionship of animals, and outdoor recreation—softball, fishing, skating, and sledding. Mary Ann Horst describes her Old Order Mennonite childhood as a happy time surrounded by family, friends, and numerous pets.[34]

Responding to a question about the deprivation of children, Mennonite Isaac Horst quips, "Oh, our poor deprived children . . . we deprive them of qualified teachers . . . of education beyond the eighth grade. We even deprive them of that greatest of educators, the television set. They are deprived of the opportunity to watch movies, exhibitions, baseball, and hockey games . . . to go to the beach, the cottage, or summer camp." Deprived of these "advantages," children are expected to "feed the chickens, sweep the floor, and fill the woodbox after coming home from school. On Saturdays and holidays they help with planting the garden and later, with picking berries and cherries, peas and beans, corn and potatoes. They drive a tractor or a team of horses for loading hay and cultivating crops. They have very little leisure time."

Horst concludes with the playful suggestion that, "the lack of TV does not seem to hamper their education." Mennonite children are bilingual, and according to him, the trades that they learn through practical apprenticeships "serve them as well as a college degree." This Old Order farmer argues that there are "blessings in deprivation." Instead of public entertainment, "our children find enjoyment in nature on the farm: the baby chicks, cuddly kittens, and playful puppies. They learn to know and appreciate the wild animals and birds that abound in woodland and meadow. They swim and fish in ponds and streams. Above all, they enjoy learning by doing."[35] This somewhat idyllic view of Mennonite children overlooks, perhaps, the struggles, feuds, and disappointments that are also part of Mennonite childhood.[36]

In the first half of the twentieth century, Mennonite youth attended rural public schools; however, the massive consolidation of public schools in the 1950s shook the stable patterns of the past. Old Order parents did not want their children bussed away to strange places where they would be taught by strange teachers and immersed in teenage culture. Moreover, parents felt that an eighth-grade education was adequate for farming families. In tandem with the Amish, Mennonite parents in some areas refused to send their children to newly consolidated schools. Clashes with public officials were sometimes harsh. These conflicts spurred the development of private Mennonite schools in the 1950s and 1960s.[37] In a 1972 case that also covered Old Order Mennonites, the U.S. Supreme Court permitted Amish youth to end their formal schooling with the eighth grade.[38]

Team Mennonites in North American operate about one hundred and fifty elementary schools for pupils in grades one through eight.[39] The schools are organized by parents, not by the church. Many schools are administered jointly with the Amish and some other conservative Mennonite groups. School houses, often located on a plot of ground at the edge of a farm, may be within a mile or so of home. An average of 32 pupils attend each school, typically a one-room operation, except in Ontario where two rooms are more typical. Several fathers serve as directors for each school, supervising curriculum, maintaining the building, and hiring teachers.[40]

A Mennonite teacher and her pupils in a one-room school. *Source:* Keith Baum

The teachers are generally women who have been trained in Mennonite schools but have not attended high school or college. Teachers develop their skills by attending teachers' meetings; reading the *Blackboard Bulletin,* a teachers' magazine published by the Amish; and learning from other seasoned teachers.

Lessons are conducted in English. The curriculum emphasizes basic skills in reading, writing, spelling, arithmetic, history, and geography. Except in Ontario, science is not taught. Sex education is taboo. Television, computers, videos, and other forms of modern technology are missing from the schools. Pupils carry their own lunch and are responsible for janitorial chores around the schools.

Although religion is not formally taught in the schools, religious values permeate the classroom and playground. The parochial schools play an important role in passing on traditional Mennonite values. They also shield youth from the values of the dominant culture and insulate them from worldly teenage culture and friendships. The schools do not prepare students for college, but they do equip them to lead meaningful and productive lives in the Mennonite community.

One Mennonite father described the teenage years as a "dangerous gap." Young people typically leave school by age 14 but are not baptized until they reach 17 to 19 years of age. They are expected to comply with the *Ordnung* of the church after baptism, but before that they have more freedom. The extent of rebellion during the "gap" between school and baptism varies from settlement to settlement. Some young people wear worldly clothing, attend movies, purchase tape players, smoke, and drink alcohol. There are also some cases of sexual immorality before marriage. Although the church officially discourages it, folk dancing is quite common at youth gatherings.

Rebellious behaviors, according to some informants, have declined in the Groffdale Conference in recent years. With many youth baptized by age 18, the opportunity for rebellion shrinks. An Ontario observer noted that smoking and drinking have also dipped among youth in his community, but some teens still disrespect church and parental authority. Despite the difficulties, the church tries, in the words of one member, "to keep young people funneled in a positive direction" so that they will eventually be baptized and fit fully into Old Order ways.

Baptism and Marriage

Baptism symbolizes the formal entry into Mennonite society. Although it is an individual decision, most of the applicants are 17 to 19 years of age. In early summer the candidates for baptism are invited to meet the ministers in an anteroom of the meetinghouse prior to a Sunday morning service. The ordained leaders, seated in order of seniority, "emphasize the need of being saved and the seriousness of life," said one bishop. "We ask them if they are willing to be shown a better way—willing to give in if someone sees something out of line in their life." The youth who answer "yes" attend six "instruction meetings" on Sunday afternoons throughout the summer months. Leaders use these meetings to instruct applicants on basic Mennonite beliefs. Ministers review three articles of the Dordrecht Confession of Faith per session, asking each applicant if they "understand and believe" the article.

In the morning service on the Sunday before the baptism, members of the congregation may raise concerns about any of the candidates. At a special meeting of candidates before baptism, the ministers ask them if they are willing to follow the *Ordnung* and want to proceed with baptism. In preparation for future leadership, the young men also promise to serve as ministers should the congregation ever call them.

During the baptismal ceremony, the applicants stand before the bishop at the front of the meetinghouse and respond to three questions: (1) Do you believe in one almighty God, who created heaven and earth; in Christ Jesus, his only begotten son; and in the Holy Spirit, who proceeds from the Father and Son? (2) Are you sorry for your past sins and willing to renounce Satan and the dark Kingdom of this world, your own will and all the satanical works of this world? and (3) Are you willing to submit to the Gospel of Jesus Christ, especially Matthew 18?[41] The passage in Matthew 18 describes the three-step pattern of discipline used by the church and in the baptismal context means that the candidate is willing to accept the moral authority of the church.

After the candidates have responded, they kneel, and the congregation arises for prayer. Following the prayer, the applicants remain kneeling. One by one, they are baptized as a deacon pours water into the bishop's cupped hands above their heads. The bishop then pronounces them baptized in the name of the Father, the Son, and the Holy Ghost. The deacon's wife removes the head coverings from the heads of the women; the bishop's wife replaces them after the baptism.

After all are baptized and still kneeling, the bishop offers the right hand of fellowship to each one as they arise to a new beginning. Then the bishop and his wife greet each male and female member respectively with a kiss of peace. The newly baptized members return to their seats, and the service ends with an admonition and prayer by the bishop. The new members are now able to fully participate in the communion services and counsel meetings of the congregation.[42]

Baptism always precedes marriage because a bishop will only marry people who are members of the church. The church does not arrange marriages, but it supervises the wedding through the bishop who performs the ceremony. Although a wedding date may be set several months in advance, it is usually secret until it is "published" or announced in a church service about three weeks before the wedding.[43] Mennonite weddings are typically held on a Tuesday or Thursday in the Groffdale Conference, and usually on Wednesday or Thursday in Ontario.

The wedding is an all-day affair, usually held in the home of the bride. Hostlers are on hand to care for horses and carriages—marking them with chalk so they are not mismatched at the end of the day. The hostlers are usually tipped for their service. Guests are often served cookies and sometimes a small glass of wine in an upstairs room before a "caller" invites them downstairs to their seats. A bridal party of several couples accompany the bride and groom, who sit directly in front of the bishop. Marriage is a ritual entry into adulthood, and the couple are expected to dress in the order of the particular church. The service lasts for about an hour and a half and includes congregational singing, Scripture reading, and a sermon. The couple responds to the wedding vows asked by the bishop and then joins their right hands as he pronounces them married. There is no kiss, exchange of rings, candles, flowers, or special music.

After the wedding, the guests gather for a large meal that may be served in five or six seatings to accommodate the numerous guests. Following the feast, guests join together in singing and visiting. The singing typically begins with German songs and shifts to English in the late afternoon. Younger couples and singles stay for an evening meal, merrymaking, games, and more singing. In Pennsylvania the hostlers may bring a blanket full of balloons and candy to throw over the couple. The groom is sometimes thrown over a fence to signal his leaving the singles and joining the married. Friends of the bride may grab her and try to "shake out her childhood." The merriment, sometimes including square dancing, may continue until midnight. The couple does not take a formal honeymoon, but they typically visit relatives on Sundays for several weeks. The bride and groom receive gifts at the wedding as well as later when visiting relatives.

Based on the biblical order of authority in 1 Corinthians 11, the church considers women subordinate to men. One Mennonite writer argues that this does not mean that women are "second rate creatures."[44] Wedding vows do not contain the word *submit*, but Mennonite women are expected to yield to their husbands who are viewed as the spiritual head of the home. Marriage roles and patterns, of course, vary with the personalities of the spouses. Mennonite marriages rarely end in separation, and divorce is simply not an option. Indeed, divorce would be cause for excommunication from the church.

Citing biblical passages, Mennonites teach that women should be silent in church services. They do not hold formal roles in congregational life and do not serve on committees. Women often speak out in council meetings regarding expectations for women's dress and behavior. Women are expected to "adorn themselves with a meek and quiet spirit" rather than with fancy fashions, outward cosmetics, and "forward" behavior.

Instead of working away from home, married women are expected to care for their families, households, and gardens.[45] Many do their own sewing in addition to other domestic duties. Most women do not have a regular source of income, but some sell vegetables or baked goods in road-side stands to supplement their household income. A growing number operate small home-based businesses that produce and sell dry goods, baked goods, crafts, and quilts. Many school teachers are single women. Other single women work for several years before marriage as domestic workers, sales clerks, and general helpers in a variety of Mennonite and non-Mennonite shops and industries.[46]

CONGREGATIONAL LIFE AND RITUAL

Sunday Meeting. Sunday services form the heart of Old Order religion.[47] Members and children riding in horse-drawn carriages converge at the meetinghouse before 9:00 or 10:00 A.M., depending on the season. The two-hour service is normally conducted in Pennsylvania German dialect. If outsiders are visiting, a minister may preach part of his sermon in English. In the Virginia Conference, English is always used. Ordained officials sit on a bench at the front of the meetinghouse and face the congregation. Men and women sit on separate sides of the simple meeting room.

Unlike Catholic and Protestant practice, there are no church school classes, offerings, choirs, musical instruments, ushers, candles, robes, altar, or printed liturgy. The congregation kneels for prayer and sings in unison at a slow and measured pace. A ten-verse hymn may stretch over some fifteen minutes. Children sit patiently with their parents during the lengthy service. A mood of lowliness, solemnity, and simplicity engulfs the service as the community yields itself up to the mysteries of divine providence.

The order of service varies slightly from community to community, but the basic format follows a twelve-step sequence.[48]

The Groffdale Conference rotates the preaching assignments of min-

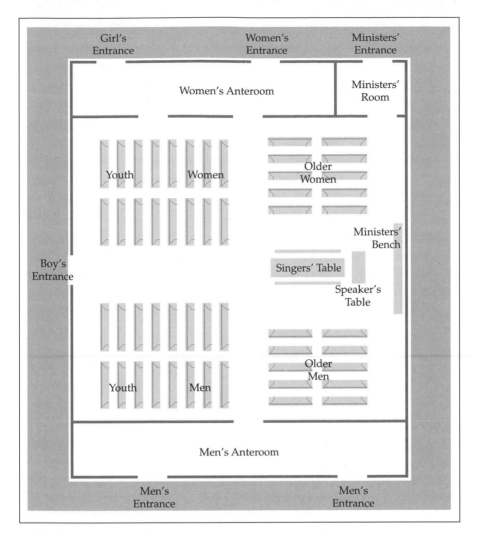

FIGURE 3.4 Seating Patterns in a Typical Groffdale Conference Meetinghouse
Note: Diagram not drawn to scale.

isters throughout the settlement. Every minister is scheduled to preach at least once in each meetinghouse throughout the year, and neighboring ministers even more frequently. "We feel very strongly," said one member, "about shuffling our ministers around so that no one knows who will preach. This keeps everything tied together." This unpublicized pattern

TABLE 3.4 TYPICAL ORDER OF A MENNONITE WORSHIP SERVICE

Consultation	Ministers meet in counsel room to pray and to assign responsibilities for the service.
Hymn	A hymn, led by song leaders seated at a table, opens the service.
Ministers	Ministers enter the assembly room and take their seats.
Hymn	A minister announces and reads the first verse of the second hymn.
Opening sermon	A 20- to 25-minute sermon, often preached by a visiting minister, may focus on Old Testament characters.
Silent prayer	The congregation kneels for silent prayer (several minutes).
Scripture text	A deacon reads a chapter from the New Testament which forms the text of the main sermon.
Main sermon	The minister preaches a 45- to 50-minute extemporaneous sermon based on the chapter read by the deacon.
Testimonies	Several ordained leaders give brief responses, testifying to the truth of the sermon.
Vocal prayer	The congregation kneels while the minister offers an audible prayer.
Benediction	The minister gives a benediction without raising his hands.
Hymn	The congregation joins together in singing a closing hymn.

prevents members from seeking after a particular minister and strengthens the solidarity of ministerial leadership across the conference.

Counsel, Conference, and Communion.[49] The fall and spring communion services are the high points in the sacred calendar. The communion service is proceeded by a congregational counsel meeting and a conference-wide meeting of ordained leaders. The counsel meeting follows a Sunday morning service when the preacher's text is always Matthew, chapter 18. The counsel sermon stresses the importance of self-examination and the purging of sinful behavior.

After the sermon, the bishop invites men and women to come in separate groups to a small cloakroom called the "counsel room" to meet with the ordained leaders. Typically only older members choose to enter the counsel room. Here they state if they have peace with God, their fellow members, the church in general, and the teaching of their ministers. They also express their willingness to participate in the communion service. Members often voice concerns for the church in the counsel meeting. One

The counsel room of a Mennonite meetinghouse. Ministers consult in this room prior to worship services and members come here to express their concerns prior to communion. *Source:* Daniel Rodriguez

bishop said, "the subject we hear the most about is pride." Some complain that others are wearing "small head coverings, ruffles on sleeves, big figures in dresses, and colored stockings or that the boys are dressing up their horses and harnesses too much."

After all the counsel meetings are conducted, leaders take any concerns arising from the meetings to a one-day conference of ordained officials in the spring and fall.[50] The word *conference* carries two meanings. It refers to the organized authority of the church as well as to the biannual meeting of ordained leaders. Conference is the highest authoritative body; the scope of its power supersedes bishops and congregations. This significant meeting, usually held on a Friday, reaffirms the authority of the church and the solidarity of ordained leaders.[51] If a major issue is stirring—the use of beepers or computers, for example—the conference gathering may approve or ban the questionable practice. In some communities, the Saturday following the conference is a day of baptism or fasting in preparation for communion. The first communion takes place on the Sunday following the conference. The communion services then rotate among the congregations over several Sundays because a bishop must preside over each one.

The communion service is part of a lengthy Sunday morning service. The sermon begins with Old Testament prophecies that point to the advent of Christ and then emphasize the suffering, death, and resurrection of Jesus. Following the sermon, the congregation sings hymns that retell the suffering and death of Christ while the bishop, assisted by the deacon, administers the communion. The bishop gives a small piece of bread to each member and also passes a common cup of wine from which members take a sip. Members then pair off, men and women in different areas, to wash one another's feet by dipping them in a tub of water and drying them with a towel. This rite of humility and service concludes as the partners greet each other with a holy kiss. Communion—when the community not only recalls the sufferings of Christ but also unites together in fellowship and support of the *Ordnung*—is the ritual high point of Mennonite life.

Ordination. Mennonites use the biblical procedure of casting lots when selecting congregational leaders. Ordained officials receive no formal theological training, and they serve without pay for the rest of their lives. They typically continue their normal work in farming or related trades. Only men are eligible to serve in the ordained roles of bishop, minister, or deacon. Although women are permitted to nominate candidates, they rarely do.

The congregation prepares for a ministerial ordination by praying for guidance weeks in advance. At the close of a Sunday service, the bishop and deacon enter the counsel room and wait for members to come forward and nominate peers who qualify for office. The nominees are said to be "in the lot." It is not unusual for half a dozen or more men to share the lot. The next day, Monday, the candidates and their wives meet with the bishops and ministers. The elders examine the candidates for their suitability for leadership and willingness to adjust their personal attire and behavior to the more exacting standards of the ministry. The ordination then takes place on Tuesday, two days after candidates first learned that they were in the lot.

At the ordination service, the candidates sit by age on a bench at the front of the meetinghouse.[52] After a sermon on the duties of the office, two deacons take a songbook for each candidate out to the counsel room. Inside the cover of one of the books, they place a slip of paper with these words, "The lot is cast in the lap, but it falls as the Lord wills" (Prov. 16:33). The deacons then shuffle the books and return to the meeting room where the bishop places the books in a row in front of the candidates.

After a kneeling prayer the bishop says, "Thou Lord, who knowest the hearts of all men, show which of these thou hast chosen." The bishop reshuffles the books and then invites the candidates to select one. Beginning with the oldest person, the bishop opens each candidate's book until he finds the slip of paper. The chosen one is immediately ordained to the office of deacon, minister, or bishop, as the case may be. In this holiest of moments, members feel the awesome presence of divinity as God reaches down from heaven to select a new leader in their very midst. Many weep as they witness the miraculous hand of Providence in the selection. Such a divine anointing confers enormous power upon leaders— power that far exceeds academic credentials or a majority vote by a congregation.

Excommunication. Members who stray from the teachings and practice of the church are reprimanded by the deacon. Persons who refuse to cooperate with the church may be "set back" from communion. If they remain stubborn and unyielding to the *Ordnung* and the counsel of elders, they will face excommunication. Sometimes a person may continue to attend services but refrain from communion if he or she participates in a forbidden practice. In the Ontario Conference, a number of persons who smoke tobacco attend worship services, but they do not commune because smoking is a test of membership. These persons participate in the life of the community but technically are outside the fold. In eastern Pennsylvania, smoking is "testified against" but is not a test of membership, and hence members who smoke are able to commune. More serious offenses—owning an automobile or divorcing a spouse—will bring excommunication if the deviants fail to repent. Mennonites generally do not shun excommunicated members as severely as do the Amish. Several independent groups of team Mennonites do practice social avoidance, but the larger groups do not. Nevertheless, excommunicated members will feel the stigma of shame.

Unlike the Hutterites, who have few restrictions on technology, Mennonites use it selectively. The most significant limitation is the taboo on motor vehicles. Mennonites see the car as a symbol of independence, individualism, speed, status, and mobility. Automatic mobility threatens a community that hopes to keep its members tethered near home. Leaders fear that the car would fragment their community, pulling it apart by encouraging greater participation in the larger society. Horse-drawn transportation effectively limits mobility, thereby enhancing social integration in the local community. The rejection of motor vehicles has also become an important symbol of ethnic identity. The horse and buggy mark a sharp separation from the larger society as well as from the more progressive Mennonites who operate cars.

Although Mennonites prohibit the ownership of motor vehicles, they do ride in them. The church permits members to hire "taxi" service from local neighbors. In fact, some Mennonite businessmen contract with outside drivers on a regular basis. This neighborly "taxi service" is also used to visit relatives and friends in far-flung settlements beyond the reach of horse-and-buggy transportation. As many as twenty-five vans loaded with friends and relatives may arrive at a funeral in an outlying area. However, church leaders urge members not "to make a habit of driving

TABLE 3.5 RESTRICTIONS ON TECHNOLOGY IN THE GROFFDALE CONFERENCE

Forbidden: Test of Membership			
Airplane (Travel)	Computers	Motorcycle	Snowmobile
Auto	Cordless phone	Musical instruments	Tape player
Camera	Driver's license	Radio	Truck
CB radio	Fax machine	Record player	Wrist watch
Computerized dairies	Large motorboat	Rubber tires on tractors	Video

Strongly Discouraged: Not Test of Membership	
Accordions	Military toys
Electronic gadgets	Posing for photos
Fashionable carriages	Smoking
Large farm machinery	Stylish furniture
Large tractors	Tobacco raising

Source: The Ordnung of the Groffdale Mennonite Conference. The restrictions vary somewhat in Virginia, Indiana, and Ontario.

A "belting" wheel on a tractor. Some farmers wrap belts of rubber around the wheel under the steel cleats so they can drive tractors on hard-surface roads. *Source:* Daniel Rodriguez

too much with taxis and using them to go where we could go with the horse."

In addition to cars and trucks, the church prohibits the ownership of motorcycles, motor bikes, snowmobiles, and motorboats. However, "small rowboats with small motors" are permitted by the Groffdale Conference. Members are allowed to travel by public transportation on bus, boat, and train. Except for extreme emergencies, air travel is also taboo.[53] Unlike some Amish communities that prohibit bicycles, the Mennonites use them widely. Young people often ride bicycles to work and social gatherings as well as to worship services.

Some restrictions on agricultural technology are tied to the automobile taboo. Tractors and other self-propelled equipment, for instance, are carefully restricted. The Groffdale Conference permits tractors for field use, but only if they roll on steel wheels. Garden tractors and riding mowers must also be fitted with steel wheels. The prohibition of rubber tires developed because leaders worried that rubber-tired tractors might be used for local errands and shopping and thus lead to pickup trucks and cars. "The line," one member explained, "is if you can ride it; rubber tires are not permitted if you can ride on something." A rototiller, silage cart or walk-behind forklift may roll on rubber because it does not carry a driver.

Rubber-tired wheels remain a temptation. In the late 1990s some shop owners placed rubber tires on fork lifts to make it easier to turn sharply on concrete floors. Some Groffdale farmers added bands of rubber to the steel wheels on their tractors to cushion the impact of the steel on the macadam, making it easier to take tractors on public roads. These "belting wheels" stirred controversy because they blurred the longstanding rule against rubber on self-propelled vehicles. With these rubber-padded steel wheels, farmers could drive tractors on the road up to 35 miles per hour. The debate over the belting wheels was so intense, according to one member, "that it almost divided the church." Although such wheels are frowned upon, probably three-quarters of the farmers now have them.

Ontario Mennonites, on the other hand, permit full rubber tires on their tractors but regulate them in other ways. The church forbids (1) tractors with more than 100 horsepower, (2) cabs and rollover bars on tractors, (3) the use of tractors for road transportation, and (4) tractor speeds over ten miles per hour. These restrictions keep the tractor under the scrutiny of the church and reduce the chance that it will lead to use of the car. Out of respect to the Groffdale Conference and mindful of setting high standards, ministers in the Ontario Conference refrain from placing rubber tires on their own tractors.

Limits on technology also help to curb the size of farming operations. The church fears that large operations will place too much wealth and influence in the hands of one person and might weaken the viability of small, family-centered farms. Moreover, large-scale technology would take jobs from Mennonite youth and push them into other occupations. Large tractors and self-propelled harvesters are "testified against" by the Groffdale Conference. Farmers are urged to "be satisfied to remain more ordinary and to use their horses more." Automatic feeders in dairy barns are also shunned in order to control the size of herds.

Said one farmer, "If we permit rubber-tired tractors and cars, it will lead to big farming operations. Putting steel wheels on the tractors and keeping the horse and buggy help to keep things small." He went on to note that, "some of our people who want bigger things join the Weaverland Conference" (a more progressive Mennonite group). In their efforts to keep things small, Ontario Conference also forbids the use of mechanical stable cleaners and silo unloaders. Such restraints keep farm operations labor intensive and provide ample work for children.

In the first half of the twentieth century, Old Order Mennonites were hesitant to tap electricity from public utility lines and to install telephones in their homes. The use of public electricity and telephones violated the principle of separation from the world and increased dependency on the larger society. The telephone provided easy access to the outside world. Electricity from public utility lines would have enabled families to use a multitude of conveniences and opened the door for radio and television. For all of these reasons, most Mennonites were not eager to install electricity and telephones in their homes.

The use of telephones and electricity was never an explicit test of church membership, however. About mid-twentieth century, some members gradually began installing them in their homes. In the Groffdale Conference, at present, fax machines, cordless phones, and answering machines are not permitted in shops or in homes. Beepers are counseled against, but "some have them," conceded one member. Indeed, in the late 1990s the use of beepers stirred considerable controversy. Some members had them because they were members of local volunteer fire companies. After first banning beepers, the conference rescinded its action and agreed to permit voiceless beepers or ones that could only receive messages from the local fire company.

Ministers, as examples of virtue, were never permitted to have telephones or electricity. Those who had them prior to ordination had to tear them out of their homes when they assumed office. The taboo on electricity for ministers began to weaken in the Groffdale Conference in 1993. By the beginning of the twenty-first century, about one-fifth of the ministers in Lancaster County had electric and telephones. In newer settlements in other states, these conveniences are even more common in the homes of ministers.

Ministers in Ontario are forbidden to have electricity and telephones in their homes. However, lay members in Ontario were permitted to install telephones, with certain restrictions, in 1989. Only black phones are permitted, and not more than one phone and one extension is allowed per family. Cordless phones, fax machines, answering machines, and other unnecessary accessories are also off-limits in Ontario.

Like other Old Order groups, Mennonites restrict media technologies that would beam outside values into the minds of members and children. Radio and television are strictly forbidden, as are citizen band radios and monitors, record players, tape players, and video cameras and players. Such devices are viewed as instruments of cultural contamination that would surely expose members to ideas that mock the ways of humility.

Regulating Social Change

Occupational changes are underway in some communities. A few members are leaving the farm for shops and small businesses. Young men sometimes work in shops before marriage or in the first years of marriage until they can purchase a farm. One leader estimated that between 75 and 90 percent of the men enter farming after they "settle down."[54] A Mennonite accountant in Ontario estimates that 95 percent of the families in his community are on farms or in farm-related occupations. Many farmers have a sideline business to supplement their farm income and to provide work throughout the winter. A growing number of people also operate small shops and enterprises independent of farming operations. Woodworking and machine shops are the most popular. It is not unusual for parents and adult children to live on the same homestead, where one family operates the farm and the other a small business.[55]

When faced with sprawling urbanization and expensive farmland in Lancaster County, many Mennonites pack their belongings and migrate to other states in order to remain in farming. The Amish in Lancaster, by contrast, have been more willing to abandon their plows for shops and small businesses.[56] "Staying on the farm for the sake of the family is the 'in thing,' " noted one Mennonite farmer. "We encourage moving out of the area so we can stay in farming."

Although Mennonites are cautious about technological change, they are not a static community. Indeed, they have accepted many technological changes, albeit with limitations, in the past fifty years. The process of social change is a delicate task of moving cultural fences without tearing them down. These adjustable fences have both practical and symbolic consequences. The taboo on automatic feeders and milking parlors limits the size of herds, but it also sets Mennonites apart from non-Mennonite farmers. Many of the cultural fences, especially clothing, are symbolic lines that distinguish Old Order Mennonites from outsiders as well as from other groups of Mennonites and Amish. As one bishop explained, "Not everything is wrong with these forbidden things, but we can't distinguish ourselves from the world without them." The technological and social restrictions help, in other words, to fortify the lines of separation and to bolster community solidarity.

Mennonites have accepted numerous changes in recent decades. Farmers are milking their cows with automatic milkers and plowing their fields with tractors. Rubber tires have appeared on farm implements that are not self-propelled. A band of rubber is also used today on carriage wheels, an exception that clarifies the rule (that is, rubber is only forbidden if the vehicle is self-propelled and can carry a rider). The transition to rubber on carriage wheels, recalled one bishop, was a very "hot issue." In other changes, electrical appliances are now common—with the exception of dishwashers, air conditioners, microwave ovens, and computers. A few families even have air conditioners and microwaves. One farmer noted that as electricity was more widely adopted, some families had it in the barn but not in the home or vice versa "depending on the husband's or wife's thinking." [57]

In a broad sense, the *Ordnung* is the throttle that regulates the speed of change. Although some details of the *Ordnung* are written down, the *Ordnung* is a broad and pliable cluster of understandings. The oral interpretation is more flexible than the literal written version. Reflecting the broad consensus of the conference, ordained leaders seek to apply the *Ordnung* consistently across all congregations.

Church leaders worry that rapid change will ruin the church. One bishop compared social change to a hole in a dike: "If a small hole develops in it, the water will eventually flood everything." The leader went on to explain that regulating social change is difficult when it comes to things like computers because "you can make a dummy out of yourself if you don't know what you're talking about." "We couldn't rule out all computers," the bishop noted, "because digital clocks and calculators are widely used and they have computers in them. But we don't want the large personal computers with screens." Consequently, in 1995 the Groffdale Conference forbade personal computers with monitors for fear they would lead to television and video games. Any computer that has a separate monitor or capability for Internet hookup is forbidden. "The Internet just doesn't fit our plain way of life—it's too hard to control," said one leader. "It makes it too easy to let worldly entertainment and pornography come into our homes." However, digital scales, calculators, and word processors with small display screens are acceptable and widely used.

The rate of social change is regulated by the "understandings" of the *Ordnung* and also by the example of ordained leaders who usually are the last to change. The ministers comply with the old ways until most of the lay people have accepted a new practice. In midcentury, as electricity and telephones were coming into homes, ministers were expected to shun them—even to tear them out of their homes after they were ordained. Finally, in the fall of 1993, a minister refused to take electrical service out of his home because, in his words, "I never promised not to use it." Some ordained leaders wanted to force him to take it out or resign. Delicately sidestepping the issue, Groffdale Conference officials decided not to bring it to a vote, thus opening the door for change.

This decision in effect permitted ministers to use electricity by default—a painful change to the conservative sector of the church. The same pattern of adaptation by default occurred with bands of rubber on buggy wheels. Lay members gradually began placing rubber tires on their buggies in the mid-1970s. By the early 1990s, one Groffdale leader estimated that 80 to 90 percent of the lay members, but none of the ministers, had rubber-wheeled carriages. Rubber is not forbidden by the *Ordnung*, but "it's just understood that the ministry should not have it," said one bishop.

Ordained officials worry that too much change, too fast, will send them down the tracks of cultural assimilation. "The train starts off ever so gradually," said one bishop, "and it gains speed slowly until it picks up more speed and then it gains and gains and gains." The list of forbidden amusements grows as new forms of entertainment bring ever more temptations. One leader, referring to the customary reading of the *Ordnung* before communion, said, "It takes twice as long to read the *Ordnung* in church today as when I was young."

The Mennonite road to heaven does not follow the Hutterite trail through the valley of shared property and cloistered living. Traveling closer to the main road, Mennonite leaders must keep their route well-posted with signs of separation lest the pilgrims lose their way and drift into the wider boulevard. For the most part, Mennonite pilgrims have heeded the signs and remain on the old trail. In many ways, the Mennonite emphasis on separation is similar to the Amish story, which we will explore next.

CHAPTER FOUR

The Amish

What makes Amish children so nice is the spanking.
—Amish mother

AMISH ORIGINS

The Amish are the largest and most visible of the four Old Order groups. Their prominence in the national consciousness has spiraled since midcentury with the rise of tourism and generous media coverage. The feature film *Witness* spread Amish images on theater screens around the world. An issue of *Vogue* magazine featured fourteen color pages of new trends in "plain" clothing worn by models framed by a variety of Amish props—buggies, hay bales, and horse-drawn machinery. *Glamour* magazine carried the story of an Amish woman who left the fold of Amish life. It is even possible to buy an "Amish" software program for personal computers, although the software, of course, has nothing to do with the Amish.[1]

Although the Amish often find themselves in the public spotlight, they prefer to live quiet, undisturbed lives. Unlike the Hutterites, but similar to the Mennonites, the Amish own private property. They live alongside their non-Amish neighbors in small villages and farming communities in some 250 settlements across North America. With more restrictions on technology than the Brethren and the Hutterites, the Amish are more similar to the Old Order Mennonites. Indeed, the Amish and Mennonites shared a common history from 1525 until 1693, when Swiss and South German Anabaptists divided into two religious streams: Amish and Mennonite.

Jakob Ammann, an Anabaptist elder, sought to revitalize the church in several ways. He proposed holding communion twice a year rather than once, which was the typical Swiss practice. Following the Dutch Anabaptists he argued that Christians, in obedience to Christ, should wash each other's feet in the communion service. To promote doctrinal purity and spiritual rigor, Ammann administered a strict discipline in his congregations. Appealing to New Testament teachings and the practice of the Dutch Anabaptists, he also urged the church to avoid excommunicated members in daily life, a practice called "shunning."

Disagreements over shunning eventually drove the decisive wedge between Ammann's followers and other Swiss-South German Anabaptists. Social and theological differences as well as personal ones led to a permanent division. Ammann's followers were eventually called Amish, while many other Anabaptists gradually took the name Mennonite after the prominent Dutch Anabaptist leader Menno Simons. Religious cousins who share a common beginning, the Amish and Mennonites have maintained distinct identities since 1693.[2]

Searching for political stability and religious freedom, the Amish came to North America in two waves—first in the mid-1700s and again in the first half of the 1800s. Their first settlements took root in southeastern Pennsylvania, but in time the Amish followed the frontier to other coun-

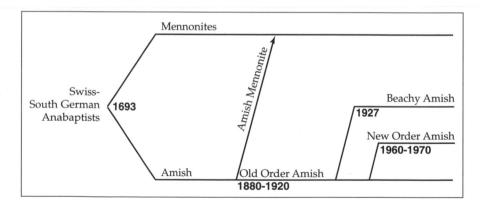

FIGURE 4.1 Formation of Amish Groups in North America

ties in Pennsylvania and then on to Ohio and Indiana as well as to other Midwestern states. Amish settlements today cluster in the mid-Atlantic and Midwestern regions of the country. Very few live west of the Mississippi or in the deep south. Meanwhile, in Europe, the last congregation dissolved in 1937.

The "Old Order" label emerged in the latter part of the nineteenth century.[3] Influenced by the rising tide of industrialization, clusters of Amish in some areas formed more progressive Amish-Mennonite churches. The conservers, who wanted to preserve more traditional Amish ways, became known as the Old Order Amish. The more progressive Amish-Mennonites eventually joined mainstream Mennonite churches.[4]

At the turn of the twentieth century, the Old Order Amish numbered about 5,000 in North America. Now scattered across twenty-five states as well as into Ontario, they presently number more than 180,000 children and adults. Nearly three-quarters live in Ohio, Pennsylvania, and Indiana. Other sizable communities are found in Iowa, Michigan, Missouri, New York, and Wisconsin.[5] With a loose federation of some 1,200 congregations, the Amish function without a national organization or an annual convention. Local church districts—congregations of twenty-five to forty families—shape the heart of Amish life. Congregations that follow similar practices and permit their ministers to preach in each other's services are considered "in fellowship" with each other. These subgroups of like-minded congregations form what scholars call an *affiliation*. Practices vary considerably from settlement to settlement and between the different affiliations.

The Amish have enjoyed remarkable growth in twentieth-century North America. Despite their tenacity for traditional ways, they have thrived in the midst of the most technologically advanced century of all time. In recent years their population has doubled about every twenty years. In the five-year period from 1991 to 1996, their population soared from approximately 135,000 to nearly 165,000.[6] This represented an increase of 199 church districts for the period, or about forty new ones per year. David Luthy (1997) reports that in the twenty-year period between 1972 and 1992, the Amish established about 145 new settlements.[7] By the dawn of the twenty-first century, new migration initiatives had scattered the Amish into more than 250 settlements in the United States and into 7 settlements in the Canadian province of Ontario, with a total population of children and adults approaching 200,000, as shown in Table 4.1.

FIGURE 4.2 Distribution of Amish Congregations in North America
Note: Montana and Washington, which are not shown, have three and one districts, respectively.
Source: Raber (2000).

DISTINCTIVE AND DIVERSE

Common dress and other visible markers create the impression that the Amish are all alike.[8] However, beneath the surface many differences abound. A distinctive Amish identity is maintained by symbols of separation that carve deep contours between the sectarian subculture and the larger society. These symbols of separation that provide easy recognition of Amish persons—clothing, horses, and carriages—also shape interaction within the ethnic fold. Such visible symbols imprint an indelible identity on the minds of members. Unlike modern youth who may wan-

TABLE 4.1 ESTIMATED OLD ORDER AMISH POPULATION BY STATE AND PROVINCE

State/Province	Congregations	Adult Membership	Children/Adults
Ohio	328	24,600	49,200
Pennsylvania	278	20,850	41,700
Indiana	219	16,425	32,850
Wisconsin	69	5,175	10,350
Michigan	58	4,350	8,700
Missouri	40	3,000	6,000
New York	34	2,550	5,100
Kentucky	33	2,475	4,950
Iowa	32	2,400	4,800
Illinois	29	2,175	4,350
Ontario	22	1,650	3,300
Minnesota	13	975	1,950
Tennessee	11	825	1,650
Delaware	8	600	1,200
Kansas	8	600	1,200
Maryland	6	450	900
Oklahoma	5	375	750
Montana	3	225	450
Virginia	2	150	300
Seven States[a]	7	525	1,050
Total	1,204	90,375	180,750

Source: Raber (2000) and Luthy (1997). These estimates assume 75 adult, baptized members and 150 adults and children per church district. Raber's directory excludes a few Old Order districts and also includes some New Order districts; thus these are estimates.

[a]The following states have one district: Arkansas, Florida, Mississippi, North Carolina, Texas, Washington, and West Virginia.

der about for years trying to "find themselves," Amish youth know who they are and to whom they belong. Their distinctive clothing and use of horses symbolize their distance from modern life and erase any doubt about their social-psychological identity. These symbols of ethnicity generate a strong sense of meaning, belonging, and identity in Amish life.

Differences between various groups are camouflaged by visible symbols of separation that provide a united public front. At least ten badges of identity are shared by most Old Order Amish across North America: (1) horse-and-buggy transportation, (2) the use of horses and mules for fieldwork,[9] (3) plain dress in many variations, (4) a beard and shaven up-

An Amish mother and her daughters enjoy a hoagie at a social gathering. *Source:* Keith Baum

per lip for men, (5) a prayer cap for women, (6) the Pennsylvania German dialect, (7) worship in homes, (8) eighth-grade private schooling, (9) the rejection of electricity from public utility lines, and (10) taboos on the ownership of televisions and computers.[10] These symbols circumscribe the Amish world, mark it off from the larger society, and bridle the forces of assimilation.

These signs of solidarity are upheld by the *Ordnung* of each community. An informal policy manual of sorts, the *Ordnung* embodies the behavioral expectations that shape Amish life. Typically unwritten, it regulates the religious and social life of Amish communities. It carries prescriptions related to dress—a prayer cap for women and a regulation hat and beard for men—as well as proscriptions—do not own a television, hold a driver's license, or attend high school. The scope of the *Ordnung* ranges from attire to the use of technology, and its particular applications vary from community to community. Children learn the ways of the *Ordnung* at an early age by observing adults and receiving parental instruction. Church leaders occasionally revise the "understandings" of the *Ordnung* as special issues emerge and new forms of technology arise. In the spring of 1996, worried about the World Wide Web's pornographic potential, the bishops in one settlement urged their members to "stay away from the Internet."[11]

The church prescribes dress regulations for its members, but the standards vary from settlement to settlement. Men are typically expected to wear a wide-brimmed hat and a vest when they appear in public. In winter months and at church services, they wear a black suit coat, which is typically fastened with hooks and eyes rather than with buttons. The men in most settlements also use suspenders instead of belts. Modern-styled, commercially tailored suits and ties are forbidden.

Amish women are expected to wear a head covering and a bonnet when they appear in public settings. Most women wear a cape over the top of their dresses as well as an apron. The three parts of the dress are often fastened together with straight pins. Various colors—green, brown, blue, lavender—are permitted for men's shirts and women's dresses, but figures on fabrics are taboo. Although very young girls do not wear a head covering, Amish children typically dress like their parents. Jewelry, including wedding rings and wristwatches, and all forms of facial makeup are forbidden, lest they lead to pride and vanity. Dress serves as a tool for individual expression in modern life; however, among the Amish it signals group loyalty and limits personal expression.

There are other distinctives of Amish life as well, but the badges of identity listed above are widely shared by most groups. What is remarkable, however, is that these badges of separation have been preserved without a centralized national structure and with nearly twelve hundred congregations afloat in twenty-five states and one Canadian province. These tangible symbols of separation have served the Amish well in carving out a distinctive public identity and in satisfying the social-psychological needs of their members.

At first glance, all Amish groups appear to be pressed from the same cultural mold. A deeper look, however, reveals many differences in practice within and between the many Amish settlements in North America. Some affiliations forbid milking machines, while others depend on them. Mechanical hay balers, pulled by horses across some Amish fields, are taboo in others. Prescribed buggy tops are gray or black in many affiliations, but white or yellow in others. Buttons on clothing, banished in many groups, are accepted in the more progressive ones. Gas refrigerators are welcomed by some groups but forbidden by others. One group insists that men wear one suspender, while most groups permit two. The dead are embalmed in one settlement but not in another.

Because primary moral authority resides in the congregation, practices vary between congregations even within the same affiliation. Some bishops permit telephones in small shops, but others do not. Artificial insemination of livestock is acceptable in one district but not in another. In some communities most of the men are farmers, but in other regions the majority work in shops and Amish industries. In the Elkhart-Lagrange settlement of Indiana, many Amish persons work in rural factories operated by non-Amish persons. Behind the common badges of identity that appear on the front stage of Amish life, endless diversity, with dozens of distinctions within and between groups, thrives.

Religious Rhythms

Worship services held in Amish homes reaffirm the moral order of Amish life. Church districts hold services every other Sunday. A group of two hundred or more, including some relatives from other districts who have an "off Sunday," gather for worship. They meet in a farmhouse, in the basement of a newer home, or in a shop or barn—underscoring the integration of worship with daily life. A fellowship meal at noon and informal visiting follow the three-hour morning service.

A plain and simple unwritten liturgy revolves around congregational singing, prayer, and two sermons. Without the aid of organs, offerings, candles, crosses, robes, or flowers, members yield themselves to God in the spirit of humility. The congregation sings from the *Ausbund*—a German hymnal without musical notations—which dates back to the sixteenth-century Anabaptists. The tunes, passed across the generations by memory, are sung in unison without any musical accompaniment. The slow, chant-like cadence creates a sixteenth-century mood. A single song may stretch over twenty minutes. Extemporaneous sermons, preached in the Pennsylvania German dialect, recount biblical stories as well as lessons from daily life. Preachers exhort members to be obedient to Amish ways and abstain from worldly vice.

Communion services, held each autumn and spring, frame the religious year. These ritual high points emphasize self-examination and spiritual rejuvenation. Sins are confessed, and each member in turn reaffirms his or her willingness to uphold the rules of the *Ordnung*. Communion is held when the congregation is "at peace"—meaning all members are in harmony with the *Ordnung*. The six- to eight-hour communion service includes preaching, a light meal during the service, and the commemoration of Christ's death with bread and wine. Near the conclusion, pairs of members wash each other's feet as the congregation sings. As members depart, they give an alms offering to the deacon—the only time that a regular offering is collected in Amish worship services.

Baptism typically occurs between the ages of 16 and 22. Prior to baptism, the candidates are instructed in the eighteen articles of faith from the Dordrecht Confession of Faith, an Anabaptist confession written in the Netherlands in 1632. These are the same articles of faith that guide the Old Order Mennonites. Baptism is a pivotal moment in the life of Amish youth because it signifies not only a confession of Christian faith but also a pledge to uphold the *Ordnung* of the church for the rest of their lives. Young men promise to serve as a minister if ever called by the congregation. Because adult baptism is central to Amish theology, they respect the integrity of each individual's decision about baptism. Those who accept baptism and later renege on their vows will face excommunication and shunning. However, people who reject baptism and drift away from the community are able to continue fellowshipping with their family and friends without the stigma of shunning.

Worship, communion, and baptism are sacred rites that revitalize and preserve the *Ordnung*. But the Amish, like other human beings, forget, rebel, and sometimes stray into deviance. Major transgressions are confessed publicly in a "members meeting" following the worship service. Violations of the *Ordnung*—using a tractor in the field, posing for a television camera, flying on a commercial airline, filing a lawsuit, joining a political organization, or opening a questionable business—are confessed publicly. Public confession of sin diminishes self-will, reminds members of the supreme value of submission, restores the wayward into the community of faith, and underscores the lines of faithfulness that encircle the community.

The headstrong who spurn the advice of elders and refuse to confess their sin face a six-week probation. Likewise, those who voluntarily confess a sin, such as fornication, will also undergo the six-week probation. Members who exhibit repentance during the probation are restored into full membership; those who remain stubborn will face excommunication. Exiles also face shunning—a cultural equivalent of solitary confinement. Members are expected to limit social interaction and financial transactions with the excommunicated. The practice of shunning is a public ritual of shaming. A bishop compared shunning to "the last dose of medicine that you give a sinner. It either works for life or death . . . but if love is lost, God's lost, too." For the unrepentant, social avoidance becomes a lifetime quarantine. One excommunicated member noted, "It works a little bit like an electric fence around a pasture."[12]

Shunning is a silent deterrent that prods those who think about breaking their baptismal vows to think twice. This practice is used to preserve the purity of the church, to clarify the moral order, and to encourage repentance. Excommunicated members can, even years later, be restored into membership upon public confession of their sins. In some instances, older persons living in exile for many years have returned to the church to repair the breech before they die.

Patterns of Social Organization

The *immediate family*, the *extended family*, and the *church district* form the basic building blocks of Amish society. Amish parents typically raise about seven children, but ten or more is not uncommon. About 50 percent of the population is under 18 years old. An Amish person will often have seventy-five or more first cousins, and a typical grandmother will easily count more than thirty-five grandchildren. Members of the extended family often live nearby—across the field, down the lane, or beyond the hill. Youth grow up in this thicket of family relations where, as one Amish woman put it, "everyone knows everyone else's business." One is rarely alone but always embedded in a caring network of support in time of need and disaster. The elderly retire at home—usually in a small apartment built onto the main house of a homestead. Because the Amish reject government aid, there are virtually no families that receive public assistance. From cradle to grave the community provides a supportive network of social support.

Twenty-five to forty families constitute a *church district* or congregation. This is the basic social and religious unit beyond the family. Roads and streams mark the boundaries of districts. Members participate in the district in which they live. A district's geographic size varies with the density of the Amish population. In smaller districts families can walk to church services, which are held every other Sunday in a different home. As districts grow, they divide. A bishop, two preachers, and a deacon share leadership responsibilities in each congregation. None of the leaders receive formal education or payment for their service. The bishop, as spiritual elder, officiates at baptisms, weddings, communions, funerals, ordinations, and membership meetings. Those unhappy with life in their district need to literally move to another one. The church district—the hub of Amish life—is church, club, family, and precinct all wrapped up into one. It is like a neighborhood parish. Periodic meetings of ordained leaders link the districts of a settlement into a loose federation.

Social life—leisure, work, education, play, worship, and friendship— revolves around the immediate neighborhood. Although Amish babies in some settlements are born in hospitals, many of them greet this world at

Amish worship services rotate among the homes in a church district. *Source:* Dennis Hughes

home or in local birthing centers. Weddings and funerals occur at home. Occasionally couples or families travel to other settlements or even out of state to visit relatives and friends. But for the most part, the Amish world pivots on local turf. From home-canned food to homemade haircuts, things are likely to be done at or near home. Social relationships are multibonded. The same people frequently work, play, and worship together. Unlike the fragmented networks of modern life, the Amish are tied into many overlapping circles of friendship. Family, friends, and neighbors interact within a thick web of ethnic social ties.

Amish society is remarkably informal. Without a centralized national office, a symbolic national leader, or an annual convention, the tentacles of bureaucracy are few. Apart from one-room schools, a modest publishing operation, and a few historical libraries, formal organizations do not exist. The one exception is a loosely organized National Steering Committee that provides a common voice for speaking with government agencies.[13] Regional committees in various areas coordinate activities related to schools, mutual aid, and historical interests, but typical bureaucratic structures are simply absent.

The organizational units that do exist in Amish society reflect the small-scale spirit of humility. By meeting in their homes for worship, the Amish limit the size of congregations to about thirty-five households. Farms, shops, and schools are also relatively small. Small-scale social units not only increase informality and participation but also prevent power from accumulating on the lap of one person. Moreover, small-scale settings assure that each person has an emotional niche within a network of social support.

The conventional marks of social status—education, income, occupation, and consumer goods—are less evident in Amish society. Their agrarian heritage had always placed most members on common footing. Today, however, the rise of small industries in some settlements and factory work in others threatens the social equality of bygone years. Nevertheless, the range of occupations and social distinctions remains relatively small. Common garb, horse-and-buggy travel, an eighth-grade education, and equal-size tombstones embody the virtues of social equality in the midst of growing economic disparity.

The practice of mutual aid also distinguishes Amish society. Although the Amish own private property, like other Anabaptists they have long emphasized mutual aid as a Christian duty in the face of disaster and special need. Mutual aid goes far beyond romanticized barn raisings. Harvesting, quilting, births, weddings, and funerals all require the help of many hands. The habits of care address all sorts of needs triggered by drought, disease, death, injury, bankruptcy, and medical emergency. The community springs into spontaneous action in these moments of despair, thus articulating the deepest sentiments of Amish life.

Amish society is patriarchal. Apart from school teachers, who are generally women, men assume the helm of most leadership roles. Although women can nominate men to serve in ministerial roles, they are excluded from these roles themselves. Women can, however, vote in church business meetings. Some women feel that, since "the men make the rules," some types of modern equipment are tolerated more readily in barns and shops than in homes. In recent years some women have taken on new roles as entrepreneurs—establishing quilting operations, craft stores, roadside stands, and food stores.[14] This development will likely alter gender roles for years to come.

Although husband and wife preside over distinct spheres of domestic life, many tasks are shared. A wife may ask her husband to assist in the garden; and he may ask her to help in the barn, field, or shop. The husband does hold spiritual authority in the home, but spouses have considerable freedom within their distinctive spheres. In the words of one Amishman, "The wife is not a servant; she is the queen and the husband is the king." The nature of the partnership between husband and wife, as in other societies, varies considerably with personalities.[15]

Passing on the Faith

"We're not opposed to education," said one Amishman, "we're just against education higher than our heads; I mean education that we don't need." Indeed, the Amish willingly participated in public education as long as it revolved around one-room schools. Under local control, small rural schools posed little threat to Amish values. The massive consolidation of public schools and growing pressure to attend high school sparked clashes between the Amish and government officials in the middle of the twentieth century. Confrontations in several states led to arrests and brief stints in jail. Finally, after many legal skirmishes, the U.S. Supreme Court gave its blessing to the eighth-grade Amish school system in 1972 in the landmark case known as *Wisconsin v. Yoder.* In the words of the court, "There can be no assumption that today's majority is 'right' and the Amish and others are 'wrong.' " The justices concluded: "A way of life that is odd or even erratic but interferes with no rights or interests of others is not to be condemned because it is different."[16]

Today the Amish operate about 1,200 private schools for some 32,000 Amish children.[17] Many of these schools are one-room operations with twenty-five to thirty-five pupils and one teacher who is responsible for teaching all eight grades. A few Amish children attend rural public schools in some states, but the vast majority go to private schools governed by the Amish. A local board of three to five fathers organizes the school, hires a teacher, approves the curriculum, oversees the budget, and supervises the maintenance of the building. Teachers receive about $25 to $35 per day. The annual cost per child is roughly $250—nearly sixteen times lower than many public schools, where per pupil costs often top $4,000. After funding the costs of their own schools, Amish parents also pay public school taxes.

Bible reading and prayer opens each school day, but religion is not formally taught in the school or in other Amish settings for that matter.[18] The curriculum includes reading, arithmetic, spelling, grammar, penmanship, history, and some geography. Classes are conducted in English, and both English and German are taught. Parents want children to learn to read German so that they can understand religious writings, many of which are recorded in formal German. Science and sex education are missing in the curriculum as are other typical trappings of public schools—sports, dances, cafeterias, clubs, bands, choruses, computers, television, guidance counselors, principals, and college recruiters.

Amish teachers, themselves trained in Amish schools, are not required to be certified in most states. The brightest and best of Amish scholars, they return to the classroom to teach, often in their late teens and early twenties. Amish school directors select them for their ability to teach and for their commitment to Amish values. Frequently they are single women, who typically stop teaching when they wed. Without the benefit of high school or college diplomas, they manage some thirty pupils across eight grades. Periodic meetings with other teachers, a monthly teachers magazine, *Blackboard Bulletin,* and ample common sense prepare them for the task. Some textbooks are recycled from public schools, but most are printed by Amish publishers.

FIGURE 4.3 Distribution of Amish Schools in North America
Note: Montana, which is not shown, has four schools.
Source: Blackboard Bulletin (1999).

With three or four pupils per grade, teachers often instruct two grades at a time. Pupils in other classes ponder assignments or, as the case may be, listen to previews of next year's lessons or hear reviews of last year's work. Classrooms exhibit a distinct sense of order amidst a beehive of activity. Hands raise to ask permission or clarify instructions as the teacher moves from cluster to cluster, teaching new material every ten or fifteen minutes. Despite the teacher's responsibility for eight grades, students receive a remarkable amount of personal attention.

The ethos of the classroom accents cooperative activity, obedience, respect, diligence, kindness, and interest in the natural world. Little attention is given to independent thinking and critical analysis—the esteemed

Amish boys trade major league baseball cards during recess at their school. *Source:* Dennis Hughes

values of public education. Despite the emphasis on order, playful pranks and giggles are commonplace. Schoolyard play during daily recess often involves softball or other homespun games.

Amish schools exhibit a social continuity rarely found in public education. With many families sending several children to a school, teachers may relate to as few as a dozen parents. Teachers know parents personally, as well as the special circumstances surrounding each child. In some cases, children have the same teacher for all eight grades. Indeed, all the children from one family may have the same teacher for all their education. Amish schools are unquestionably provincial by modern standards. Yet in a humane fashion they ably prepare Amish youth for meaningful lives in Amish society.

Parochial schools play a critical role in the preservation of Amish culture. They reinforce Amish values and shield youth from contaminating ideas afloat in modern culture. Moreover, schools restrict friendships with non-Amish peers and impede the flow of Amish youth into higher education and professional life. Amish schools harbor the young within the confines of an Amish world as they step toward adulthood. Islands of provincialism, the schools promote practical skills that prepare their graduates for success in Amish society. Some selective testing indicates, in fact, that Amish pupils compare favorably with their non-Amish peers in rural public schools on standardized tests of basic skills.[19]

Social Gatherings and Holidays

Various social gatherings bring members together for times of fellowship and fun beyond the biweekly worship. Young people gather in homes for Sunday evening singings. Married couples sometimes gather with old friends to sing for "shut-ins" and the elderly in their homes. Various frolics blend work and play together in Amish life. Parents often gather for preschool frolics to prepare the school buildings for September classes. End-of-school picnics bring parents and students together for an afternoon of food and games.

Quilting bees and barn raisings mix goodwill, levity, and hard work for young and old alike. Other moments of collective work—cleaning up after a fire, plowing for an ill neighbor, canning for a sick mother, threshing wheat, filling a silo—involve neighbors and extended families in episodes of charity, sweat, and fun. Adult sisters, sometimes numbering as many as five or six, will gather for a "sisters day" that blends laughter with cleaning, quilting, canning, or gardening.

Public auctions of farm equipment, often held in February and March, attract crowds in preparation for springtime farming. Besides opportunities to bid on equipment, the day-long auctions offer ample time for farm talk as well as gossip and friendly fun. Games of cornerball in a nearby field or barnyard often compete with the drama of the auction. Household auctions and horse sales also provide favorite times for socializing.

Family gatherings at religious holidays as well as summer family reunions link members into familial networks. Single women sometimes gather at a cabin or a home for a weekend of fun and frolic. Special meetings of persons with unique interests—harnessmakers, cabinetmakers, woodworkers, blacksmiths, businesswomen, teachers—often called "reunions," are on the rise. A network of persons in several states who have

Amish boys wearing baseball uniforms participate in a game sponsored by a public league. This practice has stirred controversy in some settlements. *Source:* Dennis Hughes

experienced bypass heart surgery circulate a letter and hold an annual meeting. The disabled have gathered annually for a number of years. These gatherings often attract persons from many states.

Leisure and pleasure have long been suspect in Amish life. Idleness is often viewed as the devil's workshop. The recent rise of small businesses in some settlements has increased the cash flow and brought more recreational activities. Said one Amish entrepreneur, "Some of us are business people now, not just backwoods farmers, and sometimes we just need to get away from things." For the rising class of business people, various forms of leisure time activity are increasing.

Amish recreation, for the most part, is group-oriented and tilted more toward nature than commercial entertainment. Indeed, most forms of commercial entertainment are taboo for members. The Amish rarely take "vacations," but their "trips" to other settlements often include visits to scenic sites and state parks. Groups often travel by chartered bus or van to other settlements for reunions, special gatherings, historical tours, or visits to a state park or city zoo.

Among youth, seasonal athletics like softball, sledding, skating, hockey, and swimming are common. Volleyball is a widespread favorite. Pitching quoits is a favorite activity at family reunions and picnics. Fishing and hunting for small game are favorite sports on farms and woodlands. In Pennsylvania some Amish men own hunting cabins in the mountains where they gather in the late fall to hunt white-tailed deer. Deep-sea fishing trips are also common summertime jaunts for men in some of the settlements. Others prefer camping and canoeing.

Some couples travel to Florida for several weeks over the winter. They live near Sarasota in an Amish village populated by winter travelers from several states. A trip to Mexico in search of special medical care may include scenic detours along the way. Although some Amish travel by train or bus, chartered vans are by far the most popular mode of long-distance transportation. Traveling together with family, friends, and extended kin, they enjoy the laughter and chatter that builds the bonds of community.

Cultural constraints shape the calendar of Amish holidays. Sharing some national holidays with non-Amish neighbors and adding others, the Amish calendar underscores both their participation in, and their separation from, the larger world. As conscientious objectors, the Amish have little enthusiasm for patriotic days with a military flair. Memorial Day, Veterans Day, and the Fourth of July are barely noticed. Even Labor Day stirs little interest. The witches and goblins of Halloween feel foreign to Amish spirits. Pumpkins may be displayed in some settlements, but without cut faces. Halloween parties are never held.

Amish holidays mark the rhythm of the seasons and religious celebrations. A day for prayer and fasting precedes the October communion service in some communities. Numerous festive fall weddings provide ample holidays of another sort. Unless they have an invitation to a wedding, families celebrate Thanksgiving day with turkey dinners and extended family gatherings. New Year's Day is a quiet time for family gatherings. Some communities add a second day to their celebrations of Christmas, Easter, and Pentecost. The regular holiday is a sacred time celebrated with quiet family activities. The following day—second Christmas, Easter Monday, and Pentecost Monday—provide time for recreation, visiting, and sometimes shopping. Ascension day, prior to Pentecost, is also a holiday for visiting, fishing, and other forms of recreation. "More visiting takes place on these springtime holidays," said one Amishman, "than at any other time."

Christmas and Easter festivities are spared from commercial trappings. Families exchange Christmas cards and gifts. Some presents are home-made crafts and practical gifts, but increasingly many are bought at the store. Homes are decorated with greens, but Christmas trees, stockings, decorative lights, Santa Claus, and mistletoe are missing. Although eggs are sometimes painted and children may be given a basket of candy, Easter bunnies do not visit Amish homes. Sacred holidays revolve around religious customs, family gatherings, and quiet festivities rather than commercial trinkets and the sounds of worldly hubbub.

Birthdays are celebrated at home and school in quiet but pleasant ways, with cakes and gifts. They are not large-scale parties with clowns, balloons, and noisemakers but casual, low-key festivities. Parents often take a special snack of cookies or popsicles to school to honor a child's birthday. Birthday celebrations and other holiday festivities in the Amish world reaffirm religious roots, strengthen family ties, and underscore the lines of separation with the larger culture.

WEDDINGS

The wedding season is a festive time in Amish life. Coming on the heels of the harvest, weddings are held on Tuesdays and Thursdays from late October through early December in some settlements. In other communities they occur throughout the year. The larger communities may have more than 150 weddings in one season. More than a dozen weddings may be scattered across a settlement on the same day. Typically staged at the home of the bride, these joyous events attract upwards of 350 guests. The three-hour service begins shortly after eight o'clock in the morning. It is followed by a noon meal, singing, snacks, visiting, an evening meal, and festivities that last into the night. The specific practices vary from settlement to settlement.[20]

Young persons typically marry in their early twenties. A couple may date for one to two years before announcing their engagement. Bishops will only marry persons who are members of the Amish church because marriage is viewed as a divinely sanctioned union for life. Divorce is not only taboo but is cause for excommunication. The church does not arrange marriages, but it does place its blessing on the pair through an old ritual. Before the wedding, the groom takes a letter signed by elders of the church to the bride's deacon. The letter testifies to the groom's "good standing" in his home district. The bride's deacon then meets with her to verify and sanction the marriage plans.

The wedding day is an enormous undertaking for the bride's family as well as for relatives and friends who assist with preparations. Efforts to clean up the property, paint rooms, fix furniture, pull weeds, and pave driveways, among many other things, begin weeks in advance. The logistics of preparing two meals as well as snacks for several hundred guests are complicated and strenuous. The day before the wedding, the groom, according to custom in some settlements, decapitates several dozen chickens. The noontime wedding menu in one settlement includes "chicken roast"—chicken mixed with bread filling—mashed potatoes, gravy, creamed celery, pepper cabbage, and other items. Desserts include pears, peaches, puddings, cookies, and doughnuts.[21] Food is often served at two or three seatings because of the large number of guests. Many guests bring dishes of candy and other sweets for the "eck," or corner table, where the bride and groom are seated.

Flowers, rings, solos, and instrumental music are missing from the wedding, which is similar to any other Amish worship service. The long service includes congregational singing, prayers, two sermons, and testimonials by ordained leaders. The bishop who preaches the main sermon marries the couple after they affirm the wedding vows. The couple holds hands but do not kiss. Single friends of the bride and groom serve as attendants; however, no one is designated maid of honor or best man. Amish brides typically make their own wedding dresses from blue or purple material crafted in traditional styles. The bride and her attendants wear white capes and aprons over their dresses. In addition to the groom's new but customary black coat and vest, he and his attendants wear small black bow ties in some settlements.

In some communities games, snacks, and singing follow the noon meal. Young people are paired off somewhat randomly for the singing. Following the evening meal, another more lively singing takes place in which couples who are dating pair off. Those who are making their first appearance together stir considerable attention. Festivities may continue until midnight or until guests gradually leave. Some guests, invited to several weddings on the same day, may rotate between the festivities.

Newly married couples usually set up housekeeping in the spring following their wedding. Until then, the groom may live at the bride's home or continue to live with his parents. Couples do not take a traditional honeymoon, but they visit relatives on weekends during the winter months. Several newlywed couples may visit together, sometimes staying overnight at the home of close relatives. During these visits, family and friends present gifts to the newlyweds, adding to the bride's dowry, which often consists of some furniture. Young men begin growing a beard—the functional equivalent of a wedding ring—soon after their marriage. They are expected to have a "full stand" by the spring communion.

OCCUPATIONAL CHANGE

Amish life is rooted in the soil. Ever since European persecution pushed them into rural areas, the Amish have been tillers of the soil, and good ones at that. The land has nurtured both their common life and their robust families. "It's been a long-standing tradition," said one leader, "that Amish families live on the farm, attached closely to the soil. And a good father provides a farm for his boys." In the words of another leader, "Good soil makes a strong church where we can live together, worship together, and work together." Until recently the bulk of Amish families were farmers.

Amish ties to the soil remained firm until midcentury, when they began to unravel. The rising cost of prime farmland, suburbanization, tourism, and the booming growth of the Amish population itself have all contributed to the decline of farming. As urbanization devoured prime acreage, farmland prices soared. For example, while in the heart of Pennsylvania's Lancaster Amish settlement land sold for $300 an acre in 1940, the same farmland sold for $8,000 to $10,000 an acre in the 1990s. If sold for development, prices often doubled or tripled. Changes in agricultural technology and government regulations—especially those related to milk production—have made it difficult for some farmers to earn a living. All of these factors, including their own rapid growth, have nudged the Amish off the farm, particularly in older settlements in Indiana, Ohio, and Pennsylvania.

The Amish have coped with the demographic squeeze in several ways. First, farms have been subdivided into smaller units with intensive cropping and larger concentrations of livestock. Second, some families, committed to farming, have migrated to the rural backwaters of states where land could be purchased at lower prices. Third, in some settlements many farmers abandoned their plows to work in small shops, rural factories, or in various trades. The occupational shift has not been easy. Even ex-farmers insist that the farm remains the best place to raise a family and hope that someday their children or grandchildren will return to the soil.

The exodus from the farm has been steady in the past thirty years in the larger Amish communities that are located near urban areas. In the Elkhart-Lagrange settlement of Indiana, the number of farmers dropped from 61 to 35 percent between 1970 and 1988. Many Amish men began working in factories, especially in recreational vehicle factories. Indeed, 45 percent of the household heads were employed in factories by 1988.[22] The Amish settlements in the Elkhart-Lagrange area as well as in Geauga, Ohio, are distinctive for their large number of factory employees.

The number of farmers in the Amish settlement in Geauga and Trumbull Counties in northeastern Ohio near Cleveland had already dipped to 30 percent by 1977. Today only 16 percent of the families in that area are engaged in farming. The remainder work in factories, shops, construction, logging, and sawmills.[23] Farming has also dwindled in the large Amish settlement located in the Holmes County area of Ohio. In 1965 about 72 percent of household heads were farming, but today fewer than 40 percent are tilling the soil.[24] Those who have abandoned their plows operate hundreds of microenterprises as well as work in factories. However, the rate of factory employment in Ohio is lower than in Indiana's Elkhart-Lagrange settlement. A recent inventory lists over seven hundred Amish-owned-and-operated microenterprises in the Holmes County area of Ohio.

A similar pattern has emerged in Pennsylvania's Lancaster County settlement. As early as 1977, the number of men farming had dipped to about two-thirds. In recent years only about 45 percent have been farming for a living.[25] Unlike some other settlements, Lancaster has had very few persons working in factories. Those who have left the farm have established hundreds of cottage industries and small businesses. More than fifteen hundred Amish-owned enterprises are thriving in the Lancaster settlement.[26]

Some Amish entrepreneurs operate retail stores open to the general public.
Source: Dennis Hughes

The rise of cottage industries and small shops marks a historic turn in Amish life. Mushrooming since the 1970s, these new enterprises are reshaping Amish ways. Amish retail shops sell dry goods, furniture, shoes, hardware, and wholesale foods. Church members now work as carpenters, manufacturers, mechanics, plumbers, painters, and self-trained accountants. Professionals—lawyers, physicians, and veterinarians—are, of course, missing from Amish ranks because of the taboo on higher education.

The new industries come in three forms. First, there are home-based operations lodged on farms or built adjacent to new homes. These typically employ a few family members and neighbors. Bake shops, craft shops, hardware stores, health food stores, quilt shops, flower shops, and repair shops of all sorts are but a few of the hundreds of home-based operations. Work in these settings revolves around the family. "What we're trying to do," said one proprietor, "is to keep the family together." A growing number of these small cottage industries cater to tourists, but many serve the needs of Amish and non-Amish neighbors alike.

Second, larger shops and manufacturing concerns are housed in newly constructed buildings on the edge of farms or on commercial plots. These formal shops with five to ten employees manufacture farm machinery, hydraulic equipment, storage barns, furniture, and a variety of cabinetry. Some metal fabrication shops arrange subcontracts with other manufacturers. The larger shops are generally efficient and profitable. Low overhead, minimal advertising, austere management, modest wages, quality workmanship, and sheer hard work grant Amish businesses a competitive edge in the public market. Some of the larger shops have annual sales that top several million dollars.

Mobile work crews constitute a third type of industry. Amish construction workers travel to building sites for commercial and residential construction. The crews usually travel in hired vehicles. In some settlements the church permits Amish contractors to use electric tools for construction if they are powered by portable generators or on-site electricity. The mobile crews represent a major change in Amish life as they travel away for work that increases contact with the outside world.

Despite the recent occupational changes, few if any Amish are unemployed, and they are rarely recipients of government benefits. In the long run, however, the rise of small industries may disturb the equality of Amish life by encouraging a three-tier society of farmers, entrepreneurs, and day laborers. Will the next generation of prosperous shop owners turn their profits back to the community, or will they spend them on lavish lifestyles? Parents worry that youth, working a forty-hour week and with "loose" cash to spare, will snub traditional Amish values of simplicity and frugality. The new industries also encourage interaction with outsiders. Indeed, Marc Olshan has argued that business involvements constitute the "opening of Amish society" because they increase interaction with the outside world—a world the Amish have been taught to avoid for some three centuries.[27]

These rather dramatic occupational changes will surely transform the character of Amish life and culture over the generations. The rise of microenterprises is an attempt by the Amish to preserve many of their traditional values. Nevertheless, the exodus from the farm will undoubtedly alter family size, child-rearing practices, and attitudes toward leisure, as well as increase interaction with the outside world. New sources of wealth will also promote status distinctions in their community. In short, this occupational shift promises to be the most consequential change in the Amish community in recent decades.

Political Entanglements

The Amish view government with ambivalence.[28] Since they regulate many of their own affairs, they have less need for outside supervision. Although they support and respect civil authority, they generally keep a healthy distance from it. On the one hand, the Amish follow biblical admonitions to obey and pray for rulers and encourage members to be law-abiding citizens. On the other hand, government epitomizes worldly culture and the use of force. Persecutors of the Anabaptists in Europe were often government officials. Moreover, when push comes to shove, governments engage in warfare, use capital punishment, and impose their will with raw coercion. In Amish eyes, the government's use of force reflects a different moral order that is at odds with the nonresistant spirit of Jesus. As citizens of another kingdom, the Amish reject the use of force, including litigation.

When civil law and religious conscience collide, the Amish are not afraid to "take a stand" and to "obey God rather than man," even if it brings imprisonment. They have clashed with government officials over a variety of issues, including education, midwifery, Social Security, worker's compensation, slow-moving-vehicle emblems, land use, sanitation, zoning regulations, wearing hard hats at construction sites, and various health-care issues. Although they are conscientious objectors, the Amish have experienced little conflict over this issue. Amish youth have received farm deferments or served in alternative service projects during times of military draft, thanks to federal provisions for conscientious objectors.[29]

The church forbids membership in political organizations and holding public office for several reasons. First, running for office is viewed as arrogant—out of character with esteemed Amish values of humility and modesty. Second, office holding violates the religious principle of separation from the world. Finally, public officials must be prepared to use legal force if necessary to settle civic disputes. The exercise of such force, to Amish thinking, mocks the meek spirit of nonresistance.

Voting, however, is typically viewed as a personal matter. Although the church may not prohibit it, few persons vote. Those who do vote are likely to be businessmen or farmers concerned about local zoning issues. Jury duty is considered part of the state's system of force and hence is off limits. Joining political parties, attending political conventions, and campaigning for candidates flies in the face of the Amish virtues of simplicity, humility, and separation from the world.

For the most part the Amish pay taxes like other Americans. They pay federal and state income taxes, sales taxes, real estate taxes, and personal property taxes. Indeed, they pay school taxes for both public and parochial schools. Scant use of motor vehicles results, of course, in fewer gasoline taxes. Following biblical injunctions, the Amish pay all levied taxes except Social Security, from which they are exempt. In some states they are also exempt from workers' compensation and unemployment insurance.

The Amish view Social Security as a national insurance program, not a tax. Congressional legislation in 1965 exempted self-employed Amish persons from Social Security. After years of conflict, in 1988 Congress also exempted Amish people who were employed in Amish businesses. Amish employees in non-Amish businesses do not qualify for the exemption, however. They must pay Social Security without reaping its benefits. Thus, most church members neither pay nor tap into Social Security benefits.[30] Bypassing Social Security not only severs the Amish from old age pension payments, but it also closes the spigot to Medicare and Medicaid.

The Amish object to government aid for several reasons. The church, they contend, should assume responsibility for the social welfare of its own members. The aged, infirm, senile, disabled, and retarded are cared for, whenever possible, within extended family networks. To turn the care of their members over to the state would abdicate a fundamental tenet of faith—the care of one's brothers and sisters in the church. Furthermore, federal aid in the form of Social Security or Medicare would erode dependency on the church and undercut its programs of mutual aid, which the Amish have organized to help members who have suffered fire and storm damage as well as onerous medical expenses.

Government subsidies, or what the Amish call "handouts," have been firmly opposed. Championing self-sufficiency and the separation of church and state, the Amish worry that the hand that feeds them will also control them. Over the years, they have stubbornly refused direct subsidies even for agricultural programs designed for farmers in distress. Some Amish farmers do, however, receive indirect subsidies through agricultural price-support programs. The Amish have a long history of caring for their own and have little need for public welfare. On the whole, they tap few public funds, and thus they can hardly be called freeloaders or social parasites. By paying their fair share of taxes and siphoning off few public dollars, they not only care for their own but also make significant contributions to the public good as well.

Growing conflicts with government agencies led to the formation of a special committee in 1967 to speak with a common voice on legal issues to state and federal government agencies.[31] The National Amish Steering Committee has worked with government officials to resolve disputes related to conscientious objection, zoning, slow-moving vehicles, Social Security, Workers' Compensation, and the wearing of hard hats at construction sites—to name but a few. Informally organized, the National Amish Steering Committee is the only Amish organization that is national in scope. Outside legal advisors volunteering on behalf of the Amish have made a significant contribution to the preservation of religious liberty for all Americans through legal precedents established by various court decisions.[32]

The federal government has acquiesced to Amish convictions on three key issues that have bolstered their well-being and helped to preserve their culture. First, the Amish have not been forced to fight in America's wars. Long-time conscientious objectors, the Amish, along with other religious objectors, have enjoyed the option of performing alternative service rather than joining the armed forces.[33] Second, the integrity of Amish mutual aid has been buttressed by their exemption from Social Security in 1965, a major feat for the Amish. Their third and most significant legal victory, however, came in 1972 when the U.S. Supreme Court ruled in favor of the Amish in the landmark case of *Wisconsin v. Yoder*. This decision sanctioned Amish schools and permitted youth to end formal schooling after eight grades.[34] The outcomes of other disputes at local and state levels are mixed, but all things considered, the Amish have thrived under the benevolent spirit of religious freedom in North America.

The prosperity that the Amish have enjoyed in the twentieth century can be partially attributed to the tolerant—or perhaps more accurately, accommodating—political conditions that they have enjoyed in North America. Although some of them have been arrested and imprisoned, all things considered the Amish have fared rather well. Three of their legal disputes were reviewed by the U.S. Supreme Court between 1972 and 1990.[35] But despite the legal wrangling, the Amish have for the most part enjoyed a tolerable political climate where they have been able to practice their faith with little state interference and often with its protection.

Unlike their religious forbears in Europe, no Amish have been executed for their faith and few have chosen to migrate for religious reasons. Indeed, the ironies of history have brought tourists by the millions to gawk and gaze at Amish ways in some of the larger settlements. So in a strange twist of fate, those who were once hunted down and burned at the stake have now become objects of public curiosity if not outright admiration and respect.

TECHNOLOGY AND SOCIAL CHANGE

Although popular images construe the Amish as organic farmers milking cows by hand and cooking food on an open hearth, most of them spoil this caricature. They do prefer the ways of nature, but they certainly do not shun all forms of modern technology. A wide array of technology aids their work and enhances their comfort in kitchens, barns, and shops. Technology is selectively used and sometimes limited or harnessed in special ways.

Among dozens of common household items, progressive Amish homemakers typically use spray starch, detergents, instant pudding, disposable diapers, Zip-lock bags, and permanent press fabrics. Modern bathrooms, the latest gas appliances, and air-powered tools are common in many Amish settlements, although families in the smaller, more conservative communities still use outhouses and do not have refrigerators. Except for a few battery-powered gadgets, electricity is missing from Amish homes. Televisions, computers, and radios, of course, are taboo. Electric clothes dryers, blow dryers, microwaves, air conditioners, and other electrical appliances, of course, are not found. Washing machines are often powered by gasoline engines, hydraulic pressure, or air pressure. Water is typically heated by gas water heaters. Homes are normally heated by kerosene or coal heaters or in some cases by wood stoves.

In the more progressive settlements, a wide array of technology supports farming operations—automatic milkers, tractors, elevators, welders, and electric cow trainers powered by batteries. Pesticides, insecticides, preservatives, and chemical fertilizers are widely used alongside modern veterinary practices. Although historically frowned upon, artificial insemination of dairy cattle is being used in some states. But there are limits here as well. Embryo transplants are taboo. The more conservative churches do not permit automatic milkers or the use of bulk tanks for cooling milk. Silo unloaders, milk pipelines, milking parlors, automatic barn cleaners, self-propelled equipment, and the use of tractors for fieldwork, with a few exceptions, do not received the blessing of the church in Old Order settlements.

Shops and cottage industries employ a vast array of mechanical equipment, albeit powered by hydraulic and air pressure. Some craftsmen work with plastic and fiberglass materials. Small 12-volt motors, electrical inverters, and diesel engines energize the shop equipment in the more progressive settlements. Inverters are used to convert 12-volt electricity from batteries into 110 volts in order to operate small electrical equipment. Electronic cash registers, digital scales, and electric calculators powered through inverters are commonplace in the progressive settlements as well. But again, there are some limits: computers and standard electrical equipment—with some special exceptions—are forbidden. Some carpentry crews for example, may use electrical tools at construction sites, but not at home.

Despite popular misconceptions, the Amish are not a fossilized relic of the past. Economic pressures prodded by farming and microenterprises have spawned many changes. Other changes have come as families sought ease, comfort, and convenience within the boundaries of Amish society. Innovations that pose little threat to Amish identity or community solidarity are overlooked. Gas grills, for example, have appeared on Amish patios in recent years. Instant coffee, plastic tricycles, and chain saws have been welcomed by many Amish groups. In other cases, ordained leaders have drawn firm lines. Fearing that computers would lead

Air and hydraulic power are used, instead of electricity, to operate large equipment in many Amish manufacturing shops. *Source:* Dennis Hughes

to video games and television, they were banned in the 1980s in many settlements.

The unwritten *Ordnung,* as interpreted by church leaders, regulates the rate of social change.[36] Once embedded into the understandings of the *Ordnung,* taboos are difficult to overturn. Sometimes new technology is accepted on top of old taboos, yielding a perplexing riddle. For example, power lawn mowers were forbidden in the 1950s in some settlements for fear that they would spawn ostentatious lawns and proud hearts and might steal work from Amish youth. A decade later farmers were permitted to mount engines on field mowers. Still later, "weed eaters" powered by small gasoline engines were deemed appropriate for lawns and gardens. Yet the taboo on power lawn mowers held firm across the years. Thus, today, some homesteads sport old-fashioned push mowers alongside modern weed eaters, chain saws, and large power mowers in hay fields.

Telephones illustrate a similar pattern. First barred from homes in the early decades of the twentieth century, they were later permitted at the end of lanes. Eventually they were permitted adjacent to barns and shops, and finally even inside shops in some progressive church districts. However, the original taboo on home phones has held firm. Although trying to respect the initial taboo, church leaders have, over the years, yielded to pressures to install phones for business purposes, resulting in a zigzag pattern of telephone use. Although banned from homes, phones are found in some settlements in various outbuildings and shops, depending on the views of the local bishop. Cellular phones, which transcend the traditional boundaries, have stirred controversy in some districts in recent years.

A ragged pattern of change has also followed the car. The original proscription against the ownership of motor vehicles has held over the decades, although leaders have gradually permitted widespread hiring of vehicles to accommodate the need for greater mobility. As settlements expanded geographically and as families moved to other areas in search of farmland, it became increasingly difficult to use horse-and-buggy transportation. The church has made a sharp distinction between ownership and use of motor vehicles. Members may not own or operate vehicles, but they may rent taxi service for business purposes and long-distance trips. The extent to which vehicles are used varies widely from settlement to settlement.

The church has firmly opposed practices that might erode traditional taboos or bring cultural contamination—microwave ovens, television, video games, video cameras, and computers. Other practices and products that pose no threat—trampolines, hot dogs, and battery-powered calculators—slip into place with little fuss. A patchwork pattern of social change often results as elders try to retain traditional practices while also nodding to pressures for change. Moreover, what is permitted varies considerably from settlement to settlement and rests somewhat on the disposition of the local bishop. Working together, the bishops in the same affiliation try to uphold the historic markers of Amish identity as prescribed by the *Ordnung*. Because moral authority ultimately rests in the local congregations, bishops vary in their interpretation and application of rules.

The lines of discretion that restrict the use of technology are drawn from many sources. Some of the limits flow from fears that large farms and shops will disrupt the order and equality of community life. Other restrictions are designed to stymie the cultural contamination that might come via computers and televisions. Other restrictions, such as the taboo on ownership of motor vehicles and the use of tractors in fields, are designed to limit mobility and encourage family-related work, which binds the community together and impedes social fragmentation. Still other guidelines rest on symbolic taboos that have, over the years, helped to preserve Amish identity. The selective use of technology reinforces community solidarity and arrests assimilation into American culture.

THE RIDDLE OF AMISH CULTURE

The growth of this unique people poses a fascinating riddle. Why is it that the tradition-laden Amish are not merely surviving but are actually thriving in contemporary society? How is it that a people who shun high school, television, air travel, computers, and the ownership of automobiles are not withering away? By what means are they able to spurn the temptations of modern society without fading into oblivion? Political toleration and their esteem as a cultural icon of sorts have surely enhanced Amish growth and vitality. Yet these are not enough. Other unusual groups who enjoy similar religious freedoms have not necessarily flourished like the Amish. The success of the Amish experiment derives from at least three factors: vigorous biological growth, social restrictions, and cultural compromises.

Because they do not seek converts, the robust Amish growth rate is produced by large families and strong retention of their young. A few outsiders occasionally become members, but very rarely, because of the wide cultural gap [37] The average family has six or seven children, but some families have ten or more. Throughout the twentieth century, the Amish gradually began using modern medicines and the services of physicians and trained midwives. These practices reduced infant mortality and encouraged their families to grow.

Children are an economic asset in an agrarian economy, and in Amish eyes they are also viewed as a blessing from the Lord. Although no official statements prohibit artificial birth control, the Amish discourage such tampering with divinely ordained means of reproduction. There is growing evidence, however, that in some settlements Amish couples, especially

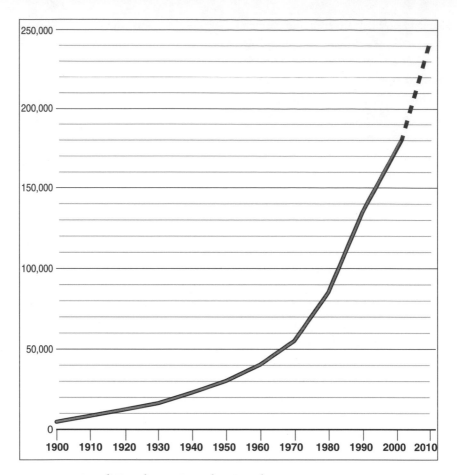

FIGURE 4.4 Amish Population Growth in North America, 1900–2010
Note: These estimates are based on the number of church districts and assume
150 people (members and children) per district.
Sources: Raber (2000), *Luthy* (1997), and various editions of *The Mennonite Yearbook.*

younger ones involved in business, are limiting the size of their families
by artificial means.[38] It remains to be seen if Amish families will shrink
in size as more of them enter nonfarm occupations. In any event, the robust size of Amish families has, at least in the past, provided a large pool
of recruits for membership.

But having children is not enough. They must be persuaded to join the
community. What attracts youth to the church, and why do adults re-

main? Retention rates vary by settlement and affiliation and also fluctuate with economic, social, and religious circumstances. In the three largest settlements, 80 percent or more of the offspring join and remain with the church.[39] As long as four out of five youth claim the church of their birth, the Amish are assured of steady growth.

But why are young people attracted to the church? Many factors—romantic, social, economic, cultural, religious—compel them.[40] Amish youth grow up in an Amish world speaking a different language. All of their friends are Amish. They are embedded in a thicket of family ties with dozens of aunts, uncles, and cousins who share not only kinship but ethnicity as well. Youth must join the church before they can marry. Young men who have been flirting with the world are often enticed to membership by prospective brides. The promise of a farm or a stake in the family business can also be a lure to remain in the community. But the largest incentive of all is the fact that the Amish world, constructed by thorough childhood training, is their primary, and often only, social world. Young people socialized into such a different cultural world "really have no other option," charged an ex-Amishman. A few, of course, choose to leave, but the overwhelming majority stay in the church.

The erection of social fences—restrictions of one sort or another—has enabled the Amish community to retain a strong sense of identity and solidarity. The church has constructed social fences, visible symbols of ethnic identity—clothing, transportation, practices—that mark the borders with the world. The community regulates interaction with the larger society by prohibiting the ownership of motor vehicles, television, radio, and higher education. The rise of Amish schools since midcentury has also helped to preserve Amish ways and cultivate a distinctive people. All of these fences enhance identity and impede assimilation into modern life. The use of shunning to preserve religious boundaries troubles tolerant modern minds. But even those who cherish tolerance are willing to expel unruly dissidents, political traitors, illegal aliens, and absentee employees.

The social fences, however, have not been overly rigid; the church has absorbed technological changes that enable members to sustain a comfortable, albeit modest standard of living. The church has negotiated numerous cultural compromises that permit the selective use of technology without abandoning traditional practice. These puzzling compromises often baffle outsiders: the use of tractors at barns but not in fields, the use of 12-volt electricity from batteries but not 110-volt electricity from public utility lines, the use of telephones in outbuildings but not in houses, the use but not ownership of vehicles. These and many other comprises show the ingenious ability of the Amish to tap the resources of technology without forfeiting their religious souls. Striking a host of cultural compromises, the church has selectively picked the fruits of progress while retaining a firm grip on traditional ways. These factors and others help to solve the riddle and explain how an Old Order people have been able to flourish in the midst of contemporary life.

There are other reasons for Amish success as well. Despite hard work and some inconvenience, Amish life satisfies many basic human needs. There are faults, failures, and cases of abuse along the way; nevertheless, membership in this distinctive subculture offers a sense of identity, belonging, and meaning. A stable community with enduring habits of care provides social and emotional security. Moreover, for young and old alike, this is the bestowed road to heaven. It is not a superhighway, but it follows a path prescribed by Scripture and forged by ancestors of old. To walk on the old road—to know where one is going and why—fills the human soul with meaning. And that is likely one reason, at least, why so many Amish youth claim their birthright church and why so many adults take this road to heaven.

CHAPTER FIVE

The Brethren

The Kiss of Peace to each we give.
—Brethren hymn

BRETHREN BEGINNINGS

The Old German Baptist Brethren, nicknamed "Dunkers," simply call themselves Brethren. Their historic practice of baptizing by immersion—dunking—in public streams and lakes, gave rise to the Dunker label. Unlike the Hutterites, Mennonites, and Amish, who descend directly from the sixteenth-century Anabaptists, the Brethren claim a mixed parentage. Blending German Pietism and Anabaptism, they see themselves as different from other plain groups. And indeed they are—even among peculiar people, they are peculiar. They are not the plainest or most unusual; in some ways, they are less strange than the Mennonites or Amish. So while they repudiate the modern world as a fallen kingdom, they also defy Anabaptist patterns of plainness in fascinating ways.

Founded in the German village of Schwarzenau, the Brethren began as a small band of separatist Pietists in 1708. They rejected not only the established Protestant and Catholic faiths of their day but also the spiritualization of the church and the individualism of the Radical Pietists. Influenced by Mennonites, whom they admired but considered spiritually lukewarm, they rebaptized each other in the Eder River. They hoped to graft Anabaptist understandings of the disciplined church onto Pietist roots of spirituality and thus to recreate the primitive faith of the early church. Believing that the "teachings of Jesus and the Apostles could actually be lived out and need not be explained away or otherwise improved upon," they embraced the New Testament as their binding norm.[1]

The movement flourished briefly in Germany, forming several congregations. Yet because of persecution, competition from other separatists, economic factors, and internal dissension, Brethren soon migrated to eastern Pennsylvania and New Jersey. They settled among Mennonites, whom they viewed as good neighbors and a spiritual field ripe for picking. By 1740 few Brethren remained in Europe.

For Brethren, the nineteenth century was a time of remarkable expansion. They fanned outward from the eastern states of Pennsylvania, Maryland, Virginia, and the Carolinas, across Kentucky, and into Ohio and Indiana. As the frontier opened up, Brethren continued westward into Illinois, Kansas, Missouri, the Dakotas, and on to the Pacific coast. Between 1790 and 1880 they grew from a small German-speaking sect of 1,500 members to a geographically extended, largely English-speaking fellowship of 58,000 members in 500 congregations.

By the 1880s, Brethren were deeply divided over the revivalistic methods of mainstream Protestantism. Their council meetings and periodicals brimmed with bickering about paying preachers, operating Sunday Schools, and holding prayer meetings and revivals. Discord over higher

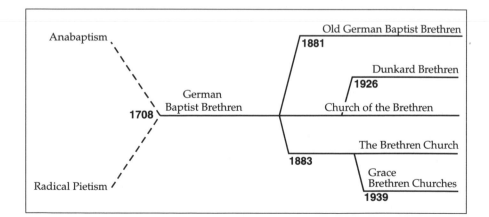

FIGURE 5.1 Formation of Brethren Groups in North America

education, church government, discipline, plain dress, and other marks of distinction widened the breach. A three-way split in 1881–82 severed the Brethren into Old Order, conservative, and progressive factions.

The first of these groups, the Old German Baptist Brethren, set out to vindicate the "old paths" and the "ancient order" of the church. Rejecting evangelistic innovations and other adaptations, they sought a return to the simpler practices of the early nineteenth century. These Old Order Brethren have experienced a great deal of change since the 1880s, but through it all they have sustained remarkable unity. In fact, unity is a precondition for remaining "Brethren" as they understand the term. Buttressing their order with a strong Annual Meeting and a close-knit fellowship, they have maintained ancient practices that other Brethren abandoned long ago.[2]

GROWTH AND ORGANIZATION

Assessing the Old German Baptists during the 1930s, one observer wrote that "they have gradually dwindled in numbers. . . . [W]ithout a feeling of responsibility for others, without a program for religious work, . . . there can be but one result. A lack of vision can mean only darkness, and where there is no vision the people perish."[3] Their numbers did decline during the early twentieth century, but forecasts of their demise were premature. Numbering about 4,000 when they formed, today the Old German Baptist Brethren count some 6,000 adult members in sixteen states from Pennsylvania to California. Adding nonmember spouses and children, the Brethren community involves about 20,000 persons.[4] The largest concentrations are in Ohio (31 percent), Indiana (27 percent), California (11 percent), Virginia (10 percent), Pennsylvania (8 percent), and Kansas (8 percent). Together, these six states account for 94 percent of the Brethren and forty-three of their fifty-five congregations. Slow but steady growth in the late twentieth century has increased their number by over 50 percent between 1950 and the year 2000.[5]

Brethren are organized into congregations with clear geographic boundaries, called church districts; they must join the district where they live. Typically, each district has one meetinghouse, and district names refer to natural surroundings (Ash Grove) or a water source used for baptizing (Falling Spring, Pigg River, Spruce Run). A district of 250 persons

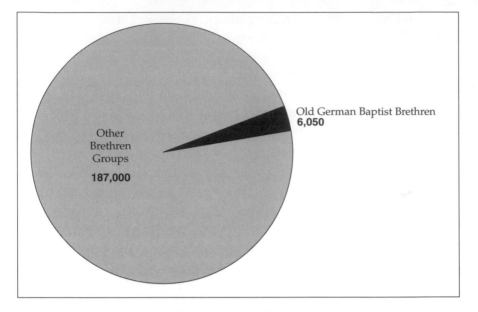

FIGURE 5.2 Estimated Adult Membership of Brethren Groups in North America
Note: Other Brethren groups include Church of the Brethren, the Brethren
Church, Dunkard Brethren, and the Fellowship of Grace Brethren Churches.
Source: Yearbook of American and Canadian Churches (2000).

would likely have about 85 members and 165 children and nonmember
adults.

New districts are formed in one of two ways: by geographic migration
or by district repartitioning. The first occurs when families relocate to a
new area. Once a core of several families is established, a new district will
form. A fledgling fellowship may remain under the oversight of an existing district until it can oversee its own affairs. In some cases, ministers
travel great distances to nurture such congregations. Under the watchful
care of ministers from central and southern Ohio, a new congregation in
Michigan grew from 12 to 18 members between 1985 and 1993. Groups
of Brethren have also recently founded districts in Wisconsin, Georgia,
and Washington state. The growth in Washington was fueled by an
exodus of Brethren from California.

District repartitioning occurs when an established congregation opts
to divide. Brethren redraw district boundaries in such a way that both
groups retain a strong nucleus of members and ministers. In recent divi-

sions in Ohio and Virginia, parent districts continued to share a meetinghouse with their daughter congregations, holding services on alter-
nating Sundays. Some members attended both services, enabling the fellowship to continue despite the partitioning.

Such intermingling is typical in dense settlements where strong chains
of support link neighboring congregations. The chain is social, devotional,
and practical. If a district has difficulty resolving an issue, it calls upon *adjoining elders* from neighboring districts for counsel and support. When
it holds a meeting to select a new minister, adjoining elders oversee the
process.

Worship is staggered among neighboring districts, typically every
other Sunday. Off Sundays provide an opportunity to worship with kindred Brethren in a neighboring district. Visiting ministers are often in-

FIGURE 5.3 Distribution of Brethren Congregations in North America

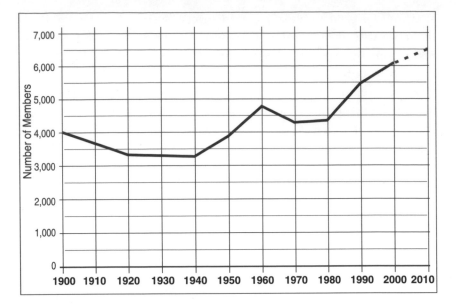

FIGURE 5.4 Growth of Brethren Membership in North America, 1900–2010
Sources: Yearbook of American and Canadian Churches (2000) and *Directory of Officials of the Old German Baptist Brethren Church* (2000).

vited to preach. In some locations visitors are so common that members rarely hear their own ministers. After singing the final hymn, visiting Brethren spend the afternoon eating lunch and fellowshipping with members of the host congregation. In fact, Sundays become a dynamic interplay of hosts and guests. Yet Brethren would describe it more simply. It is the gathering of the spiritual family—brothers and sisters uniting for a season of worship and fellowship.

Biological kinship matches spiritual lineage. Common surnames such as Bowman, Brubaker, Skiles, Denlinger, and Metzger reflect the church's Germanic heritage. Members from neighboring districts and distant states are likely to be cousins, or at least cousins of cousins. But the circle of kinship is porous—names such as Clark, Davis, Montgomery, Rogers, and Robinson reflect a legacy of intermarriage with outsiders. A Virginia congregation illustrates the pattern. Its membership includes thirty different surnames, yet the three most common—Bowman, Layman, and Montgomery—account for over half of its membership.

Many typical Old Order fences are missing among the Brethren. First, they speak the language of the broader culture. Few know any German, and neither did their grandparents or great-grandparents. The Brethren legacy of German hymns was nearly extinct by the time the Old German Baptist Brethren formed in 1881. Despite the fact that Hutterites, Mennonites, and Amish do not carry the appellation "German," they are encircled by a linguistic fence. Ironically, only the Old *German* Baptist Brethren are thoroughly Anglicized.

Second, Brethren are not residentially segregated. Most live in small towns or rural areas, interspersed with Mennonite, Lutheran, and Methodist neighbors. Brethren own their own homes and farms. While the white-framed farmhouse is typical of their past, the housing development on the edge of town may typify their future. They shop in malls and mega-chains and eat in family restaurants.

Third, Brethren not only live near mainstream Americans but also work alongside them. Brethren are plumbers, teachers, electricians, social workers, contractors, nurses, auctioneers, and assembly line and postal workers. Skilled trades are common, as are small agriculture-related enterprises such as orchards, nurseries, and farm equipment stores. Few Brethren pursue graduate study to become doctors or engineers, but occupations that require technical training such as nursing, realty, or accounting are on the rise. In their roles as supervisors, employees, or business associates, Brethren interact daily with persons who know little of their faith and who espouse values that are foreign to them. Thirty years ago most Brethren were farmers; today fewer than one-quarter make their living this way.

Fourth, their standard of living appears typically middle-American. Homes are often decorated in a "country living" style, with adornments ranging from flowers, to scenic vistas, to devotional poetry. The look is distinctly nonmetallic. Couches are pillowy soft. An abundance of chairs testifies to afternoons of warm fellowship. A dining room table with only sixteen seats might be considered too small to welcome guests. Modern appliances such as dishwashers and microwaves are common. In the driveway sits one or more large cars or vans—generally new and well-equipped. Yet Brethren rarely own brightly colored vehicles. Sports cars, convertibles, and flashy accessories would raise eyebrows and questions.

A Brethren dressmaker at work in her home surrounded by family.
Source: Roanoke Times

Vans are valued because they permit more than one family to travel to-gether. Brethren like to travel for educational and recreational reasons, but they love to travel to visit distant Brethren.

Fifth, many Brethren children attend public schools. Furthermore, it is hard to distinguish their dress from the church-going children of Baptists and Methodists. Like other youth, some excel at sports and some at aca-demics. A generation ago physical education was frowned upon because shorts were required. Now it is even possible to find Brethren cheerlead-ers. Brethren teenagers own and drive cars and enjoy socializing with Brethren and non-Brethren friends.

Sixth, Brethren have no bishop or group of leaders invested with the power to discipline members. No ladder of authority exists whereby church officials make or enforce a church *Ordnung.* Even though the frontiers of worldliness are carefully patrolled, there is little disowning or disfellowshipping. Great patience is shown toward violators. Elders ad-monish members time and again to put away televisions, fill in swimming pools, put on broadbrimmed hats, or lower hems before firmer measures are taken by the council meeting of the local congregation.

Given all these similarities with mainstream culture, why are Brethren included in a book on Old Order groups? They do not live in communes or speak a distinctive language. They are neither economically nor socially segregated from society. Their homes are no more plain than their technologies are primitive. They are more likely to be seen on a Boeing 747 than in timeless buggies.

And yet Brethren are more distinct in appearance than Old Order Mennonites. Their bearded men and plainly dressed women are often mistaken for Amish. Brethren homes are devoid of pianos, guitars, radios, televisions, stereos, tape recorders, and VCRs. Radios are stripped from cars and vans. While Brethren are permitted to marry outside their faith, they may neither divorce nor remarry once divorced.[6] Even with nonmembers, Brethren do not attend the weddings of divorcees and are discouraged from letting such couples sleep together as guests in their homes. In fact, by the standards of most Americans, Brethren weddings are hardly weddings at all. They are held outside of church sanctuaries and without corsages, adorning objects, special singing, instrumental music, or candles.

Christmas trees, stars, and tinsel are considered idolatrous distractions of sacred events. "Worldly amusements" such as movies, skating, and water skiing are prohibited. The use of public recreational facilities is discouraged. Swimming in public is disallowed. Members who tried to avoid public immodesty by installing private pools were recently required by the church to fill them with dirt. Brethren eschew extensive involvement with outside clubs and associations. They counsel against voting and other forms of political involvement and strictly prohibit military service and filing lawsuits. They own and operate all manner of businesses, but they may not advertise them on radio or television.

About half of their children are home-schooled or attend private schools run by members of the church. Brethren do not sponsor Sunday schools or missions. Their ministers are unsalaried, and their meetings are as plain as they were in 1880, even though their meetinghouses have been upgraded. Brethren reject offerings, benedictions, postludes, pulpits, steeples, stained glass, fancy oratory, revivals, and ecumenical cooperation. Nonmembers are excluded from communion, and wayward members are disciplined for violating the church order. The list goes on and on.

Despite some missing cultural fences, Brethren are distinctly Old Order. These pilgrims are not on the main road to heaven, but their path also departs from the route taken by other plain groups. In this sense, Brethren are doubly strange. To understand their peculiar peculiarity, we must unlock their Pietist legacy.

GRACE IN THE HEART

Viewing a religious group from the outside, one's gaze often falls on the external veneer of faith. Tangible markers such as dress, language, and demeanor are highlighted, while the spirit of distinction goes unnoticed. To dismiss or downplay the spirit, however, is to miss the inner logic of the Brethren. Their extensive interaction with the world demands that Brethren nurture a *spirit* of distinction if they are to remain distinct at all. Such a spirit, planted deep in the heart of each member, is less crucial for Amish, Mennonites, and Hutterites, where barriers of buggies, geography, or language wrest them more neatly from the grasp of the world. But where daily life turns worldlings into neighbors and associates, as it does for many Brethren, a sectarian spirit may be the only secure foothold against the slide toward modern life.

Brethren thus struggle and pray for inner transformation—in their own words, for "a deeper work of grace in the heart." The Holy Spirit's inner voice, they believe, whispers to every believer, but it can only be heard by those who willingly sacrifice self-will to God's will. God's work of grace, then, depends upon receptivity to the Spirit, which requires a constant struggle against selfish and worldly concerns.

Such talk is more than theological slogans in an occasional tract. Spiritual awakening and singleness of mind are things Brethren genuinely think and talk about. When the concerns of daily life threaten to consume them, they pray that their vision might turn heavenward. They heed the scriptural teaching "Be not conformed to this world" but are even more attuned to being "transformed by the renewing of your mind, that ye may prove what is that good, and acceptable, and perfect, will of God" (Rom. 12:2, KJV). Spiritual transformation is the core of the Brethren faith, the axis from which all else radiates. Conforming to the order and rejecting worldly habits is well and good, but if not inspired by the right spirit, it is only "dead works." To be credible in Brethren eyes, a peculiar practice must spring from God's work of grace in the heart.

Unity and Love

The fruits of spiritual awakening are gentleness, peace, love, and unity with Christ as well as with one's brethren. Love and unity are especially important. Brethren maintain a deep, almost mystical, understanding of each, believing that one is impossible without the other. To be in Christian love with a brother or sister is to cherish visible displays of like-mindedness, for these reveal that Brethren are guided by the same spirit. Disunity, on the other hand, testifies to spiritual confusion and threatens the peace and love of the body. Christian unity, as the Brethren understand it, is both spiritual and tangible. It is visible in dress and lifestyle, heard in what is spoken and unspoken, and sensed in gentleness of spirit, genuineness of affection, and in the twinkling of eyes as Brethren meet. It is confirmed by the sound of a cappella hymns with simple harmonies, sung slowly and fully.

> *Lo! what an entertaining sight*
> *Are brethren that agree,*
> *Brethren whose cheerful hearts unite*
> *in bands of piety. (Hymn 299)*[7]

> *Keep us, Lord, still in communion,*
> *Daily nearer drawn to thee,*
> *Sinking in the sweetest union,*
> *Of that heartfelt mystery. (Hymn 176)*

If unity is the Spirit's fruit, then love is its flower. Only a deep love for God and the Brethren sustains a willingness to subordinate personal interests to those of the church. When love grows cold, Brethren believe, patience disappears, discipline loses its gentleness, and believers justify their self-will. It is love that causes members to grieve for the sins and celebrate the virtues of their brethren. Love softens discipline but also undergirds it by binding the church into a single unbroken chain. And heartfelt love makes submission possible; without it a brother's admonition reaps only resentment. Like unity, love is a recurring theme in Brethren hymnody:

> *Love is the golden chain that binds*
> *Believers all in one;*
> *And he's an heir of heav'n that finds*
> *His bosom aglow with love. (Hymn 237)*

> *Love is the fountain whence*
> *All true obedience flows;*
> *The Christian serves the God he loves,*
> *And loves the God he knows. (Hymn 244)*

> *And when we parting leave this place,*
> *Let us in love remain—*
> *Still strive to grow in Jesus' grace,*
> *Until we meet again.(Hymn 43)*

In short, intense unity and love nourished by the Holy Spirit are the heart of the Brethren faith. Habits of gentleness, patience, self-denial, and devotion flow from this divine essence; pride and moral lethargy grow in its absence. Where the true Spirit resides, violence and deceit are dissolved by God's love. This is what Brethren mean when they speak of being born again.[8]

After nearly three hundred years, the Old German Baptist Brethren still model themselves after their vision of the early church and embrace the New Testament as their only creed. Beneath their Old Order veneer, they are a deeply religious people with a strong spiritual sensitivity. This sensitivity, which shapes polity, doctrine, and discipline, is most clearly reflected in the symbolic content of their ordinances—baptism, the Love Feast, and the holy kiss.

BRETHREN BAPTISM

Brethren follow Jesus' teaching that if one is not "born of water and of the Spirit, he cannot enter into the kingdom of God" (John 3:5). They make a doctrinal issue of baptism and turn to Scripture for the specific mode. There Christ instructs them that believers, not babies or young children, should be baptized: "He that believeth and is baptized shall be saved" (Mark 16:16). Likewise, the admonition to baptize "in the name of the father, and of the son, and of the Holy Ghost" signals a threefold immersion. So Brethren baptize in a free-flowing stream by dunking believers three times forward. This "trine immersion" symbolizes the burial of the carnal nature and the birth of a new creature in Christ.[9] This mode of baptism is firmly defended and practiced.

The age of baptism varies. Some children are baptized at the age of 12, and some wait into their twenties or later. While there are no firm guidelines, 14 is still considered young; 16 through 20, normal; and the mid-twenties, late. Until the late 1970s, most Brethren children attended public school and waited until after graduation to join the church. They thus avoided ridicule for their clothing because plain dress is required only after baptism. Presently, about half of the youth attend private schools operated by church members or receive home-schooling. With the threat of ridicule reduced for these youth, the age of baptism has declined. Brethren remain watchful that the trend does not dip to child baptism.

Two children and a young member of the Brethren. The head covering and traditional dress is worn after baptism. *Source: Roanoke Times*

Outsiders, of course, may join the church at any age, as may Brethren who decide to wait.

Never ones to lure or entice potential converts, Brethren wait until someone—including their own youth—approaches them before discussing membership. Ministers then pay a private visit to candidates. All applicants must promise to refrain from participating in warfare, going to law, voting in political elections, taking oaths, and using profanity. They must also express their unity with the order of the Brethren by agreeing to follow church rulings and the uniform standard of dress. In the words of an 1848 ruling that still prevails, they must accept "the principles of being defenseless, nonswearing, and not conforming to the world."[10]

If satisfied with the candidate's response, the ministers ask the congregation if it will receive the new member. Matthew 18:10–22—the church's rule for dealing with offenses between members—is read and explained to the applicant.[11] If the candidate accepts these rules of governance, baptism may proceed.

At the designated time, Brethren gather at a customary spot on the bank of a river or dammed stream. Two persons descend into the flowing water. The applicant, facing downstream, kneels. Then the minister, wet to his hips, solemnly poses three questions: "Dost thou believe that Jesus Christ is the Son of God, and that He has brought from heaven a saving Gospel?" The applicant replies, "I do." "Dost thou willingly renounce Satan, with all his pernicious ways, and all the sinful pleasures of this world?" Barely audible at times over the current, the applicant agrees. "Dost thou covenant with God, in Christ Jesus, to live faithful until death?" . . . "I do."

After this third and final commitment, the minister responds, "Upon this, your confession of faith, which you have made before God and these witnesses, I baptize you for the remission of sins. . . ." The applicant closes his eyes. "In the name of the Father. . . ." The minister dips his head. For an instant, his entire body is submerged, and then his head reappears. "And of the Son. . . ." The applicant is dipped again and then catches his breath. "And of the Holy Spirit." After the third dipping, all present close their eyes while the elder offers a prayer for the new member, his hands placed on the dripping head. The new member then stands, and the minister greets him with a holy kiss, symbolizing the fact that everything has changed—a new relation exists with all who are watching.

Believer's baptism, like other Dunker rituals, touches the entire community, not just the two in the water. Its ripples of significance spread across the stream and up the bank to the gathered assembly. In one sense all are rebaptized as they silently reconsider their own vows, yet all are baptizers, coauthors of the decision that this applicant should become a brother or sister. Baptism is not a single event, but a chain of smaller ones.

One of these smaller rites, the holy kiss, is so important that Brethren consider it secondary only to baptism and the Lord's Supper as a major church ordinance. If baptism is the gateway to the Lord's pasture, and communion to the feeding of the sheep, the holy kiss is the repeated reminder that one belongs in the fold.

THE HOLY KISS

The kiss of peace to each we give—
A pledge of Christian love:
In love, while here on earth, we'll live,
In love we'll dwell above. (Hymn 237)

When Brethren meet—at home, at church, or in other private settings—they greet each other with the right hand of fellowship and a kiss on the lips. Men greet men and women, women. Variously called the salutation, the kiss of peace, the holy kiss, or simply "the kiss," this greeting symbolically separates members from nonmembers, dividing the world into Brethren and non-Brethren.

The rite is grounded in Paul's instruction to the Christians at Rome, Corinth, and Thessalonica, "Greet one another with an holy kiss." Brethren believe the admonition applies to apostolic Christians of all times and places.[12] When Brethren asked in 1974 if they could bestow the kiss upon outsiders, the ruling was, "We feel it is not right according to the Scripture, nor Church order, for members to greet other fraternities with the holy kiss. However . . . there is a difference between the holy kiss, and a friendship or relationship kiss."[13] While a kiss of friendship binds socially, the holy kiss joins spiritually. It is the symbolic rite, the Brethren believe, that seals the true love of God that unites the hearts of his children.

A visit to a Brethren home reminds outsiders of these distinctions. You are greeted warmly at the door and ushered into the living room, where

Two members greet each other with a holy kiss at a church gathering. *Source: Roanoke Times*

a circle of Brethren stand to greet you with handshakes. After introductions, they listen with interest as you share stories of your life, and they respond with theirs. Fifteen minutes later the doorbell rings and an Old German Baptist Brethren enters the room. All rise again, but this person moves around the circle greeting everyone of the same gender with a kiss until they come to you. Then the kiss suddenly cools to a handshake.

Five minutes later another Brethren enters. Again everyone rises to receive the kiss except you. Throughout the evening the ritual boundary line is redrawn again and again. The visitor remains inside the circle of conversation but outside the circle of intimacy. Brethren who are barely acquainted will exchange the kiss, for it expresses a holy love for all brothers or sisters in the faith, not a feeling toward a specific individual.

This marker of membership also confirms baptism, communion,

church council, and other symbolic moments that reaffirm Brethren unity. In the case of baptism, the kiss symbolically seals one's altered relationship to other members. In the case of communion, it confirms the peace and unity of the congregation before partaking of the Eucharist.

THE LOVE FEAST

Though most observers would place Old German Baptist Brethren and Catholics at opposite ends of the Christian spectrum, they share one thing in common: communion is a moment of intense spiritual drama in which every detail flows with precision. For both traditions the emphasis is plainly liturgical, yet it is Brethren, not Catholics, who have crafted a plain liturgy. With Brethren, it seems, things come in threes. Members are baptized thrice, and communion involves a threefold service known as the Love Feast, a term from the church's Pietist heritage.[14] Occurring once per year in each district, the Love Feast is the spiritual peak of the congregational calendar. Although the event lasts from Saturday morning to Sunday afternoon, the focal point is the Saturday evening reenactment of the Last Supper—a service of *feetwashing*,[15] the *Lord's Supper* (an evening meal), and *communion* (the bread and wine). Love Feasts are staggered across congregations over several weekends to encourage visiting. Preparation, begun weeks ahead, commences with *the visit*.

The Visit. A few weeks before Love Feast, the ministers and deacons of a congregation designate pairs of "visiting Brethren" to pay a "yearly visit" to the home of each member. Members are asked three questions: "Are you of the same mind as when you were received into the church by your baptism?" "Are you still willing to receive and give counsel according to the gospel order?" and "Are you, as far as you know, in peace and union with the church?" These probes provide an opportunity to reaffirm baptismal commitments and to acknowledge the mutual discipline of the saints.

After the member responds, the visit continues: "There is now liberty given to you should you see or have any knowledge of anything among your dear members which would be out of order, and contrary to sound doctrine, now is your time to make it known." This is not an invitation to gripe or raise conflicts of a personal nature (unless an effort has already been made to work them out in private). Rather, it is an opportunity to identify actions and attitudes that undercut church teachings. The visit ends with encouragement to remain diligent in prayer, devotion, and attendance at church gatherings. Members are called to greater faithfulness. With that, the visitors move on to another home.

Visit Council. After all visits are completed, the congregation holds a visit council—a meeting for collective examination. "How do we measure up against church doctrine?" "Where could we do more or better?" General admonitions are given and, if necessary, individual ones. If individual charges are raised, the member typically knows in advance and is asked to respond publicly during council. This response usually takes the form of confession and asking forgiveness.

Unrepentant offenders may be "set back from communion and the kiss" until matters are resolved. If the problem involves general discord in the church, Love Feast might even be postponed until the issue is settled, though such drastic measures are rare. More typically, the visit council is a forum for positive instruction designed to strengthen the faithful. All are encouraged to examine themselves, paying special attention to concerns raised during the visit—"Let us put forth all our effort to purge from our lives that which is not pleasing to the One we profess to serve."[16]

A few days before Love Feast, practical preparations are made. Sisters and children clean the meetinghouse kitchen and prepare the entire building to seat and feed a large assembly. Some of the men, usually deacons, purchase the beef, bread, butter, apple butter, pickles, fruit, coffee, and tea for the meals. Another small group, including ministers, their wives, and interested members, gathers in a home to bake communion bread. And well in advance, one of the brothers has prepared wine for the occasion.[17]

Saturday Morning. Finally, the day of Love Feast arrives. The cars of members, friends, and neighbors fill the parking lot on a Saturday morning. Families from neighboring congregations, even from out of state, have come. Men drift toward the door on the "brethren's side" of the plain meetinghouse, greeting each other with a kiss of love. Sisters greet similarly outside the sisters' door. Children dressed in modest "worldly" clothing play about the grounds. (Uniform dress, reflecting the unity and discipline of spiritual life, is expected only of members.) While the tone remains spiritual, the event is also social. Visiting Brethren lodge with members of the local congregation—everyone knows they will have a place to stay and will be warmly received. Pleasure is taken in large numbers. Just before 10 A.M., the crowd files inside.

The view from the back, with everyone seated, shows a plain white ceiling and walls decorated with broadbrims and bonnets hanging on evenly spaced hooks. Stretched on one side is an assembly of men clad in plain, dark uniforms. Their hair, untapered but cut short in the back, draws a stark line across the backs of their necks, well above the "standing collar" of their coats. Many necks are framed on the sides by the silhouette of an untrimmed Dunker beard. These Brethren men, however, have a shaven upper lip. A mustache detracts from the holy kiss and is traditionally associated with military affairs.

On the sisters' side is a sea of white head coverings, each pleated on top, reaching down to just below the ears and drawn snugly under the neck with a thin white tie. The sisters' dresses display a mix of dark and pastel colors, many with small floral prints, yet the cut of their dresses could not be more uniform. Cut plain and gathered around the waist, each is adorned by an integrated cape of the same color as the dress. Pointed in the middle of their backs, the capes wrap around their shoulders and descend in front nearly to their waists, to a point on each side.

At the front of the meetinghouse, beyond the rows of benches and people, sits a long table. Around it are seated anywhere from six to twenty local and visiting ministers. Also at the table, with their backs to the congregation, are the deacons, who will lead singing, read Scripture, and generally assist in the service. Replacing the altar of some denominations, the table symbolizes fellowship, simplicity, equality, and hospitality— attesting to the fact that worship is a spiritual feast.[18]

Worship. A minister begins the service by calling out the number of a hymn and then *lining* it by reading a verse aloud. Pulling from their purses or pockets a small black book labeled simply "Hymns," the congregation joins in singing. They pause between verses while each one is lined. The hymnbook contains no musical notes; a deacon or minister selects a melody known to all. Many hymns follow the ancient style of metrical psalms, written in a defined meter and adhering to a scriptural text. The hymn's meter determines the tune. In theory, any hymn written in long meter can be sung to any tune of the same meter, yet tradition has assigned certain tunes to certain hymns, and these are the ones selected by the leader. Even though members carry personal hymn books with them, the tradition of lining persists. Melodies from the eighteenth and early nineteenth centuries provide a slow, sweet manner of singing that predates faster gospel rhythms.

The slow, sweet music must be heard to be fully appreciated. Imagine a song sung so slowly in English that it is not understandable, or a familiar hymn such as "Rock of Ages" paced so slowly that it is beyond recognition. No musical instruments embellish the simple melodies; all one hears is the full sound of God's people lifting their voices in unison and methodically digesting each word.

After the hymn, one of the ministers stands to read the fifty-third chapter of Isaiah. Then another briefly "exhorts to prayer." There is a stir throughout the church as everyone kneels. When the prayer is ended and Brethren resume their seats, those near the front hear what outsiders might interpret as confusion among the ministers—"Be free, brother." "No, not I . . . you brother, will you take the text?" "Be free, brother; don't lay the burden upon me." "No, brother, you take the liberty."

This deferential custom of *extending the liberty* reflects neither confusion nor lack of preparedness. Many of the ministers have a sermon ready, and most have a good idea who will "take the liberty" to give it. It is an intentional rite of humility that underscores each brother's reticence to put himself forward, preferring to wait for a call to preach. It also invites the Holy Spirit to guide the proceedings by refusing to fix the speaker and the topic in advance.[19]

Despite the ostensible openness in extending the liberty, factors such as age and geographic distance establish an unspoken chain of priority. Ministers who have traveled the greatest distance are given first liberty. If several come a similar distance, the oldest and most experienced have the first opportunity to speak. Thus, an older minister traveling from a distance expects to preach, while a younger, local minister is rarely chosen. The popularity of visiting, coupled with the fact that most districts have three or more ministers, means that a minister may only preach four or five times a year in his own district. Indeed, he may have more opportunities in neighboring districts. In congregations with fewer visitors, an informal rotation of its own ministers sets the sequence.

There are different styles of preaching. Some prefer an expository style, interpreting a scriptural passage as they work through it. Others focus upon a scriptural topic or theme, selecting additional scriptures to amplify the message. While both are carefully considered ahead of time, topical sermons rely more on advanced preparation, while expository preaching is more extemporaneous. Some ministers rely only upon memory and the leading of the Spirit; others use notes or a printed outline.

The process of extending the liberty takes only a few moments. The minister who accepts the burden names a passage from the New Testament, and another stands to read it. After another hymn, the speaker begins his discourse. On the Saturday morning of Love Feast, sermons usually center upon Christ's suffering and death. New or novel interpretations are frowned upon, but old truths in new dress are welcomed. When the sermon is ended, another hymn is sung. Then another minister offers commentary on the first brother's discourse. Other ministers may add their testimony as the Spirit moves. As noon arrives, a minister closes the service with prayer and a final hymn.

As the smell of coffee drifts in from the kitchen, the two-hour meeting concludes. Dinner is served to the crowd, and Brethren enjoy a time of visiting. Attendance at the afternoon service is lighter because some have farm chores, and the youth attend a "young folks" gathering of singing, games, and informal fellowship.

Saturday Evening. At about 5 P.M., all return to the meetinghouse for the climax of the weekend: the threefold service of feetwashing, the Lord's Supper, and communion. Rows of long tables are covered with white cloths. Brethren sit on one side of the room and sisters on the other, ministers sit together, and spectators (children and nonmembers) take a place to the side. When everyone is seated, a brother reads the eleventh chapter of First Corinthians.

Then a half hour is devoted to *self-examination,* "for he that eateth and drinketh unworthily, eateth and drinketh damnation to himself, not discerning the Lord's body" (1 Cor. 11:29). During this time, ministers underscore the seriousness of the evening's events, the necessity of being in unity with God and every member, and the importance of living an exemplary life. The aim is to stir repentance and increase resolve. Brethren are encouraged to forgive and forget past differences and to strive for greater love and union. The examination service ends with singing as the deacons distribute basins, towels, and tubs of warm water among the tables.

Feetwashing. After a few moments, a minister stands to read from John 13: "If I then, your Lord and Master, have washed your feet; ye also ought to wash one another's feet. For I have given you an example, that ye should do as I have done to you." Then the *server* (the officiating minister) instructs that in order to commune, all must have their feet washed, for servants are no greater than the Lord Jesus, their master. "If ye know these things, happy are ye if ye do them." While some denominations accent humility and servanthood as the primary message of feetwashing, the Brethren emphasize spiritual cleansing, a precondition for communion.

Other ministers speak on the importance and meaning of the ordinance. Then two members at each table rise from their seats, one taking a towel and the other a basin. Moving down the row, they wash and wipe the feet of several members. As each act of cleansing is completed, the serving sister or brother grasps the hand of the one being served and places a holy kiss upon his or her lips, quietly whispering a word of love and encouragement. After several are washed, the two who are washing take their seats and two more take up the task. Thus, the service continues until all are washed.

The Lord's Supper. After feetwashing, local deacons remove tubs, towels, and basins as others bring in the supper. Tables are set, a hymn is sung, and the server offers thanks for the meal. Brethren believe that the Lord's Supper in the early church was exactly what the name implies: a meal. Being spiritual in nature, however, it is not intended to fill the hungry. In fact, any who were hungry have already eaten so that natural appetite does not detract from the spiritual experience.[20] Brethren believe the meal offers a foretaste of the heavenly banquet, the marriage supper of the Lamb, when Christ will feast together in heaven with his bride, the church. Those who are dressed in the white linen of righteousness will have a place at the table, but "foolish virgins" who have frittered away their days will be barred from the celebration.

Brethren eat quietly and solemnly during the meal, meditating upon their own spirituality, the events of the Last Supper, and their hope of reunion with the bridegroom. Both Christ's Last Supper and the prospect of his second coming remind them of the uncertainty of mortal life and the hope of eternity—this meal may, indeed, be their last supper together. From a common bowl they eat a "sop" of bread soaked in broth. There are also slices of beef and bread with apple butter. Some members claim that "the apple butter never tastes better than at Love Feast." Glasses of water are distributed at regular intervals and shared among members seated nearby. These symbolic details—dipping from a common bowl, sharing a glass of water, deferring to others in the taking of food, and even the shared silence—evoke for many an almost mystical awareness of the bonds that unite Brethren with Brethren, and Brethren with their Lord. When all are finished eating, the quiet is broken by the server, who lines a hymn and offers a prayer.

The Lord's Supper highlights a theological difference between the Brethren and other Anabaptists: their strong millennial hope. A Dunker elder explains: "The Amish believe they are already in the millennium—already living in the Kingdom—we see ourselves as part of the *spiritual* Kingdom, but looking forward to the millennium." Accepting Jesus' word that they will know neither "the times or the seasons," Brethren do not predict end-time scenarios. They cannot properly be called premillennialists or postmillennialists, yet they are millennialists and suspect that Christ may return sooner rather than later. It is something that they think and read about. Their metaphor for the church is "the bride," whom the Lord will collect only if she is faithful and ready. Brethren assurance of Christ's return translates into lack of worldly confidence—"We will meet again next Lord's day, *if* the Lord tarries."

Communion. The entrance of the officials bearing the bread and wine announces the climax of the evening services: holy communion. A minister reads a scriptural account of the crucifixion, and another stands to interpret. His comments recast the familiar story in a fresh and immediate fashion, as if Christ were being crucified before their eyes. Yet rather than dwelling upon death, the focus soon shifts to resurrection, resulting in "smiles through tears—after agony unspeakable joy . . . !"[21]

Before partaking of the elements, Brethren seal the unity of their fellowship with the right hand of fellowship and a holy kiss. The server begins by greeting the brother to his left. The brother then greets the brother to his left, and so on, until the kiss makes a complete circuit to its point of origin. The chain of love is similarly sealed on the sisters' side, with the exception that the server, who is male, greets the first sister with only a handshake. She then greets her sister with a kiss, and so forth, until the circle is complete.

With unity thus established, the server stands, quotes from 1 Corinthians 11, and offers a prayer for the symbol of the bread. Breaking a piece from a large strip, he hands it to the brother beside him, saying, "Beloved brother, the bread which we break is the communion of the body of Christ." The brother lays the small piece on the table, takes the larger strip from the server, and breaks a piece to the brother beside him, repeating the blessing. While the brothers break bread among themselves, the server moves to the sisters' tables. There he moves from sister to sister, breaking the bread and offering a piece to each one. After returning to his seat, the server invites everyone to partake of the bread. All eat simultaneously as they meditate upon the cost of their redemption.

After a few moments of silence, the server prepares the fermented wine by mixing it with water from another bottle. When all is ready, he proceeds as he did for the bread—reading Scripture, offering thanks, passing the cup to the brother beside him, and saying, "This cup of the New Testament is the communion of the blood of Christ." The brother takes a sip, repeats the blessing to the next brother, and so on. The server moves to the sisters' table and offers the cup to each in turn. Again, the formula for brothers and sisters is identical except that the sisters do not pass the wine among themselves.

When all are served, the server and the local elder in charge offer a few closing remarks, followed by a hymn and dismissal. As many as five hours may have passed since the beginning of the service, yet sacred time is not linear, and no one watches the hour. Brethren leave the premises spiritually filled, knowing what it means to strike the deepest chords of affection and devotion.

Sunday. After an early breakfast at the meetinghouse, members and guests visit until about 9:30 A.M. The crowd may swell even beyond the previous day. Brethren hope that the best preaching has been saved for Sunday, and they are rarely disappointed. Five or six visiting ministers deliver sermons on topics such as the lost condition of man, the evil state of the world, the importance of self-denial, obedience to Christ, and remaining faithful. Sermons are gauged by their earnestness and sincerity; artfulness and sophistication of expression are avoided. Brethren tarry over the morning service beyond the customary two hours. The final common meal is followed by additional visiting.

Why do so many come from so far for Love Feast services that have barely changed during the lifetime of most members? In the words of brother Fred Benedict, "To people who maintain a separation from many pleasures of society, Christian fellowship becomes pleasure. To those who don't attend the drama of the theater, the beauty of the ordinances, crowds of worshippers, and powerful preaching are drama enough. To those who don't belong to secret societies, the church becomes the center of their lives, and invites their undivided loyalty. To people who don't go to war, mutual aid, sharing of Christian love, and the peace of Christ are all their theme. To people who don't have radio and television, the Bible has a central part in their lives and affections."[22]

In the same way that the holy kiss links everyday greetings to the special unity of communion, the Love Feast ties each district into covenant with the entire brotherhood. Unlike the Hutterites and Mennonites, whose structures divide them into separate conferences and endow bishops or ministers with disciplinary authority, Brethren ground their order in the unanimous consent of the members, ritually sealed by a national Love Feast to which all members are invited. All of this occurs every spring when the Old German Baptist Brethren travel to their Annual Meeting, the largest gathering of plain people in the world.

ANNUAL MEETING

Annual Meeting is many things to the Brethren: a time to travel across country, a season of preaching and spiritual growth, a time to renew friendships, and a forum for resolving differences. Held annually at Pentecost to celebrate the outpouring of Christ's spirit, Annual Meeting draws Brethren families from across the nation. As many as four thousand men, women, and children join in four days of meetings. A gathering of this size sounds routine in an age of convention centers and grand hotels, but the Dunker convention center is a pasture, their hotels are their homes, and their restaurant is a large canvas tent. Add free room and board for whoever needs them, and there is the makings of a rather unusual gathering.[23]

Preparations. Preparations for Annual Meeting begin two years in advance. Members in the host district select a farm with suitable terrain, outbuildings, and convenient access. After underground electric and water lines are installed, up to twenty-five acres are seeded in grass and reserved for the conference. As the time draws nearer, outbuildings are adapted for a baggage room, first aid station, and nursery. Large restrooms are constructed to accommodate the crowd. Local Brethren form committees to purchase groceries, lumber, and hardware and to arrange for refrigeration, electrical, telephone, and plumbing service.

Members from across the country visit at the Annual Meeting of the Brethren.
Source: Roanoke Times

Additional committees provide for everything from sanitation and garbage disposal to traffic control, construction of outbuildings, and even relations with the press. Among other things, they may purchase 5,000 pounds of beef, 2,000 loaves of bread, 550 gallons of peaches, 200 gallons of pickles, 160 gallons of apple butter, 2,000 pieces of lumber, 10 water heaters, 2 freezers, porcelain sinks, pressure tanks, over 1,000 pillows, bath towels, and washcloths, 500 foam mattresses, two 1,000 lb. capacity wagons, and 18 sets of volleyball poles and nets.[24] All costs are borne by the host district, which recoups part of its outlay in a public postconference auction. The meeting rotates annually to different regions of the country.

The Thursday morning before conference is tent-raising day. Men arrive early to drive posts, arrange the canvas, and build dozens of wooden tables and benches. By noon a large dining tent is erected and outfitted to serve lunch to the workers and watchers. The tent, measuring 60 × 110 feet, has tables constructed on site, 13 for men and 13 for women. A long center table provides a supply point for the servers. With 32 people at each table, the tent accommodates 832 at one feeding. Attached to one end is a kitchen. A supply building is constructed nearby for storage and distribution.

Approximately 12,000 individual meals are served free of charge over the four-day period. During peak attendance, as many as 1,800 persons are served per meal, requiring two full shifts and a smaller one to feed the servers. The massive meals are dispatched like clockwork by volunteer laborers without the convenience of disposable plates or plastic spoons. Area congregations assign volunteers to designated tables. In about forty minutes between each shift, the volunteers clear the tables, wash 832 sets of plates and silverware, and reset the tables for the next feeding. The menu, similar to that served at love feast, is always the same: bread and sop, slices of beef, brown and white bread, butter and apple butter, pickles, sliced peaches, and coffee. Brethren eat heartily and converse during the meal, opening and closing each feeding with a hymn and a prayer.

On Thursday afternoon before the conference, a second, even larger tent is raised. Shaped in a 101 × 136 foot oval, it seats 2,400 people on backless wooden benches. Spaced conveniently throughout the tent are wooden racks for bonnets and broadbrims. A long table that will accommodate approximately forty bearded elders sits in the center. To amplify the preaching, loudspeakers were added for the first time in 1986. Before then, many had difficulty hearing, especially after the tent was enlarged in 1980. Even with the larger tent, several hundred people must stand on the periphery. On Saturday and Sunday a second service is held simultaneously in an adjoining building—sometimes in a barn—to accommodate the crowd.

Friday is a final day of preparation. Local members ready meals and beds to host large numbers of guests. Host families may use trailers for additional bedrooms or clear a garage and set it with tables, cafeteria style. Families with large houses often host ten to twenty guests; those with the largest accommodations may invite as many as seventy for Saturday evening dinner. Brethren arriving without prearranged lodging go to the Annual Meeting baggage room and ask for a ticket. Color-coded by date, the ticket names the host family and gives directions to their home. Each ticket represents one bed in the home of a member.

Worship and Fellowship. On Saturday morning Brethren arrive early at the conference grounds. Large numbers of children testify to the youth and vitality of families. Young folks gatherings, held throughout the weekend at a nearby location, alternate worship with recreation. Volleyball is especially popular. During these gatherings, 700 to 800 youth build lifelong friendships with Brethren from distant states. More than a few meet a future spouse.

Conferees anticipate the preaching at Annual Meeting, for it features esteemed elders from the far reaches of the brotherhood. On Saturday, Sunday, and Monday, services are held from 10:00 to 12:00 in the morning and 2:00 to 4:00 in the afternoon. There are also early morning worship services on Sunday, Monday, and Tuesday. Preaching services follow the format of the Saturday morning of Love Feast weekend described above. Men and women sit separately; they kneel for prayers, which always end with the Lord's Prayer; the liberty is extended among ministers; multiple ministers speak; and the unaccompanied hymns are lined. The music is slow and beautiful. The melodies drift out over open fields as some 2,500 voices join in song.

A brotherhood-wide Love Feast is held on Sunday evening, culminating a weekend full of fellowship and worship. Duplicating local patterns, the Love Feast begins at 5 p.m. and continues for five hours. All members are invited, but the lure of visiting and lack of seating keep many away. From the preliminary self-examination to the serving of bread and wine, the ordinance adheres closely to the historic pattern. Despite the fact that participants come from across the country, each knows the exact protocol. As the hours unfold and dusk gives way to darkness, a sense of peace and unity settles upon the meeting. By the end of the evening, the darkness beyond the tent matches the mystery and solemnity within.

Although such a service may seem detached from the business meetings that occupy Monday and Tuesday, it is closely connected. The Love Feast proclaims the spiritual unity of the membership, thus ordaining the business council with legitimate authority.[25] Having sacralized their agreement in a Love Feast, it is difficult for Brethren to ignore the rulings of the same meeting. Whether the issue is dress, entertainment, computers, union membership, or bankruptcy, the decisions of Annual Meeting are neither set in stone nor handed down from above by church officials. They are sacred covenants, entered into voluntarily and renewed annually by the total membership. The procedures of the business sessions conform entirely to this understanding.

Ruling by Unanimous Consent. Decisions on churchwide business are made by the unanimous consent of some 600 participants without a formal vote. The process begins early on Monday morning when 110 "messengers"—two lay-delegates from each local congregation—travel to a local meetinghouse to organize the conference business. After brief exhortation and prayer, they file one by one into a separate room. Here they present to a committee the *queries* (concerns) raised in their local congregations, as well as their choices for twelve ordained elders to comprise the "Standing Committee," the most esteemed leadership role in the church. After stating their concerns and choices, they return to the conference grounds and the worship service already in progress.

At the end of the worship, a spokesman reads the names of those selected for Standing Committee. As each name is called, the elder indicates his presence in the crowd. Despite an open selection without ballots or candidacies, Standing Committee membership is very stable from year to year. Members are replaced only for illness, death, or a serious breach of ethics. The character of these leaders must be beyond reproach. According to one leader, "They are hard working, successful farmers or businessmen, apt to teach, who uphold all the order of the church, are usually patient with variations, temperate and moderate." At present, they are "united and bent conservatively," their temperament and behavior epitomizing what it means to be Brethren.[26]

Even so, Standing Committee's conservatism is not without criticism, as indicated by a 1992 query requesting a more frequent turnover in its membership. The request was denied because "[t]here is stability in the continuity of leadership as we now practice. We find no scriptural record advocating a frequent change of leadership in the early Church."[27]

Standing Committee selects its officers, including the Annual Meeting "foreman," or moderator, and begins addressing many matters related to the faithfulness of the churches. Its most pressing concern is to oversee the shaping of responses to queries. Toward this end, it groups similar queries together and forms subcommittees to draft responses to each concern. Most queries deal with matters of daily life or church procedure, and all responses are tentative, subject to approval the following day.

On Tuesday the entire church considers the queries, seeking to discern the Spirit's leading on each question. Distinctions between ministers, messengers, and ordinary members blur. Every brother has an equal voice in the final decision. Each query and answer is read aloud. A messenger from the district that sent the query speaks, followed by someone from the committee that drafted the response. After the issue is explained, members are free to speak their minds. Speeches are made and opinions aired, all with a generous quoting of Scripture, but Brethren try to convince without being forward or aggressive. They seek to preserve a prayerful attitude throughout.[28]

The moderator or "foreman" monitors the open discussion. When he thinks that agreement is near, he calls for a voice on the matter—a verbal "yes" or "no." The verbal votes are not counted in a formal fashion. The moderator always seeks the "voice" of the congregation—the common mind on an issue—rather than a formal vote. The church can pass the committee's answer, amend it, send the query back without an answer, or "lay it down" for lack of agreement.

If the prevailing sentiment favors passing the proposed answer, the foreman will ask whether everyone can accept this solution. If a significant minority says "no," the discussion continues, focusing on the objections. The foreman again calls for a voice. If the "sense of the meeting" is clear and unity prevails, those who differ will accept the common voice as the leading of the Spirit. A vote is never taken, for Brethren believe that voting encourages factions and divides the membership, transforming brothers and sisters into winners and losers. Rather than voting, Brethren work and pray for *unanimous consent*.[29] If this is not possible, they lay the matter down and reconsider it the following year.

Even with unanimous decisions, differences remain. As one elder comments, "If God had meant for all of us to be clones or water buffaloes, he would have made us all alike, like buffaloes, but we were all made different." Rather than celebrating differences in modern fashion, Brethren labor to overcome them, understanding that the Spirit leads toward common applications of Scripture. Like-mindedness requires that small minorities give ground, submitting to the discernment of the larger body. Yet even here Brethren emphasize the loving nature of concession. In the words of the same elder, "I like the term *acceptance* better than *submission*. When the voice on an issue begins to go one way, we like to see the others accept it, not submit to it. That sounds too stubborn."

The crux of all this is that church authority and discipline are grounded in the consent of the governed. Annual Meeting rulings originate with ordinary members who bring concerns to their local council. Standing Committee members, while wielding tremendous influence, have neither the authority to introduce queries nor to rule on them. Conference decisions rest on the council of the whole on the last day of Annual Meeting. Nothing is accepted as a church position until the members in attendance unanimously accept it. Once decided, however, rulings are binding upon all members, present and future, until modified or reversed by subsequent Annual Meetings.

Practicing these principles is not always easy. Lofty ideals of unanimous consent sometimes shatter on the concrete of vested interests.[30] Despite their less-than-perfect realization of saintly ideals, Annual Meetings are generally remembered for their unity. Brethren leave for home reflecting fondly upon "a pleasant and memorable season of fellowship, worship, and council."

CALIBRATING THE ORDER

Similar to the *Ordnung* in other Old Order groups, the Order of the Brethren is the set of "understandings" that regulates congregational and personal behavior. Since many elements of the Order are not reduced to black or white, variations from established patterns abound. Such is the complexity of the Brethren's Order and their understanding of what it means to be "Old Order." But the flexibility does not imply that clear standards blur into an endless montage of grays. Instead, gentle counsel and persuasion restrict variation to a generous assortment of off-whites.

With Annual Meeting as its foundation, the Brethren's Order is subject to regular review. Not inclined to reckless revision, Brethren respond cautiously to change. They adapt and reassess, blending faithfulness and flexibility as best they can. While some practices remain constant for decades, others are continually calibrated, as the following examples illustrate.

Citizens Band Radios. Throughout the twentieth century, Brethren have spurned mass media, which provide direct access to worldly values. Radios, televisions, compact disc players, phonographs, tape players, and VCRs are expressly taboo. A nonmember spouse or child may occasionally own one, but not members. Offenders are asked to dispose of the item, and the congregation monitors their response.

The first ruling against radios, passed in 1925, was reaffirmed in 1943, 1946, and later. In 1975, however, the issue of citizens band radios surfaced. Could Brethren own and use CBs in their vehicles and farm machinery? Hoping to tap their benefits without violating the ban on mass media, Annual Meeting ruled that CBs could be used "where needed for business purposes only." However, the flexible response went awry. A query two years later complained that members were using CBs for non-business reasons, "violating highway laws" in their communications, using "false and fictitious names" instead of legal call numbers, and speaking a "peculiar language . . . unbecoming to our profession."[31]

So Annual Meeting reversed itself, ruling: "We cannot tolerate the use of the Citizens Band radio." But the fact that CBs were formerly sanctioned muddled enforcement. Could Brethren be disciplined for using devices purchased with church approval? If so, to what extent? In 1978, Brethren agreed to disfellowship members for owning a CB, but only after repeated admonitions. The matter rested quietly for fifteen years until a 1994 query noted that the ban posed a safety hazard for members involved in logging operations and also precluded certain types of employment. So Annual Meeting changed course again. CB radios could be used only when absolutely necessary and only when approved by the local congregation.[32]

Silicon Strictures. More recently, computers have tested the church. A guest in a Brethren home in the early 1980s might have been surprised to find a computer. How could Brethren who could not own pianos or radios use computers? "The church," a member explained, "accepts technologies that aid members in their work." Some Brethren are even employed as computer programmers.

But just because Brethren own and program computers does not mean there are no limits. Bearded brothers are not clinging to joysticks. Indeed, a 1988 query objected that members were allowing children to use home computers for games of entertainment: "These are mind captivating and may tempt them to play other video games of a base sort and encourage them to desire television."[33] Annual Meeting encouraged members to guard against such evils, but encouragement was not enough. So a ruling four years later set new guidelines: "Our members can use computers in their homes or places of business for serious and worthwhile personal, business and occupational endeavors only. Any member allowing non-member persons or children to play games or other forms of entertainment on such computers should be reported to the official body. The official body should investigate and handle the matter according to church order."[34]

But the technology kept exploding. By 1994 multimedia systems and soundboards had enabled computers, in the words of a query, "to display moving video images and sounds such as are played by tape recorders, radios, televisions and VCRs." Such advances threatened the mass media taboo and raised broader questions of separation from the world. Reasoning that video images are essential for business use, a query proposed that the church take a stand against soundboards. "This would allow the use of the computer for almost all of our desired purposes and yet maintain our very important and necessary positions against recorded entertainment." The request was granted. Computers with sound capabilities were prohibited, with the exception that the physically handicapped or visually impaired could use them if approved by the local congregation.[35]

In spite of their efforts to deal with the issue, the Brethren still struggle to preserve the boundary between acceptable business uses of computers and unacceptable entertainment and commercial uses. Technological developments have increasingly integrated sound into business software and welded soundboards onto system motherboards, rendering church rulings on soundboards problematic. The Internet—with its rapid access to businesses, persons, information, and advertisements of all kinds— poses a particular challenge. Prior to the Internet, distinctions between productive, entertainment, and communication technologies made sense and could be reasonably maintained. But the World Wide Web poses a critical challenge to Old Order life precisely because it blurs advertising, entertainment, and productivity in ways that elude traditional Brethren strategies for blocking out the popular culture.

Relations with Outsiders. Other examples of Brethren recalibration reach far beyond concerns about consumer products. Relations with outsiders, for instance, always require monitoring and adjustment. Although there are no firm rules against participation in business or professional associations, many members voluntarily limit such involvements. An elder who has done well in the oil and gas business reports, "I have gone to the meetings of these energy corporations, and I see differences between the way we do business. I don't go to play golf, and I don't go for the happy hour—the meeting is to *learn* something. One of the things we know is that you have to be aggressive in this business to do well, but there is a

Many Brethren youth attend public schools and interact with outsiders on a regular basis. *Source: Roanoke Times*

difference between being aggressive and getting ahead by stepping on the other man." He concluded, "There really are big differences between the way we think about things and the way other people do. We don't believe in putting ourselves forward or making a show or display of things." Although he attends the meetings, "business as usual" means something different for Brethren.

Even Brethren who work with outsiders forty hours a week and live miles away from other church members socialize primarily with Brethren. When members invest their energy in outside groups, "they tend to pull away from the church," noted one brother. "Our primary world—those who come into our homes and who we socialize with—are German Baptist Brethren, almost to the point of being an exclusive enclave."

Labor Unions. While some boundaries are drawn informally and voluntarily, problematic ones often surface at Annual Meeting. Involvement in labor unions stirred discussions from the early 1940s to the 1960s. Grounded in coercive methods, unions were considered inappropriate for defenseless Brethren. Annual Meeting ruled in 1941 that members who joined should be considered transgressors. Even so, some members salvaged their jobs by paying union dues without actually joining the ranks. A 1953 decision rejected even this limited role, risking the jobs of such Brethren and sparking a flurry of concern.[36]

In response, the church established a Labor Relations Committee to negotiate with the unions. Agreements were reached with two international unions—Brethren would be exempt from paying dues if an equal amount were paid into public charities. The Labor Relations Committee would certify the payment by issuing a card to its members. In effect, the church card served as a union card, securing access to union shops for Dunker employees. The agreement offended many members, who wondered how a church committee could negotiate with unions when Brethren were to avoid them. By 1960 the Labor Relations Committee had dissolved, and the Brethren embraced a simpler strategy: seek employment elsewhere.[37]

In 1961 Annual Meeting repealed the 1950s rulings and returned to its 1941 position—Brethren were not to join unions, and "all cards issued by the Labor Relations Committee under which members have been working, or are holding, will be null and void." The 1961 decision faulted church elders for failing to enforce the union ban and admonished them to do so. Finally, it permitted Brethren to work in union shops provided they did not have to join the union, participate in union activities, or pay dues into union charities, and if they were able to "conduct themselves as Christians." Over the course of two decades, the Brethren position on unions had shifted from nonassociation to active negotiation and back again to separation.[38]

The Gideons. An outside organization that has posed a dilemma for Brethren is Gideons International—an ecumenical group that distributes Bibles. A 1990 query asked, "Will this beloved Brotherhood please give her voice concerning brethren joining and holding office in religious organizations such as the *Gideons International*, etc. Are we making compromise with principle when we bind ourselves with other professing Christians?" Annual Meeting responded, "We do not feel to judge the efforts or sincerity of any religious organization, but feel our members shall not join any organization, or be a part of their efforts in spreading the Gospel."

While this was consistent with their legacy of noninvolvement with other religious organizations, it was difficult for some Brethren to swallow. They were already serving on hospital boards, hospice committees, and fire and rescue squads. They contributed to service organizations such as the Red Cross and Mennonite Disaster Service and were gainfully employed in a variety of service occupations. How was Gideons International different? How could the church set members back from communion for handing out Bibles? Some wondered which organization would be next on the list.[39]

In 1994 two congregations dispatched queries seeking an adjustment.[40] Although both tried to lift the embargo, one carried a typical tone of respect, and one did not. The first was framed in this fashion: "With appreciation for the cautious stand of the Brethren . . . we ask this Annual Meeting . . . [i]f any member is, or wishes to be, involved in this association's efforts, could he not submit a request for permission . . . ? This request could then be . . . brought before the local church district according to Brotherhood practice, and the Church would be voiced as to whether the requesting member's endeavor is consistent with good church order." This petition affirmed basic Brethren tenets of caution in external relations and upheld the moral authority of the church.

But the second query was different: "Some . . . would promote the idea that the Church has the obligation to determine what occupations or goodwill involvements are 'right' or 'wrong.' They imply that the Brethren have the duty to determine for each of us what is appropriate in areas of daily living which, by Scriptural standards, are neither wrong nor sinful. Such determinations only result in inhibiting each brother's Scriptural freedom to make his own necessary choices in life. . . . We pray that these many good works, whether volunteer or by employment, should be left to individual discretion, and not be interfered with by other Brethren."

This query attacked conservative precautions as unbiblical. It displayed little regard for concerns about separation from the world and the divided opinions that multiple affiliations might produce. Rather than questioning outside involvement, it seemed to question *church* involvement in the moral decision making of members. One minister confided that had the second query not appeared, the first might have been granted. But the "un-Brethren" tone of the second divided the meeting. After trying repeatedly to reach agreement, the issue was deferred for a year, with the Gideon embargo remaining in place. The following spring another minister from Virginia commented, "It's all we talked about after the meeting—I'm sure we'll do the right thing now that members have had a year to digest it."

Outward Appearances. No single topic has inspired more discussion over the years than the specifics of Brethren dress. Outsiders' reactions on seeing Brethren vary from nostalgia, to bewilderment, to a confident gleam of recognition—"*We* know who *you* are," they sometimes blurt out. "You're *Amish*, aren't you!" To which Brethren patiently respond, "No, we're Old German Baptist Brethren." The outsiders' smug certainty dissolves into confusion; their media-based wisdom fizzles. Many worldlings possess mental categories, no matter how distorted, for Amish and even Mennonites—but Old German Baptist Brethren? Sometimes outsiders are so confident that even the word of a member fails to deter them. One brother recalled such an event. The outsider, thinking he was

A family dressed in traditional garb enjoys a summer swim. *Source: Roanoke Times*

out of earshot, muttered under his breath, "In spite of what he says, I *know* he's Amish." Brethren can do little more than chuckle.

Insiders' understandings of dress vary as well. Some are snug and unwavering; others comply but adapt to the setting; still others continually test the limits. Expectations for dress have changed little since 1881,[41] yet the order is tested by fashions of the times. In 1921 a "college coat" borrowed from outsiders posed a problem. During the 1940s some brothers sported gold wristwatches and tapered haircuts. By the early 1950s some sisters, in the words of Annual Meeting, were sampling "bonnets too small; prayer coverings too small and thin; dresses too short, low necked, form fitting or without gathers; fine apparel; toeless shoes; sheer and flesh colored stockings; shawls with rounded corners and without fringes"; and men were still getting tapered haircuts (referred to unflatteringly as shingled or "roached hair").

By the 1970s short skirts were causing concern—even a few of the "old sisters" were taking up their hems. Others began to justify women's slacks and pantsuits by arguing that they were more decent than shorter skirts. For men, fashionable plain coats, pants with zippers instead of broadfall openings, shrinking hat brims, and, yes, tapered haircuts, continued to raise questions.[42] In almost every instance, Annual Meeting encouraged greater conformity to the order, preferring patient counsel to stronger measures.

Some items, however, clearly cross the line. Swimsuits, for instance, have been sharply denounced. Members who wear them in public "fall into the judgment of the church." Neckties are similarly rejected, even when required by an employer. A 1965 ruling cleared the way for Brethren to become airline pilots, which a California brother did. He encountered turbulence, however, over his tie. The airline insisted that a necktie was part of a pilot's uniform; the church insisted it was not part of theirs. Asked whether neckties could be permitted when jobs make them mandatory, Annual Meeting responded with a firm "No." As a result, the pilot abandoned his job and eventually the Brethren. Such an outcome is not unusual. Those who fly too high or become too progressive often leave of their own accord, no longer feeling at home in the Old Order world.

Neither the broadbrim, nor the beard, nor any single item is absolutely essential, yet—at least until recently—there has been a clear bottom line: male members must be recognizable as Brethren in public settings in which non-Brethren are likely to be present. Such recognition might be supplied by an untrimmed beard, the cut of hair, a broadbrimmed hat, or a plain vest and coat—whatever it takes for the brother to be recognized as "family" by insiders and as "peculiar" by outsiders. Sisters must wear the covering in public at all times, even if their work requires a specific uniform. Whenever possible, they are expected to wear the plain-cut dress with cape. In spite of consistent counsel, divergent congregational enforcement of plain attire for males has yielded considerable variation in practice.

In some congregations the long, untrimmed beard and distinctive garb are still worn by males in virtually all public settings. In others, "casual" attire is replacing plain attire (except for attendance at church meetings and religious services). In dress at least, unity represents more of a Brethren ideal than a tangible reality. In all congregations, clearly fashionable clothing like the necktie still result in church discipline if a brother ignores the counsel of the church to put it away.

FLEXIBLE DISCIPLINE

Here is revealed the beauty of discipline.
It provides a means for guilty man
to suffer chastisement on earth
instead of having to wait for
the day of judgment.[43]

Brethren have a strong but flexible understanding of discipline. Members must bow to the will of the church—preferably at their own initiative. Admonition is discipline's first and foremost tool. Old German Baptist Brethren admonish, then wait, admonish, wait, and then admonish and wait again. The full force of their dense network of informal relations bears down upon wayward members. Encouragement, counsel, and what moderns would define as gossip abound, but so do patience and forbearance. While the disciplinary system is slow and flexible, it is neither loose nor lethargic. Brethren care about their brothers' and sisters' conformity to churchly ways, and they say so—not aggressively, but by raising questions and concerns. When all these measures are spent, Brethren ratchet it up another level.

The next stage of discipline involves "setting someone back" from council, communion, and the kiss. Disciplined persons may continue to attend services and interact with Brethren, but deprived of the kiss with every greeting, they know they are out of favor. To be barred from communion by a people who treasure the Love Feast is no small penalty. And the fact that being "set back" is enacted by congregational consensus doubles the shame—all of one's peers participated in the censure. All of this occurs against a backdrop of Annual Meeting agreements. The Gideon dilemma, for instance, was sparked by concern about the activities of a brother who had been a Gideon for years. Responding to a query on the matter, Annual Meeting decided against Gideon membership. As a result, the local church had to ask the brother to withdraw. He refused, forcing the congregation to choose between setting him back and defying Annual Meeting. As loyal Brethren, they "set him back," even though privately some questioned the wisdom of Annual Meeting.

Setting persons back ends the matter only if they leave the community. As long as they remain, the faithful members will urge them to reconsider. If the wayward member returns to council, confesses, and promises to change course, the congregation joyfully restores them to full fellowship. The Brethren form a large circle and greet the returned member with a kiss or a handshake to symbolize his or her restored status. Afterward, Brethren are instructed to "go and mention no more."

"Gross sins" such as fornication, adultery, and drunkenness evoke the sharper response of swift and inevitable excommunication. For such flagrant offenses, even repentant members are disfellowshipped for a short time to render a clear judgment on their behavior. After a period of separation, they are restored if they are repentant and prepared to change their ways.

Until midcentury, some Brethren practiced "avoidance," or what the Amish call shunning. Grounding themselves in the apostle Paul's instruction, "with such a one, not to eat," Brethren did precisely that—they ate separately from wayward sinners, hoping to spur repentance. Apart from meals, they could carry on normal relations. In 1950 Brethren reaffirmed their conviction that avoidance is biblically sanctioned in extreme cases.[44] Yet today even ministers seem puzzled at its mention. Annual Meeting rulings aside, avoidance is no longer practiced, and little memory of it remains. In a rare case, one sister recalled that in her youth a minister's daughter was shunned for fornication.

While Brethren discipline remains in force, its foundation may be softening. In recent years a trickle of Annual Meeting queries have questioned its role. Does the church have the right to "interfere" with matters of private conscience? Are rulings on weddings, wardrobes, and Walkmans worthy restrictions of a community of faith or mere quibbles with details of lifestyle? How much must Brethren really separate themselves from other professing "Christians?" While members voice their reservations gently, some are clearly wondering about the role of discipline as recent queries make clear:[45]

> QUERY: "Will this Annual Meeting please say that . . . every repentant sinner has direct access to the forgiveness of God?"
> QUERY: "We appeal to this Annual Meeting to . . . reaffirm . . . that the Word of God is our only creed and doctrine."
> QUERY: "We are concerned about an attitude that 'Brethren have the duty to determine for each of us what is appropriate in areas of daily living. . . .' "

More than petitions on specific topics, these questions chip away at the bedrock assumptions of church authority. They assert the moral autonomy of individuals to receive direct forgiveness, interpret Scripture for themselves, and direct their own activities. If these queries play to their logical conclusions, little will remain of the church's role as moral interpreter in the daily lives of members.

So far Annual Meeting has rejected such arguments. If anything, the tendency during the early 1990s was to crack down. Yet the Brethren remain in dilemma—too much rigidity undercuts their historic focus upon the whisperings of the Spirit. Too much rigidity threatens a model of governance grounded in the unanimous consent of the members. And too much rigidity hardens the spirit of gentleness, patience, and love that Brethren have labored so long to cultivate.

Yet too much acceptance would dash their doctrines of nonconformity and separation. Too much acceptance undermines church unity and makes consensus decisions impossible. And too much acceptance transforms concrete standards into amorphous, abstract principles. So the Brethren continue their Anabaptist experiment—an experiment in submission without hierarchy, nonconformity without social segregation, and spirituality with a substantive twist.

Their handling of beards says it best. While long, unshorn beards are the "full order" for men, they are required only of ministers and deacons. Although few do, a clean-shaven brother can remain in fellowship for years without raising objections. But suppose young brother Bucher "raises" a beard and grows it long and full. And suppose after several years he shaves it off. He will likely receive a visit. Members will question his spiritual welfare and his relationship with the church.

While all of this might seem inconsistent to outsiders, to Brethren it makes perfect sense—there is more to a clean shave than meets the eye. To grow the beard in the first place signaled a spiritual leading to come into greater unity, to embrace the full order. The brother understood this as well as everyone else. To shave it off suggested that he was spiritually confused, acting capriciously, or falling away from the church, any of which are reason for investigation. In other words, whether brother Bucher's beardlessness is cause for concern depends less on his face than on what lies behind it.

Such shades of subtlety that mix strong patterns with ample latitude reflect the delicate balance of Brethren pilgrimage heavenward. It remains to be seen how well they can sustain the balance without veering off to one side or the other. Relations with outside groups, the challenge of the Internet, and inconsistent patterns of congregational discipline threaten their treasured unity and the fragile boundaries separating them from mainstream variants of conservative Christianity. For the moment, however, they remain decidedly Old Order, even though their backroad is fraught with hazards that make it hard to stay on course.

CHAPTER SIX

Common Convictions

Bigness ruins everything.
—Amish carpenter

From social relationships to making a living, from technology to religious rituals, Old Order communities share much in common. Beneath abundant differences lies a bedrock of common commitments. We begin by looking at four common themes that are woven throughout Old Order life: *Ordnung, Gelassenheit,* nonresistance, and nonconformity. We then explore common understandings of social relationships, daily living, technology, and religious ritual.

ORDNUNG: A RECIPE FOR ORDER

Old Order life is regulated by the *Ordnung*—a German word that roughly means 'rules and discipline.' Each group has a cluster of regulations that defines expected behavior and imparts the group's distinctive identity. These "understandings," as one Amish man called them, set forth both prescriptions and proscriptions for Old Order life. An *Ordnung*, for example, might stipulate certain forms of dress, place restrictions on technology, and also prohibit immoral behavior. Indeed, all the groups forbid wearing jewelry, owning a television, or filing for divorce.

Some groups have a written *Ordnung*, but many communities simply pass on their "understandings" by oral tradition and practice. For the Brethren, the minutes of the Annual Meeting serve as an equivalent of a written *Ordnung*.

The *Ordnung* is mostly taken for granted—simply understood as the way things are supposed to be. Children growing up within the *Ordnung* come to accept it as the bestowed way of life—the normal way that "our" people live, or as "just the way things are." In the same way that boys in modern society learn that men wear ties, young Hutterite women learn to wear bandanas, and Amish boys learn to wear their hats in public. At baptism young adults confess their Christian faith and pledge to obey the church and to comply with the *Ordnung* for the rest of their lives.[1]

The *Ordnung* embodies the tradition of the community and regulates, among other things, gender roles, dress codes, the use of technology, worship practices, recreational activities, and relations with the outside world. Some aspects of the *Ordnung* are revised as groups adapt to changing conditions in the larger society. Metaphorically, the *Ordnung* can be visualized as a body of concentric circles. At the center are core understandings that are firmly held and rarely challenged. On the periphery are guidelines that are ambiguous and more easily violated. Core expectations, if violated, bring harsh sanctions. The purchase of an automobile in some of the groups will trigger excommunication unless the deviant quickly repents. Attending a theater may bring a milder sanction because it involves a more peripheral taboo.

Expectations differ in the various communities, but all of them hold clear standards for prospective members. Mainline churches, by contrast, are often easier to enter because members practice their faith according to personal preference. And because such churches have few behavioral standards, they rarely expel people. Old Order groups, however, do not hesitate to excommunicate or "disfellowship" those who violate the *Ordnung*. All of the groups bar excommunicated persons from participating in communion. The Amish and Hutterites also shun errant members in the hope that they will eventually return to the fold.[2] Wayward souls can be restored to membership if they express remorse and show a compliant attitude, but the belligerent, haughty, and arrogant—those who intentionally transgress the *Ordnung*—are banned from fellowship. Thus baptism and the ban serve as the front and back door respectively in Old Order communities.

GELASSENHEIT: GIVING UP AND GIVING IN

The culture of Old Order groups rests on the bedrock of *Gelassenheit*—a German word that roughly means 'yielding and surrendering to a higher authority.' *Gelassenheit* is a broad concept layered with many meanings—self surrender, resignation to God's will, yielding to others, gentleness, a calm spirit, contentment, and a quiet acceptance of whatever comes.[3] *Gelassenheit*, in brief, is the opposite of assertive individualism; it signals the primacy of the group over the individual. Although the word itself is rarely spoken, its meaning is woven into the fabric of Old Order life and underscores the most fundamental difference between Old Order culture and modern values.

The ways of *Gelassenheit* are difficult to comprehend in a world saturated with personal ambition, padded résumés, and dreams of self-fulfillment. Whereas modern culture values personal achievement, advancement, and recognition; *Gelassenheit* calls for hesitation, slowing up, backing down, and giving up—giving up one's stubborn will for the welfare of the community. Regulated by the virtues of *Gelassenheit*, the community, not the individual, is the primary social unit. Contemporary culture's focus on individual rights and personal ambition flies in the face of *Gelassenheit*.

Gelassenheit is embodied in the rituals and symbols of community life. It means not only giving oneself up, but also giving in—to siblings, leaders, and tradition. The code words for yielding are obedience, humility, submission, and lowliness. The metaphor is the lamb. The meek and lowly Jesus, the Lamb of God who went to the cross without balking, provides the model for communal behavior. Early Anabaptists were willing to follow the teachings of Jesus even when it brought suffering and persecution. Indeed, a martyr's death was the ultimate expression of *Gelassenheit*—the moment of complete yieldedness to God's will.[4] The virtue of submission regulates the entire spectrum of Old Order life, from body language to social organization, from dress to religious ritual, from personal speech to symbolism. Indeed, to resist the authority of the church is to resist God. This merits repeating—to resist the church is to resist God, for community norms reflect divine precepts.

The principle of *Gelassenheit* integrates the moral order of Old Order communities. The logic of surrender undergirds diverse practices ranging from taboos on lightning rods to banning solos in church services, from

Plain dress symbolizes simplicity as well as separation from the larger society. These Mennonite women are shopping at a public market. *Source:* Jan Gleysteen

the rejection of photographs to the rites for ordaining leaders. Restrictions on clothing, jewelry, and photographs flow from the belief that unbridled vanity will disrupt community. And while it is foolish to read *Gelassenheit* into everything, it is nonetheless the thread that binds together the fabric of Old Order life. The commitment to yieldedness shapes beliefs, harnesses personal behavior, molds cultural values, regulates religious ritual, governs symbolic expression, and guides social organization. The ethos of submission is ultimately grounded in, and legitimated by, religious values—a commitment to the ways of a meek and lowly Savior.

The words of an Old Order Mennonite hymn capture the sentiments of *Gelassenheit*:

> *Humbleness, oh beauteous virtue*
> *Christian's glory and renown . . .*

Humbleness is not contemptuous
Like the haughty world displays . . .
After meekness follows gladness
with the blessings of God's Grace . . . [5]

The expression of *Gelassenheit* includes plainness, simplicity, obedience, humility, lowliness and meekness. These themes are often paired in Old Order culture against their opposites—fanciness, complexity, disobedience, pride, haughtiness, and assertiveness. Such vices are detested because they disturb the harmony of an orderly community.

Yieldedness is the supreme virtue of an obedient life. Growing up in large families, children learn to give up and give in at an early age. Hutterite toddlers learn that even their toys are not their own, but belong to everyone. Children are expected to obey parents and teachers without question. Wives are expected to submit to their husbands, women are expected to listen to men, who in turn follow the guidance of church leaders. And young ministers heed the counsel of senior elders or bishops. Obedience to authorities reflects a yielded heart that is fully submitted to God's will. Disobedience is tantamount to rebellion against God.

NONRESISTANCE: THE MARKS OF PEACE

Based on Jesus' words, "Resist not evil," Old Orders object to using force to solve problems. Nonresistance—not resisting—embodies the essence of *Gelassenheit*, for it willingly accepts whatever comes—verbal assault without retort, bodily injury without retaliation, property damage without revenge, and financial exploitation without litigation. In the final analysis, nonresistance is defenselessness—a willingness to absorb malice and leave vengeance up to God. Nonresistant beliefs prohibit not only the use of litigation but also holding public office with its implied use of force. Indeed, Old Order members can be excommunicated for such activities. There are, of course, lapses from these ideals, and Old Order groups use force themselves when they spank their children and excommunicate members. Nevertheless, they totally reject lethal force and admonish members again and again to uphold nonresistant habits.

They seek to follow Jesus' instruction to "resist not evil" but to turn the other cheek, to walk the second mile, and to love those who would harm them. Rather than contending for personal empowerment and individual rights, they teach the virtue of suffering. Members are urged to yield and submit even in the face of evil. Retaliation, in their eyes, should remain in the hands of God. Obedience to God requires even the sacrifice of self-defense.

Old Orders are conscientious objectors, meaning they will sit in jail before joining the military. Their commitment to peace prevents them from filing lawsuits, which are viewed as tools of coercion. Many are even reluctant to defend themselves in court. Noncoercion also means they cannot hold public office, for political power is ultimately backed by force. Serving as a police officer is unthinkable and would be cause for excommunication. Members are urged to avoid labor unions because of their complicity in strikes and other coercive tactics. Incidents of physical aggression in interpersonal relations are rare; homicide is virtually unknown. Divorce is taboo. As shown in Table 6.1, nonviolent commitments in all these groups extend far beyond shunning military service to a broad spectrum of public and private activities.

Given their opposition to force, outsiders may wonder how gentle people can use "force" to excommunicate wayward members. To Old Orders this is a matter of church discipline, not force, since members may return whenever they confess their sins and agree to follow the *Ordnung*. Such discipline, in Old Order eyes, is designed to maintain the purity of the church and encourage the wayward to repent. Indeed, leaders contend that the disobedient excommunicate themselves by their behavior. In any event, physical violence is not at issue—despite the fact that moderns might want to call excommunication emotional or psychological violence. Spanking and other forms of physical punishment are seen as consistent with nonresistance because parents believe that they have a God-given duty to raise their children in the fear of the Lord.

Despite their nonresistance, Old Orders stubbornly resist government regulations that encroach upon their religious practices. But again, Old

TABLE 6.1 COMMONLY RESTRICTED ACTIVITIES
THAT INVOLVE THE USE OF FORCE

Divorce	Political office holding
Law enforcement	Practicing law
Lawsuits	Self-defense
Military service	Union membership

Orders see this more as a matter of following God than of resisting government. Scripture instructs them to "obey God rather than men" (Acts 5:29), so they are willing to face incarceration if the state intrudes upon sacred turf.

NONCONFORMITY: SYMBOLS OF SEPARATION

Old Order groups draw sharp lines of separation between themselves and the larger society. Many mainstream cultural values are considered a threat to Old Order faith and practice. Separation from the world, or "nonconformity" as it is sometimes called, is based on biblical teachings such as "Be not conformed to the world," "Love not the world neither the things that are in the world," "Come out from among them and be ye separate, saith the Lord," and "Be not unequally yoked together with unbelievers."[6] The word *world* refers, in the sectarian mind, to the larger social system—its values, vices, and practices—all of which can corrode sectarian faith.

Nonconformity is grounded in the idea that persons who are baptized into the Christian faith become members of a redemptive community that stands apart from the larger society. Separation from the world is maintained by distinctive practices as well as by special symbols. These cultural fences remind insiders and outsiders alike of the borders between the sectarian enclave and the decadent dominant culture.

A variety of symbols articulate separation from the world in Old Order communities. The horses and carriages used by Mennonites and Amish are, of course, prominent symbols of nonconformity. All of the groups require their members to wear a distinctive garb that symbolizes separation as well as compliance with community norms. In all the groups except the Mennonites, adult men wear a beard. Men also wear prescribed hats and coats when attending worship services and public events. Women are expected to wear a head covering or, in the case of the Hutterites, a special bandana. In modern society dress is an individualistic tool of self expression, whereas in Old Order communities, common garb signals the rejection of individual choice and the endorsement of communal standards. These different understandings of dress reveal a cardinal distinction between the individualism of modern life on the one hand, and the communalism of Old Order life on the other.

A full beard is an important symbol of separation for men in all the groups except the Mennonites. These Amish men pay careful attention to an auctioneer. *Source:* Keith Baum

These practices serve as flags of sorts that announce sectarian loyalties and mark the boundaries of ethnic turf. The principle of separation from the world, upheld by all the groups, regulates the rate of social change, the use of technology, and leisure activities that intersect with the larger society. Old Orders not only share common convictions about the outside world, but they also treat insiders in special ways.

RELATIONS WITH INSIDERS

Family. Home base for most Old Orders is a strong, stable, and sizable family. Children, cousins, grandparents, and other extended kin envelop members in a thick web of support and obligation. Thinner family arrangements common in the larger society—single parent, one child, divorced, and remarried—are rare in Old Order communities. Divorce is strictly taboo and is cause for excommunication. With the exception of the Brethren, Old Order marriage is always endogamous, but even Brethren usually marry within the church.

Beyond the immediate family, the extended family provides a broad network of support. With six children per family, it is not unusual for a person to have as many as sixty first cousins living nearby. Add relations by marriage, and members may be loosely related to every member of the settlement. Some Hutterite colonies include only two or three extended families. Whereas moderns routinely face strangers in daily interaction, Old Orders rarely do. Extended family ties weave stability and trust into the fabric of these communities.

All members, whether related or not, are treated as brothers and sisters in the faith. On a practical level, this means that many things outsiders would consider private are open to comment and inspection. Although the family is the foundational unit in Old Order communities, it is always monitored by the church. Husbands and wives sit separately in worship services. This blends families into the larger church and also underscores the accountability of individuals to the church. The faith community coordinates weddings, prescribes gender roles, and admonishes couples about birth control and the proper training of children—continual reminders that the family is under the thumb of the church. Moreover, these are patriarchal societies. Fathers are the authoritative head of the home; although they listen to women, they defer only to *their* fathers and to other older males.

There are some differences in the role of women within Old Order communities. An attorney who handles legal transactions for Old Order Mennonites and Amish in Pennsylvania noted that Amish women participate much more than their Mennonite counterparts in financial and legal affairs. "When we sit down for a real estate settlement, the Amish women raise questions and offer their opinions; the Mennonite women are much more reserved." This particular difference in gender roles has been noted by other observers as well.

Children. Relationships with children also depart from the cultural mainstream. While modern culture encourages children to explore, experiment, and express themselves, Old Orders bid their children to be quiet, obedient, and cooperative. Obligation and dependence is emphasized rather than personal rights and independence. Childhood socialization is the most effective form of "conversion" because the images and worldview that are imprinted in childhood last a lifetime. Old Order communities recognize the significance of immersing their children in their distinctive pool of values. Each group stresses the importance of obedience as well as respect for God, elders, parents, teachers, and the church. Disobedient children are physically punished because parents feel responsible to correct them. Learning obedience to authority in early childhood is critical for shaping compliant and cooperative adults. Early and thorough socialization is the most effective means of persuading youth to join their birthright community.

The virtues of self-surrender and the habits of submission are taught at a tender age. This training is critical for a church that requires compliant adults. Children who overdevelop skills of independent thinking, assertiveness, and self-expression eventually leave the church or wreak havoc within it. Such expressions of individualism are like cancers that eat away at Old Order commitments. Habits of respect, obedience, deference, and submission, on the other hand, underwrite the unity and order of the community. Unlike modern parents, who rush their children toward independence, Hutterites, Mennonites, and Amish call for "breaking the child's will"—hoping their children will mature into quiet and cooperative adults.

One mother said, "What makes Amish children so nice is the spanking. The more you spank, the better the result." Said another, "If you spank them a lot, you break their will and they become like you want them." Old Order parents are not afraid to say no to their children, not afraid to set limits and enforce them, not afraid that these measures will injure self-esteem. These parents have developed confidence in child rearing without ever reading a how-to-do-it manual.

Mennonite and Amish religious training is entirely informal except for instruction prior to baptism. Brethren do not even hold baptismal classes. The Hutterites have a German school, but there are typically no Sunday schools or religion classes in the private schools of these communities. Instead, children acquire their beliefs and values by participating in family, church, and community life.

The importance of childhood socialization is underscored by the attention that Old Order communities lavish on their children's schooling. Since the mid-twentieth century the Mennonites and Amish have established small private schools. The Hutterites hold their German school on a daily basis. Hutterite youth also attend a public school on the colony where both teacher and curriculum fall under the scrutiny of colony elders. In recent decades Brethren have joined the exodus from public schools; about half of their children now are schooled at home or in private schools operated by members.

The private schools of all the groups are vital agents in their protest against progress. They transmit alternate values and insulate youth from Enlightenment notions of moral relativity, evolution, critical thinking, and individualism, all of which challenge Old Order ways. Equally important, the schools provide a cradle of ethnic friendships and minimize ties with outside peers.

From spanking to private schools, Old Order habits of child rearing extol tradition, restrict choice, and set their people apart from the larger world.

Other Members. Old Orders also relate in a different fashion to members outside their extended family. Rejecting modernity's sharp cleavage between public and private spheres, Old Orders constrict the private until, in the case of a Hutterite child, it may shrink to a small box or trunk for secret belongings. In Hutterite colonies it is not even necessary to knock on the door before entering the apartment of another family. Thus, realms that many moderns would consider private are open to community members. Describing the porous cocoon around private space, one Amish woman said, "Everything is everyone else's business." Private things stay in the family, but "family" expands to nearly the whole fellowship. The free flow of information would astound outsiders. But what others might denounce as gossip or meddling, Old Orders see as brotherly and sisterly concern.

In the broader culture, to question a neighbor's newly bought gadget, leisure activity, or occupational choice is considered intrusive. Indeed, employers or church officials who do so might be charged with abuse of power. Even close friends hesitate to cross these lines. One's "private" domain of home, lifestyle, and leisure is "no one else's business." Among Old Orders the interpersonal walls are more porous. Members are not as free to follow their hearts and do whatever they please—to dress in any fashion, to enjoy any leisure activity, or to purchase any product. To be sure, all of these communities grant space for personal choice, but it is remarkably smaller than the private arena of modern life.

Less privacy brings more social intimacy, something Old Orders enjoy in abundance. Unlike moderns, who have many casual acquaintances, Old Order networks are inverted. They enjoy many close, familiar ties.

Most of the people they know, they know very well. Intimate bonding beyond their family circle is reinforced through social similarity, neighborly interaction, church functions, and old-fashioned visiting—the favorite pastime of Old Order groups. Some Brethren could virtually discard their public phone directories because their calls so predictably go to church members. In Old Order communities social ties overlap because work, play, education, and worship unfold within the same social circle, many of whose members are also family. Such overlap creates a densely woven social fabric.

Another remarkable difference between Old Orders and the larger world is the absence of bureaucracy within their fellowship. Old Order social ties are informal and personal.[7] Bureaucratic structures with written procedures and impersonal protocols are missing within the redemptive community. Instead, tradition reigns, and authority is embodied in the person of "Grandma," "Brother Kurtz," or "Bishop Brubaker." Newcomers to these communities have much to learn about how things are done and who does them, but little of it is written down. The grammar of community is taught through gentle counsel, warm smiles, rebukes, and questioning stares. And all of it is done on a small scale in familiar circles.

Relations with Outsiders

Informal Ties. In the same way that tradition and submission regulate internal relations, they mold external ties as well. But while the insider-effect builds bridges, the outsider-effect erects fences. How one handles strangers in many ways defines the community. Although Old Orders emphasize separation from the world, they are willing to shake hands with their neighbors. Neighborliness flows to outsiders in daily gestures of friendship as well as when disasters strike. Farm sales, benefit auctions, and yard sales are common venues for mixing. Old Orders who are involved in business deal with outsiders every day. Mennonites and Amish sometimes serve as volunteers with Mennonite Disaster Service, aiding outsiders who are victims of floods, tornadoes, and hurricanes.

Hutterites are the most cautious about external ties. The minister is usually informed when someone leaves the colony for an errand, and first-time visitors may receive a cool welcome. But among established

Two Hutterites stop their large combines to talk with a visiting salesman.
Source: John Wipf

neighbors, Hutterites develop routine cordial friendships related to farming and business. Residential segregation minimizes individual Hutterite
contact with other outsiders. The pattern for Amish and Mennonites, on
the other hand, is mixed. The most conservative fellowships, like the
Swartzentruber Amish, keep to themselves and initiate outside contact
only for business. Brethren, meanwhile, interact rather freely with nonmembers, especially in their vocations. Yet even here, social life generally
remains focused within the faith community.

Equally telling, outsider relations carry a distinctive flavor. They are
generally friendly without being familiar, cordial without being close.

With the exception of the Brethren, romantic ties with worldlings are forbidden. Old Orders would feel uncomfortable hugging an outsider. A visitor to an Amish home proudly announced to some non-Amish friends that he was almost to the "hugging stage," an expression that would have certainly amused, if not repulsed, his Amish friends.

In short, Old Orders want to be open to outsiders without being overwhelmed, to be separate but not insular. Differences in personality yield different degrees of comfort with outsiders. Yet the distinction between "our people" and "the rest of the world" remains clear and is continually reinforced by patterns of speech, behavior, and dress. The outsider is always a neighbor and sometimes a friend, but is never a brother or sister. Old Orders are kind toward them, but not responsible for them. The kiss of peace is withheld, and the communion table is barred; only members of the spiritual family—genuine kindred spirits—have a place at the table set for the Lord's Supper.

Formal affiliations. Affiliations with outside organizations are cautiously curtailed. Using the biblical image of a yoke holding two oxen together (2 Cor. 6:14), Old Orders frown upon members becoming "unequally yoked" with nonbelievers. Business partnerships with worldlings are typically discouraged, as are holding stock in public companies and purchasing commercial insurance.[8] In more conservative communities, such ties would be cause for excommunication. All the groups strictly prohibit membership in "secret societies" such as the Masons that require an oath of allegiance.

The typical Hutterite never joins an outside organization. In progressive communities, an Amish contractor might join a local builders' organization, but such involvements are rare. Because many Old Orders are involved in farming and related businesses, they have little interest in professional associations. Even small business owners rarely join commercial organizations. In some communities Amish and Mennonites serve as volunteer firemen and assist with community benefit auctions, but that is generally the extent of their civic involvement.

When it comes to joining, the Brethren are an exception. Surprisingly open to business associations, they also participate in a wide array of charitable and civic organizations—the Red Cross, volunteer rescue squads, hospice committees, hospital boards, public schools, and disaster relief services. Even so, membership in service organizations, art clubs, and leisure associations are rarely considered. These are simply beyond the orb of Old Order life. Apart from having little interest in such affiliations, most Old Orders would feel like cultural strangers in these settings.

But even the Brethren draw the line when it comes to religious affiliation. Unlike mainstream churches, which pride themselves in ecumenical achievements, Old Orders shun broader religious ties. They rarely participate in ecumenical projects and worship services in the local community. Individual members may occasionally attend a mainline church service, but they may not formally participate, and Old Order churches would never sponsor or encourage such cooperation. To do so would risk not only exposure to questionable doctrine, but a split of allegiance as well. Old Orders are expected to pledge their sole allegiance to the heavenly kingdom as embodied by *their* church. Anything more could open endless debates about which outside groups are acceptable and which doctrines are safe.

DAILY LIVING

The contrast between faithfulness and worldliness extends throughout many domains of Old Order life—work, possessions, personal demeanor, and technology to name a few. In each of these areas, Old Orders endow with deep significance many things that moderns consider routine. More than just a matter of earning a living, work becomes an expression of sacred vocation. More than a simple question of lifestyle, possessions testify to spiritual values. More than just an accident of personality, demeanor points to peace or turmoil within. Given these meanings, each domain of daily life reflects adherence to ancient patterns, submission to the church, and separation from the world.

Work. Unlike professional employment, work is not pursued to pile up personal credits; it is a calling that contributes to the common good. Résumés are largely unknown in these communities. Within their communal system Hutterites carry no personal obligation to earn a living. Individual effort is only noteworthy as it contributes to the colony good. Old Order work is often a cooperative activity that binds generations, neighbors, and families together.[9] In some communities, however, this integrative function of work is beginning to dwindle as new technologies individualize tasks.

The Hutterites assign occupational roles based on community need as well as on individual skill. Mennonites, Amish, and Brethren permit members to select their own occupations within certain limits. The Mennonites, for instance, discourage members from working as horse or cattle jockeys who buy and sell animals. Such jobs make it "too easy to cheat and be dishonest." Members may, however, operate retail stores and sell manufactured products for a living.

All of the groups forbid members from entering occupations that would violate the *Ordnung* of their community. Selling televisions, for instance, is strictly taboo. Working in an amusement park or as a bartender are out of the question. Practicing law or serving in law enforcement are off-limits—the mantle of justice and the weapon of force contradict the gentle ways of *Gelassenheit*. Many vocational restrictions remain unstated, however, for there is little need for taboos where educational limits erect natural fences.

Old Orders prefer practical things. Labors that produce a tangible result are valued; those that manage information, relationships, or emotions are suspect. Even among the Brethren, who span a broader range of occupations, practical skills and services are favored. There are more nurses than secretaries, more plumbers than strategic planners. Brethren view higher education cautiously and accept it only when it leads to a specific skill or trade. The classical liberal arts, focused on the development of the mind, threaten Old Order ways.

All things considered, Old Order communities encourage their members to work within the corridors of ethnicity rather than among outsiders. Family considerations also play a role. Long-distance truck driving or other work that disrupts family life is discouraged. Work that weaves the community together, in or near the home, is always esteemed.

Possessions and Leisure. While moderns may be hard-pressed to connect faith and material consumption, Old Orders quickly link the two, calling for restraint instead of accumulation. Rather than personal promotions and possessions, the marks of status in these communities are commitment, integrity, consistency, and a cooperative spirit. Personal possessions, they are quick to point out, have a practical function and should not be used in a vain or conspicuous manner. Among Hutterites personal possessions are, of course, limited to a few household items. The other three communities permit personal property but with certain restrictions. All of the groups have a special affection for traditional objects. From books to quilts, decorations to furniture, older styles are preferred, and heirlooms are cherished. These are, in the end, communities of production, not communities of consumption.

Members of Old Order groups had little time for leisure so long as they were tilling the soil. As some of them leave the farm, more leisure activities are developing—especially travel to other settlements and to scenic areas of the country. All of the groups have longstanding taboos against attendance at movies, fairs, carnivals, and other forms of public amusement. Such worldly activities not only appeal to vanity and the "lusts of the flesh" but also are viewed as a deplorable waste of time. Except for an occasional mouth organ or accordion, musical instruments are deemed unnecessary. Recreation that builds relationships within the community is favored over spectator sports that focus on personal competition and gratification. Singings, softball, volleyball, table games, homespun fun, and old-fashioned visiting are favorite pastimes of the young.

Appearance and Demeanor. Everyone remembers Old Orders for their distinctive dress. Moderns, of course, go to great lengths to cultivate a distinctive look, but as a statement of individual identity, not a badge of uniformity. For Old Orders, dress visibly marks the foundational categories of life: sacred and profane, male and female, adult and child, insider and outsider. It is the language of belonging and identity, reminding insider and outsider alike of who they are and to whom they belong.

Dress is at once the most public and most personal symbol of yieldedness to the church's moral order. It is a daily reminder of one's duty, loyalty, and identity. It lifts the burden of daily choice from the individual. Members who carefully dress within the prescribed order have fewer anxieties about dress than moderns. They are not confronted every morning by a closet brimming with different looks; there is only one look—the same yesterday as it will be tomorrow. Thus, ironically, the Old Order focus on dress *frees* them from focusing on dress. Moderns must shop incessantly to update their wardrobes and keep abreast of the latest fashions.[10]

Yet even Old Orders sport subtle variations. Tiny clues signal compliance or bending of community guidelines. For example, a Dunker sister, pulling several dresses from her closet, said, "This one is for shopping," pointing to the largest floral print. The second, a slightly more subdued pattern, was for visiting. Smiling sheepishly, she held up the most muted print of all—"This one is for worship." In all of the groups, the size of a head covering, length of a covering string, width of a hat, cut of the hair, length of dress, presence of pockets, and shade of gray communicate differences of attitude and outlook that are virtually imperceptible to outsiders. However, in the eyes of church leaders, these fine distinctions signal a submissive or rebellious heart.

The importance of dress varies from group to group. It is less important among Hutterites, whose living arrangement shields them from outsiders and also reminds them to whom they belong. With the groups who mingle more freely with outsiders, especially the Brethren, dress takes on greater significance. All the groups strictly forbid any form of makeup or jewelry. Wedding rings are taboo. Any adornment that highlights the self and draws attention to the individual is considered pretentious and ostentatious. Only those with rebellious hearts would wear such things.

As noted earlier, Old Order demeanor is marked by reserve and deference to others. Members would never attend a seminar on assertiveness training. The gregarious styles and confident handshakes so common in modern culture would bring rebuke in Old Order life. Habits of humility, on the other hand, are championed. Members are expected to yield and to wait on one another rather than to contest and contend. In speech and body language, gentleness and patience are esteemed. Members pause before speaking, preferring one another, waiting in deference for the other. The grammar of *Gelassenheit* is slow to speak, hesitant to judge, and comfortable with silence. A quiet spirit is unimpressed by verbal eloquence and rational argumentation. A too-ready display of one's knowledge is viewed as arrogant. Indeed, too much knowledge, even too much biblical knowledge, "puffeth up." One Old Order paper refuses to print ads for books that promote "positive thinking and how to get smart."[11]

Coping with Technology

Production. While technology can be conceptualized on many levels, we focus on three: technologies of *production, consumption,* and *communication.* Old Order communities have the fewest restrictions on productive technology and the most on communicative technology. The Hutterites and Brethren have virtually no constraints on productive technology for farming or other economic pursuits. Amish and Mennonite restraints on productive technology often relate to the size of operations as well as to the fear that technologies like the tractor will lead to the car.

Other cultural restraints also impinge on earning a living. Mennonites and Amish emphasize the importance of small-scale operations. They worry that large farms and businesses will disturb the equality of community by piling too much wealth and power on the lap of one person. Some Amish have indeed been excommunicated because they refused to downsize their businesses. Restrictions on technology encourage small-scale operations. Milking parlors and automatic feeders are prohibited by the Amish and Mennonites for fear they will spur large-scale operations. The restraints on productive technology not only limit the size of operations but also draw symbolic boundaries with the outside world. The Amish taboo on electricity is, of course, a striking protest against progress.

Consumption. Technologies of consumption are more restricted. Constraints on household appliances and gadgets of convenience vary from group to group. The Amish and Mennonites regulate consumptive technologies the most; the Brethren, the least. The range of acceptable appli-

Brethren use state-of-the-art technology for farming and business.
Source: Roanoke Times

ances varies by group. Amish homes are the most austere because their taboo on electricity eliminates a host of modern conveniences: cof-feemakers, toasters, hairdryers, microwaves, dishwashers, and air condi-tioners, to name but a few. Some of these appliances are gradually being adopted by the other groups. The Brethren embrace of such devices is linked to their historic insistence that technology in itself is not bad; its use is what matters. The symbolic meanings that contribute to identity are also important around the home. A progressive Amish woman wor-ried that her new sofa and her house in general looked "too English." An "Amish-looking house," she noted, should "have darker colors and look more plain and simple."

The Hutterite pattern is again unique because communal control of consumptive technologies benefits everyone. Although many colonies have modern appliances in their communal kitchens, some do not have automatic dishwashers. Indeed, acceptance of productive and consump-tive technology in some cases rides on gender relations. Since men regu-late the rules of technology, they sometimes are more friendly to changes that benefit farm and business than to those that add convenience at home.

Communication. All the communities, including the Brethren, place tight controls on communication technology. This is especially true in the case of external ties. Television, of course, is prohibited because it would open a direct channel to the vices and values of the outside world. Other avenues of mass media—radios, stereos, video players, and tape recorders—are strictly forbidden. Teenagers sometimes have radios and CD players on the sly, but baptized members do not. Such devices would bring cultural contamination as well as alter the structure of Old Order life. Reading, knitting, singing, talking, and traditional games would yield to quiz shows, talk shows, and thumping rhythms, all of which would dis-turb the pace and peace of Old Order homes.

Telephones, which enable easy ties to the outside world, are now used by all the groups, though often with some restrictions.[12] In some com-munities the advent of cell phones has blurred traditional lines of usage and stirred discontent. The Old Order Amish continue to forbid the in-stallation of private phones in homes. Hutterites limit external phone use to ministers and colony managers. In the case of some colonies, the min-ister monitors outside calls. The Mennonites discourage their ministers from placing phones in their homes.

Brethren, on the other hand, use telephones to strengthen the bonds of community. A member in Ohio tells the story of a council meeting to elect a minister. A member left the meeting early and called the results to a friend in California. The California family called a Pennsylvania family, who in turn called an Ohio family living near the council meeting. Consequently, some Ohio Brethren knew the ministerial choice—via California and Pennsylvania—before their neighbors had even left the meeting!

The Amish often make a sharp distinction between *ownership* and *use* of questionable forms of technology. This distinction is particularly true with computers and motor vehicles. Both Mennonites and Amish permit hiring motor vehicles for taxi service, but ownership is taboo. Although Hutterite colonies own trucks and vans, individual members may not. Brethren may own cars, but they monitor their color and extract the radios so as to remain immune from the world as they motor through it.

The Language of Symbols

Technological restrictions not only make a substantive difference in Old Order life; they also construct symbolic identities. Each domain of everyday life—work, possessions, demeanor, and technology—has symbolic as well as practical import. Work is not just a way of getting something done; it makes a statement about one's faith and identity. Technology is more than a matter of reaching out, plugging in, or speeding up; it tells a story of connections and commitments. Possessions, in particular, become signposts of personal priorities. Old Orders speak a different symbolic language. To moderns, for instance, a Christmas tree can symbolize joy, family, and giving—a seasonal reminder of values that rise above the daily routine. However, in Old Order eyes the tree is a pagan distraction, diverting attention from the manger and the God whose miraculous gift should rivet their Christmas affection.

For moderns and Old Orders alike, dress tells a tale of identity—to whom you belong and how you envision yourself. Plain dress sends different signals to different people. For those who wear it, plain attire testifies to a spirit of self-sacrifice, love for the faithful, and Christian separation and witness. Unable to hear these spiritual messages, outsiders deride the garb as mindless conformity. Thus, while the tools of daily living signal deeper commitments, the message rests in the mind of the receiver. Whether it signals virtue or vice depends on whose side of the cultural fence one is on.

Old Orders have a keen awareness of the coding that links purchases, possessions, and daily pursuits to sacred realms. Sensitized to the symbolic, they see weightiness and moral consequence where moderns see only lifestyle and routine. The earnestness of their manner is burdensome indeed to outsiders, who value spontaneity and a freewheeling style. Whether we consider the beard, the horse and carriage, simple meetinghouses, steel-wheeled tractors, soundboard restrictions on computers, mealtime routines, or a holy kiss greeting, Old Orders symbolize their unity and separation in visible, daily ways that mark the boundaries between church and world.

RELIGIOUS RITUALS AND SYMBOLS

Rituals. Even though a sacred canopy covers all of Old Order life, certain corners are more hallowed than others. And it is these corners that are extremely resistant to change. It is here that reverence for tradition, yielding to community, and separation from the world run deepest. Of all the domains of Old Order life, this is the most "peculiar," the domain of greatest distinction. Mainstream Anabaptist groups—the Mennonite Church and the Church of the Brethren—have completely remodeled their worship routines; Old Orders have not. It is here, in the area of religious ritual, where Old Orders remain most ancient. It is here where their identities are ultimately etched and preserved.[13]

In a quiet but clear voice, religious ritual enunciates a community's most treasured commitments. Each liturgy of faith, repeated again and again, reminds participants of who they are and why they exist. For Old Orders, the communion service is the alcove in which they store their deepest meanings of membership. Occurring twice yearly for the Mennonites and Amish, and once a year for the Hutterites and Brethren, communion articulates and symbolically reenacts their most cherished values.[14] A self-examination service or visit, depending on the tradition, purges sin and purifies the community in preparation for holy communion. All the groups except the Hutterites practice footwashing in the communion service (or in the Love Feast in the case of the Brethren). The ancient ritual of footwashing reminds members that they serve one another in the spirit of humility.

Other rituals also speak the language of *Gelassenheit*—kneeling for prayer, the holy kiss, baptism, public confession, and the ordination rites for leaders. Baptism is the monumental rite of passage to adulthood—the irrevocable step that signals lifelong commitment. Except for the Brethren, and Mennonites in Virginia, the use of a Germanic dialect links Old Orders directly to their ancient heritage. While the form and flavor varies from tradition to tradition, Old Order rituals share much in common. By translating ethereal values into visible symbols, these dramatic rites remind participants that they are strangers in a foreign land.

For every backroad ritual embraced, a mainstream one is ignored. Old Order rituals of worship depart from Protestant patterns as shown in Tables 6.2 and 6.3. Written orders of service are scorned, but informal ones are scrupulously followed. The classical strains of German chorales and the lively gospel rhythms are kept at bay; the slow, simple cadence of a cappella singing brings a quiet assurance of divine presence. Standing for prayer is typically rejected in favor of kneeling—a meek and lowly expression of reverence. The drawn-out singing, lengthy sermons, extensive Bible reading, and the laborious service itself teach the skills of patience and waiting. The kiss of peace, practiced by all but the Hutterites, signifies the sacred bonds of fellowship that both unite the community and separate it from outsiders. All of these rituals of reverence speak the language of humility.[15]

Symbols. The physical setting of Old Order worship perfectly echoes the rituals within. This is especially true for the Amish, who worship at home. The meetinghouses of the other groups embody a stark simplicity. Notably absent are stained glass windows, steeples, organs, altars, carv-

---

TABLE 6.2 COMMON OLD ORDER RELIGIOUS RITUALS AND PRACTICES

A capella singing	Kneeling for prayer
Adult baptism	Multiple ministers lead in worship
Excommunication	Ordination of lay leaders by lot[b]
Fermented wine in communion	Public confession
Footwashing[a]	Segregation by sex during worship
Holy kiss[a]	Self-examination prior to communion

[a]Not practiced by the Hutterites.
[b]The Brethren do not use the lot.

Table 6.3 Worship Practices Commonly Rejected by Old Order Communities

Acolytes	Presentations by lay members
Altar calls	Reciting of a creed(s)
"Amens" and other verbal reactions	Special music groups
Candles, flowers, and other decorations	Spontaneous public sharing
Choirs	Standing for hymns or prayers
Drama	Use of videos or overhead projectors
Formal collection of offerings	Ushers
Four-part singing	Written liturgy or worship guide
Musical instruments	Written sermons[a]

[a]Hutterite ministers typically read ancient sermons.

Table 6.4 Commonly Rejected Religious Symbols in Sanctuaries

Altars	Offering plates
Candles	Raised pulpits
Carpeting	Robes
Chancel areas	Stained glass
Crosses	Statues
Flags	Steeples
Flowers	Worship centers

ings, paintings, banners, flowers, crosses, and raised pulpits. Indeed, as the name meetinghouse suggests, these plain buildings are little more than large rectangular houses with benches sufficient to seat the faithful. Like the pattern of a home, a table is the centerpiece of the family gathering. Traditional Brethren structures even have a kitchen to prepare the Love Feast and a sleeping loft for visitors, extending the sense of meeting-*house*. As shown in Table 6.4, the symbolic inventory of modern sanctuaries is simply missing. The community in worship is *the* religious reality, not other material forms of symbolism.

In their dramatic departure from mainline motifs, the religious forms of Old Order communities ground them in a radical and distinctive heritage. This symbolic inheritance is experienced as a simple, timeless treasure, one that follows a different rhythm and that accents different virtues than those embraced by mainstream churches. It values repeti-

The basement of an Amish home prepared for Sunday morning services. *Source:* Dennis Hughes

tion. It symbolically lowers the individual and elevates the community.[16] And it very intentionally rejects the symbols of popular faith that in Old Order eyes distort a Christian spirit of humility.

LEADERSHIP PATTERNS

While moderns often subject their leaders to painstaking scrutiny, Old Orders typically smile in quiet admiration at the mere mention of their leaders' names. Rather than probing for hidden flaws, they lift them up, relying upon them for instruction and counsel. They seek not human sophistication, but leaders who will lead "in weakness, in fear, and in much trembling" (1 Cor. 2:3). They do not thrill to enticing words but want to hear "the wisdom of God in a mystery." Leaders are selected for their spiritual esteem and moral credibility, not for their professional credentials and training. Moreover, they serve for life without pay. Their ministry is a sacrificial labor added to their everyday efforts to earn a living. As such, members support them with a spirit of gratitude. They may not appreciate every minister's style, but they are slow to criticize. When the burden of ministry is shared, the limitations of one are redeemed by the strengths of another.

Most important, ministers receive the blessing of divine legitimation. This blessing comes in a rather dramatic way by the casting of lots in Hutterite, Mennonite, and Amish communities. It is not the people but God Almighty who reaches down from heaven and makes the final choice from among several candidates. Among the Brethren no ballots, majority votes, or other human devices are used; the Holy Spirit's direction is sought through prayer and the private "voicing" of each member. A ministerial election may even end without "calling" anyone if the Holy Spirit does not give clarity. Such methods of selection highlight the hand of God and augment the authority of leaders. Not merely servants of the congregation, they are divinely selected servants of God. When they speak, they speak for the Lord. To slight their counsel is to snub the advice of the Almighty.

Yet none of the leaders have absolute power. Ordained officials in all the communities must bend to the voice of their people as well as the wishes of their ordained peers. The amount of power a leader can wield varies by personality and from community to community. Hutterite ministers exercise considerable influence. Mennonite and Amish bishops have a strong hand in enforcing the *Ordnung* of the church.

At the other end of the spectrum, Brethren elders, although highly respected, work in a more democratic fashion. Their Council Meetings are open to all members. Although women do not speak in public deliberations, they have equal input when a "voice" is taken. It takes a consensus of all members present to reach a decision. In Hutterite, Mennonite, and Amish settings, decisions are confined to a smaller circle. In Hutterite colonies, a small group of men hold the reins of power. Among Mennonites, ordained men meeting in semiannual conferences chart the paths of holiness, but even their decisions are tested in local congregations. All the groups ground their patterns of authority in traditional assumptions related to age, wisdom, and patriarchy.

Lack of specialized training leads to a lack of specialized systems, as shown in Table 6.5. Bishops and elders do not spend their evenings in

Table 6.5 Specialized Religious Roles and Functions Rejected by Old Order Groups

Congregational budgets	Revival meetings
Full-time, specialized leaders	Salaried leaders and officials
Missionary and evangelistic programs	Sunday school[a]
Organized lay leadership	Weddings in church buildings[b]
Professionally educated ministers	Youth programs and clubs

[a]A very small number of Amish districts have Sunday school.
[b]Hutterites are an exception as well as the Old Order Mennonites in Virginia.

committee meetings, budget deliberations, or planning sessions. Neither do they record their hours, number of sermons, and hospital visits in order to boost year-end evaluations. There are no Sunday school programs to plan, choirs to orchestrate, committees to chair, or youth programs and ecumenical activities to coordinate. Ministers simply serve the flock as time permits and needs arise. They work informally, responding to concerns as they emerge, meeting in homes, shops, or barns. Being "housekeepers" rather than evangelists or managers, they discuss matters of faithfulness and discipline rather than strategic planning, corporate goals, and techniques of growth.

When it comes to deference, seniority reigns. Unlike members of mainstream churches, who crave messages from youthful ministers brimming with enthusiasm, Old Orders cherish the wisdom of the elderly. Younger ministers look to those of prior generations for counsel, and these in turn look among themselves to the oldest. The longest ordained bishop typically serves as moderator of the Mennonite conference. Leaders in all the groups typically sit by seniority in sacred services. The oldest visiting minister receives "first liberty" to preach among the Brethren. In communities that preserve ancient truths, the eldest becomes a bridge between the bygone and the present. With few written records, the memories of the elderly become repositories of time-tested truth, tradition, and story. Old Orders are as interested in nailing down the past as moderns are in predicting the future. Thus, the values of age are inverted; older ministers become community treasures, the wielders of influence. Basing authority on age provides an additional brake on social change within these communities.

The spot where backroad and mainroad religion diverge most sharply is surely at the fork of church discipline. Older mainline understandings of discipline that issued "tickets" for communion, required public displays of penitence, and excommunicated the wayward have long disappeared from Protestant groups. Even among American Catholics, discipline has fallen out of favor. A progressive Brethren denomination has written off the word *discipline* as "negative, unloving, and punitive."[17] Mainstream religion treats individuals as seekers with their own moral compasses—more in need of support than direction, empowerment than admonition. Such groups focus on abstract themes of faith, righteousness, and redemption, letting members work out the specifics themselves. Even when clear deficiencies are detected, mainliners welcome the sinner in, promoting their church as a hospital for sinners, not a refuge for saints.

Old Orders see it the other way. The church is a "royal priesthood" and a "peculiar people . . . called out of darkness into marvelous light" (1 Pet. 2:9–11). It is a hospice of sorts, but one designed for "pilgrims and strangers" who abstain from "fleshly lusts," not for the terminally ill. Christ himself instituted church discipline by giving Peter the keys to the kingdom and authorizing him to bind (prohibit) sinful activities and to loose (permit) virtuous ones. So Old Orders find it hard to imagine a community of true disciples without discipline. If the line between light and darkness is to endure, if believers are to yield to the will of God, if the church is to follow the ancient paths, then there must be a means to ensure it. Discipline, Old Orders agree, is the means of finding the desirable mix of freedom and community constraint.

Discipline and the *Ordnung* go hand in hand. All the communities have a moral order of behavioral expectations as well as taboos. Much of it is taken for granted, learned by osmosis as children grow up in Old Order surroundings. Those who live by the *Ordnung* receive a variety of social rewards that foster a sense of satisfaction for righteous living. Disobedient members face sanctions that may include a brotherly visit, being "set back" from communion, excommunication for grievous offenses, seclusion among the Hutterites, and shunning among the Amish.

Such means of control swing into action whenever the sheep stray beyond the *Ordnung*'s protective fence. The shepherds of the flock use various means to return lost lambs to the fold. The procedures tend to be slower and more flexible among the Brethren, yet all groups exercise forbearance and patience—hoping the wayward will repent and confess their sins rather than provoke a sterner censure. Those who stray are first admonished to comply. If willing to repent, they may be asked to make a public confession—a ritual of shame that highlights the church's moral authority. Those that persist in disobedience are excommunicated. In the case of the Hutterites and Amish, they may be shunned in one fashion or another. All the communities welcome the expelled back upon a proper confession of sin.

The principle of excommunication, or "disowning" as the Brethren sometimes call it, is linked to adult baptism. In the Anabaptist tradition, baptism is a voluntary decision that entails an adult confession of Christian faith as well as a covenant with the community. Baptism symbolizes not only salvation but acceptance of the *Ordnung* and a rejection of the world. To renege on that vow later in life is a serious breech of integrity that, if not confessed, merits exclusion from the Lord's Supper and community life. Unlike modern churches, where persons sometimes drift in and out with little notice, Old Orders pay careful attention to membership status.

FIVE MARKS OF FAITH

Old Orders believe that their corporate life in one way or another embodies the will of God. They have few doubts about the reality of a transcendent God. They see life on earth as preparation for life eternal. But millions of Christians in numerous traditions also believe in a real heaven and a hot hell. What distinguishes Old Order faith and sets them apart theologically from mainstream evangelicals and fundamentalists?

First, Old Order faith is remarkably *relational*. Salvation has as much to do with social relationships as with a vertical encounter with the divine. It is a badge of faith for mainstream evangelicals to respond with a confident "yes" when asked the billion-dollar question, "Are you saved?" Old Orders would likely answer, "That is for God to judge, not me," or, "If you really want to know, ask my wife and some of the brethren." To the evangelical questioner—convinced that salvation is a state of grace grounded in a personal relationship with God—these words almost sound like a foreign tongue. A questioner might drop the matter in confusion or presumptuously conclude that the plain-faith practitioner needs saving. The Old Order sister, meanwhile, might turn away in sadness, wondering, "How can people be so convinced they are saved when they reflect so little of the gospel of humility?"

While mainstream evangelicals see salvation first as a gracious gift, Old Orders see it as a journey. They strongly oppose what some evangelicals call eternal security—the idea that the faithful can never fall into perdition. Like modern understandings of love, Old Order salvation is something that can grow stronger or weaker, be fallen into and out of. It certainly includes personal faith, but it is more expansive because it involves the entire community of faith.

Similar to their expansive view of salvation, Old Orders see love, membership, and communion in a different light than the individualized versions afoot in the broader culture. Moderns, for instance, tend to view love as a personal feeling or as something that exists between couples and in families. Old Orders highlight these as well, but they also cherish the bonds of intimacy in community. Brethren, in particular, are constantly assessing the "peace and love" of the fellowship.

Similarly, when Old Orders think of membership, an individual's desire to join is only part of the picture. Equally important is the community's decision to accept the person; church purity hinges on each baptism and each act of discipline. What a person feels and whether he or she believes in Christ is important but not conclusive. In mainline liturgy, communion centers on the transcendence of God and the believer's personal decision. Old Orders add a relational dimension, believing true communion is impossible without a right relationship among the brotherhood. Even use of the term *brethren* to refer to fellow members—common to all Old Order groups—highlights spiritual kinship, close relations, and a transparent lack of privacy.

Personal, subjective experience is downplayed in other ways as well. Charismatic expressions and personal testimonies are considered dangerous in Old Order thinking. Fresh interpretations of Scripture are not encouraged because the church relies on traditional wisdom. Members do not receive direct calls to the ministry but must wait for God to beckon them through the voice of community. Even in shunning, whether one eats or converses with another member is beyond the realm of personal preference.

A Mennonite quilt maker embodies the virtues of Old Order faith. *Source:* Jan Gleysteen

Second, Old Order faith is exceedingly *practical.* One's manner of living outweighs concerns about proper belief. Faithful adherence to the *Ordnung* paves the road to heaven. One is not saved by grace alone but also and especially by responding to grace through daily acts of obedience. Outward displays of humility and compliance evince Christ's spirit within. This practical tilt means that religious education occurs through observation and apprenticeship rather than through books and formal instruction. An informal system of training only works, however, when children live in an extended family ensconced in a stable community.

Expressing this practicality, Old Order faith is in many ways more a matter of habit than of systematic inquiry or theological reflection. Every pattern is not pondered, every sermon not scrutinized. It is acceptable to repeat today what you did yesterday without always assessing if you should do it differently tomorrow. In this sense, Old Order faith is less reflexive than modern culture, where thought and action continuously interact as people weigh multiple options. Old Orders do not feel compelled to give systematic reasons for all their behaviors or to make them appear logically consistent. Such burdens are modern preoccupations.[18]

On the backroad to heaven, tradition is still reason enough; it does not have to be dressed up in the fancy garb of theological rationale. This is not to deny that Old Orders readjust their practices along the way; ample evidence of that abounds. They do not, however, constantly reexamine their core commitments and the broader contours of their faith. When specific rules change, the adjustments are often practical responses to patterns that have emerged gradually over time. That is to say, there is rarely a formal rationale. "It is permitted," or "We no longer see any harm in it" are reason enough. The authority of Scripture, the bishop, or Annual Meeting supplies the rest.

Lack of systematic reflection also means that the Bible is allowed to speak for itself. Higher criticism, formal theological speculation, and systematic theology are considered frivolous and even dangerous. There is little need to reinterpret the Scriptures anew for every changing circumstance. The timeless wisdom of the ages is sufficient. Commitment to ancient answers dispels interest in progressive revelation.

Third, Old Orders love constancy. In contrast to moderns, who are fascinated by novelty, the implicit nature of their faith means that Old Orders delight in repetition, in seeing patterns repeated day after day in place after place. They even enjoy the similarities that stretch across plain communities—Brethren are pleased to know of the Amish, and Amish enjoy having Mennonite neighbors. While their plain coats and head coverings may differ, the common sentiments and practices outlined in this chapter signal a spiritual kinship. Each group knows that theirs is not a solitary protest.

Generally speaking, young people absorb the constant patterns as the bestowed ways of life, not as burdens. Dress is old-fashioned, worship patterns are ancient, and songs are old—but that is simply what it means to be Old Order. Those who find drudgery rather than delight in such habits will likely leave the fellowship. Without the consistent patterns, Old Orders would be drawn into the endless modern ritual of explaining and justifying every action. But having chosen to limit choice, each gathering, each communion, and each greeting becomes a rite of repetition, performed the same way each time. And each repetition evokes recognition: "We are with our own and in touch with our ancestors." Whether Old Orders travel around the bend, to the next county, or to an adjoining state, their unreflective habits reassure them that they are one people united in a common faith.

Fourth, in contrast to the confident and aggressive posture of many evangelicals, Old Order faith is remarkably *gentle.* A quiet and humble spirit is cherished. Loud celebrations, speaking in tongues, "holy laughter," arm-waving, hand-clapping, and other vibrant displays are unthinkable. Old Order spirituality is solemn, not jubilant. It is a peaceful stream, not a bubbling rapid. Elated praises and testimonies of personal religious experience fail to impress them.

What *does* impress is gentleness, steadfastness, and devout living. Old Orders are not evangelists bent on converting the world, but simple people whose devotion to God and treatment of their neighbor is their witness. Their theological humility rules out aggressive programs of mission and witness. While they are convinced of their own sources of truth and of the world's moral depravity, Old Orders are very reluctant to judge specific denominations and outsiders. They are most critical of their own members who, although knowing better, wander from the faith. They welcome converts who sincerely want to embrace Old Order ways, but few are able or willing to make the cultural leap.

Finally, our analytic separation of various dimensions of Old Order life, while useful for analysis, masks the *tightly woven* character of their faith. For all of these groups, religion flows through every aspect of life, lifting each moment to a loftier plane. It is neither confined nor compartmentalized. The color of carriages and cars, the length of dresses and beards, leisure activities, and dozens of other behaviors fall beneath the shadow of their religious canopy. All of life is sacred. Some parts, of course, are more sacred than others. But all things considered, Old Order faith is woven throughout their total fabric of life.

One way of thinking about Hutterites, Mennonites, Amish, and Brethren is to simply add them to the ethnic mosaic of American culture. Like African Americans, Japanese Americans, Hispanics, or Jews, they share a culture that sets them apart. But the Old Orders are doubly different. Most ethnic groups tend to embrace core American values—individual rights, moral autonomy, competition, success, participation in government, national defense, and the yearning for progress and material improvement. Old Orders, on the other hand, reject the cultural core, calling it "carnal." They are an ethnic group that defines itself not merely as different, but as opposed. More than just a subculture, they are a *counterculture*—a group that turns mainstream commitments on their heads. The biblical metaphors that Old Orders use to describe themselves—strangers and pilgrims, a peculiar people, and a gathered remnant—highlight their foreignness.[19] Unlike many ethnic groups, Old Orders are more interested in being left alone than in "making it"; more interested in a quiet life than in political success.

In place of the cultural canon of progress, Old Orders look to the ancients. In place of personal rights, they stress accountability. Instead of inclusive diversity, they treasure exclusive unity; for unity bespeaks clarity, and clarity, from their cultural pedestal, bespeaks divine inspiration. As we have seen in this chapter, each of these commitments permeates every layer of their existence, transforming families, work, education, consumption, recreation, technology, worship, and even casual encounters into domains of distinction.

To Old Order thinking, a church that merely mirrors the surrounding culture has not only lost its way but has forfeited its very soul. All four groups veer away from mainstreet religion. Yet while each shares much in common with the others, there are also peculiarities that distinguish them from each other. There are, in fact, several backroads to heaven. It is these different pathways that we will now explore.

CHAPTER SEVEN

Four Roads to Heaven

The pilgrim's path doth lead him on, / to his dear home beyond the tide.
—Brethren hymn

DIFFERENT ROADS

"Amish, Mennonite, Hutterite, Brethren—they're all alike! They all drive buggies, dress in black, brainwash their kids, and think the rest of us are going to hell." These reckless remarks of a college professor illustrate the popular impression that all Old Orders are "cut from the same cloth." Even "authoritative" sources can compound the problem, as did this recent posting on the World Wide Web: "Old Order groups all drive horses and buggies rather than cars, do not have electricity in their homes, and send their children to private, one-room schools. Children attend only through the eighth grade. After that, they work on their family's farm or business until they marry." There you have it: Old Order reality is as simple as their dress.

Such accounts suffer from a "they all" premise that glosses over much of what is interesting about Old Order groups. In spite of their common concerns, what is permitted by one Old Order group is often rejected by another. Moreover, their social structures differ substantially, as do their language, clothing, and modes of transportation. The further we probe, the more striking the differences and the more foolish the depictions that fail to penetrate the simplistic veneer of "they all." Each group walks on a different road; each has a different story. How are they different, and what can we learn from their differences?

Tight and Loose Textures

Some of the differences can be conceptualized on a two-dimensional scheme anchored on separation and control. *Separation* indicates the degree of social distance between the ethnic social system and the larger society. The greater the interaction with the dominant culture, the lower the level of separation. The concept of separation provides a gross measure of social distance from the larger society and encompasses both culture (language, values, norms) and social structure (institutional and organizational arrangements).

Control, the second dimension of our grid, reflects the extent to which a group regulates the development of the self and its expression. Strong measures of social control limit choices and stifle the articulation of the self. Low levels of control, on the other hand, grant greater personal freedom and individual expression. In a sense, low control is also a matter of separation, because it permits greater separation from others *within* the group.

These two dimensions—external separation and internal control—reflect social differences between Old Orders and mainstream American society, and within Old Order groups themselves. The first dimension measures the degree of distance between social systems; the second reflects how the sociocultural system is experienced by the individual. Low control encourages individualism and grants greater personal freedom. Generally speaking, the two dimensions interface with each other so that the greater the separation, the higher the control. This interplay typically occurs because stronger means of control are necessary to maintain sharper boundaries of separation.

The combination of separation and control yields communities with different textures, as shown in Figure 7.1. Some are woven together snugly, others more loosely.[1] Groups such as the Hutterites that combine high control and high separation produce tightly textured communities. Social arrangements among the Brethren, on the other hand, have a much more pliable texture. The fabric of Amish and Mennonite life lies some-

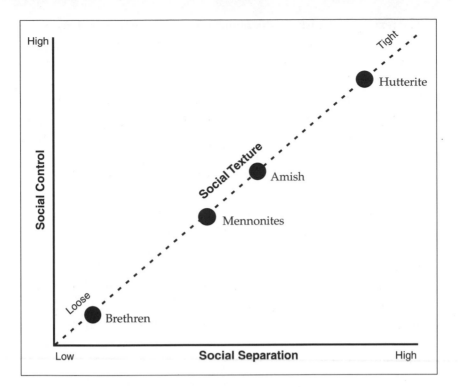

FIGURE 7.1 The Social Texture of Old Order Societies

where between the Brethren and Hutterites. Although the social fabric of the groups differs in how tightly they are woven, all things considered, all four of them are relatively tight compared with the loose weave of modern society.

A tightly woven community like the Hutterites separates itself sharply from the outside world at the systemic level. It tends to be more institutionally complete, providing many of its own institutional support systems for members throughout the life cycle. Hypothetically, a high level of separation could lead to self-sufficiency, but this is certainly not true even for the Hutterites, whose commercial activities are well integrated with the larger economy outside their colony. Tight-texture societies regulate personal behavior with explicit expectations and firm measures of social control. Role expectations are routinized and standardized. Individual creativity and freedom of expression are not prized, and the self is defined primarily by its identity with the group and explicit social roles.

The texture of Amish and Mennonite society is similar in some ways, but Amish patterns are more tightly woven. All things considered, the Amish show more signs of control and separation than the Mennonites in several ways: more explicit shunning; a greater emphasis on distinctive clothing; smaller congregational units; more restrictions on electricity, telephones, and tractors; and more frequent conflicts with the state. All of these factors underscore the ways in which the Amish social fabric is more tightly woven than that of the Mennonites.

The Brethren have the most loosely textured system of any of the groups. As we have seen, the Brethren certainly carry the marks of an Old Order society, yet their social fabric is woven together more loosely than that of the other groups. The Brethren fabric is stitched more directly into the larger society in virtually every way: social integration is especially enhanced by their use of English and motor vehicles. The flexible Brethren structures create more space and freedom for individual thought and expression, which in turn generates greater diversity of lifestyle and more latitude for personal behavior. Role expectations are more pliable, and community governance relies more on extemporaneous process than on the rigid protocols of Hutterite life.

It is overly simplistic to assume that high separation and high control are always associated as suggested in Figure 7.1. Indeed, in certain domains it may be the opposite. Because of their strong geographical separation, the Hutterites can loosen up a bit on their use of technology. In the case of the Brethren, greater integration with the outside world means they must tighten up their control on ritual practices in worship. Each group has certain *control points* that become increasingly important as they compensate for adjustments in other domains of their social system. Thus, while it is often true that greater separation follows greater control, it is not a simple relationship. Geographical isolation, a rather extreme form of control, is used by the Hutterites to assure separation. Without the benefit of geographic isolation, the Amish have had to emphasize shunning, technological restrictions, and symbolic forms of dress to maintain the lines of demarcation with the larger world.

For the Mennonites, technological restraints and distinctive dress have played a lesser role, but a centralized conference structure and a written *Ordnung* help them maintain uniformity. The Brethren strategy for achieving separation has focused less on technology and more on gentle admonitions to persuade doubters, on the written minutes of Annual

A Mennonite watches an Amish man play table shuffleboard. Differences in dress signal group affiliations. *Source:* Dennis Hughes

Meeting for authority, on a spirit of consensus, and on distinctive rituals such as Love Feast. So while the Hutterites and Brethren may ostensibly look similar in their use of productive technology, they nevertheless are at opposite ends of the spectrum in terms of their grip on social control. The Brethren grant individuals considerable freedom to own and use technology, whereas the Hutterites use it but keep ownership out of individual hands.

DIMENSIONS OF DIFFERENCE

Social Organization. Variations in social organization are displayed in Table 7.1. The fundamental point of divergence is communal property, embraced only by the Hutterites. Although Mennonites, Brethren, and

TABLE 7.1 DIFFERENCES IN SOCIAL ORGANIZATION AMONG THE FOUR GROUPS

	Hutterites	Amish	Mennonites	Brethren
Communal property	Yes	No	No	No
Institutional completeness	High	Moderate	Moderate	Low
Network overlap	High	Moderate	Moderate	Low
Personal restrictions	High	Moderate	Moderate	Low
Residential segregation	Yes	No	No	No
Role prescriptions	High	Moderate	Moderate	Low

Amish live among worldlings, they are typically within easy reach of fellow believers. Mennonite and Amish groups have their own set of residential constraints because they seek to live within carriage-driving distance of other families in their congregation. Members of both groups would never consider living in a large city, and they will only establish a new settlement if a cluster of families joins them in the venture.

The groups vary in their dependency on outside institutions. Virtually all the functions of Hutterite life—education, leisure, work, worship, and death—are anchored within the colony, ranking them high on institutional completeness. All of the groups, however, reach outside their own circles for economic resources, technical help, and trading partners. The Brethren are the most dependent on outside institutions—for education, insurance, and jobs—but even the Brethren are much more institutionally complete than typical mainline religious groups.

The social networks in a Hutterite colony are overlapping and multifunctional. The same persons are involved in many different activities throughout the day and week. The degree of network overlap varies somewhat within the other groups depending on their local orientation and mobility. The overlap of networks is the thinnest among the Brethren, which creates a looser social texture. Some Brethren, for example, may live in one town and drive to work in another.

The groups vary in the extent to which social and occupational roles are prescribed. Among the Hutterites, assigned roles and daily surveillance by leaders produce tight role prescriptions. Role identities, expectations, and transitions are firmly fixed in colony life. Role prescriptions loosen among the other groups—especially among the Brethren. Occupational choices, which are governed carefully by the Hutterite colony, are more relaxed in the other groups, but they are not without limitations. For example, Brethren, Mennonite, or Amish persons could not work as police officers.

These features of social organization have major consequences for individual privacy and freedom of choice. The sphere of privacy and personal choice shrinks among the Hutterites, whose self-identity is completely overshadowed by the group. Private space, self identity, and personal choice expand among the other groups, especially among the Brethren.

External Relations. Differences in external relations among the groups are shown in Table 7.2. Brethren mobility is of course high because of their widespread use of motor vehicles. Mennonite and Amish mobility varies depending on how frequently they hire "taxi" services provided by English neighbors. Hutterites travel in colony vehicles for commercial reasons and to visit other colonies, but the average colonist has little need to travel because colony life is largely self-contained.

The Brethren use of English as the language for home, work, and worship opens the door for greater outside contact. Although all the groups

An Amish carriage passes Mennonite women on a backroad in Pennsylvania. Bicycles are forbidden in some Amish settlements. *Source:* Keith Baum

TABLE 7.2 DIFFERENCES IN EXTERNAL RELATIONS AMONG THE FOUR GROUPS

	Hutterites	Amish	Mennonites	Brethren
Conflict with state	High	High	Low	Low
Exogamy	Low	Low	Low	Some
External interaction	Low	Low	Low	High
Higher education	Low	Low	Low	Some
Mobility	Low	Moderate	Moderate	High
Nonfarm occupations	Low	Moderate	Low	High
Use of English	Low	Low	Low	High

speak English, the Germanic dialects of the Hutterites, Mennonites, and Amish continually underscore their cultural boundaries with the outside world. The use of English, coupled with greater mobility, makes it easier for Brethren to enter nonfarm occupations. All of these factors accelerate the mode and frequency of Brethren interaction with outsiders. Individual Hutterites, by contrast, have much less contact with strangers and nonethnic neighbors.

In terms of government relations, the Hutterites and Amish have experienced much more conflict over the years than either Mennonites or Brethren. For the Hutterites the conflict is typically related to the legal complications of communal property and to land acquisition. Among the Amish, education, slow-moving vehicles, and zoning, among other issues, have spawned numerous episodes of conflict.[2]

The Hutterites, and especially the Brethren, are more open to education beyond the eighth grade than Mennonites and Amish. In some more progressive colonies, Hutterite youth take specialized technology courses at the high school level, and a few have been permitted to attend college in order to prepare to teach in colony schools. The Hutterites can afford the risk because members who take a course in diesel mechanics will continue to work under the supervision of the colony. The Brethren do not categorically oppose higher education; consequently, many of them have completed high school and a few even college and graduate school to prepare for practical vocations such as nursing or accounting that require licensure for practice.

The growth of microenterprises among many Amish and some Mennonites will surely increase their interaction with outsiders in years to come. The rise of these commercial ventures is in some ways a graphic denial of separation from the world because business owners depend on sustained interaction with outsiders for their very survival.[3]

Unlike the other three groups, the Brethren permit members to marry outsiders who are not members of the church if they are Christians and sympathize with Brethren values. In almost every way, the Brethren have the most relaxed boundaries and the Hutterites the tightest ones in their linkage to the larger world.

Technology. As shown in Table 7.3, differences abound among the groups in their use of technology. Chief among the differences is the Mennonite and Amish rejection of motor vehicles. Although Hutterite colonies own trucks and vans, members cannot use them for personal purposes. The Brethren, standing apart from the other groups, permit the ownership and free use of private vehicles.

By rejecting the ownership of motor vehicles, the Amish and Mennonites remain more tightly bound to a specific locale. In an age when some Americans routinely fly around the globe, many Amish have traveled very little from their birthplace. Traffic snarls frustrate modern drivers whose daily routines depend on motors, motion, and efficiency. Horse-and-buggy travel alters more than perceptions of distance; it creates radically different conceptions of time. The Amish and Mennonites are accustomed to a slower, more patient pace—one that measures each mile by the cadence of hoof beats and the rise and fall of the sun. Even if they wanted to run with the surrounding world, they literally could not keep up. What is more, their technology of transportation, or what mod-

TABLE 7.3 DIFFERENCES IN PERMISSIBLE TECHNOLOGY

	Hutterites	Amish	Mennonites	Brethren
Cameras	Some	No	No	Yes
Computers	Yes	No	No	Yes
Private vehicles	No	No	No	Yes
Private telephones	No	No	Yes	Yes
Public utility electricity	Yes	No	Yes	Yes
Radio	No[a]	No	No	No
Self-propelled machinery	Yes	No	Yes	Yes
Television	No[a]	No	No	No
Tractors in field	Yes	No[b]	Yes	Yes

[a]In a few cases Hutterites permit radios and use television for educational purposes in schools.
[b]There are a few exceptions in some Amish communities.

erns might consider an absence of it, underscores their sense of separation, of being a people apart.[4] The buggy creates a mental script that reads, "We are different. Our ways are slower. We are outside the frenzy, more attuned to God's calm voice and gentle spirit."

Masters of mainstream technology, Brethren cannot rely on the rhythms of hoof beats to send a message of distinction. Their cars and vans carry them not only across town to work, but across country for business meetings and church-wide gatherings. In other words, a car is more than a car; it is a gateway to jobs, opportunities, and contacts that are off-limits to Mennonites and Amish. Were the Brethren to go back to buggies, it would not only slow them down and narrow their horizons, but it would also radically alter their social contacts.

Over the years they have grown accustomed to working and interacting with distant Brethren and with non-Brethren neighbors and associates. And while the car may facilitate contact with outsiders, it does not necessarily guarantee it—as highlighted by the story of the first Dunker to show up for religious services in a car. When challenged that "your car will take our members to movies, theaters, and all manner of carnal amusements," the brother replied, "It only goes where I tell it." This quip, however, signaled a significant shift in moral authority from the group to the individual. Transportation technologies expand or constrict the range of opportunities for interaction, but members, acting as agents of moral discernment, must decide if they will realize them.

Many of the differences over farm machinery have already been noted in earlier chapters. The Hutterites and Brethren have few if any restrictions on farm and shop equipment. They use the largest and most modern field machinery as well as computers in their barns and shops. Although Amish farmers in most settlements may use tractors for high-power work at the barn, tractors typically do not pull equipment in the fields. The Amish also place restrictions on self-propelled equipment.

The patterns of telephone and electrical usage are complicated and diverse. All the groups have come to rely on telephones in one way or another, but the Hutterites and Amish do not permit the installation of private phones in their homes. Some of the progressive Hutterite colonies permit phones in family apartments for intercolony communication, but outside access is monitored by colony leaders. The Amish generally limit electrical usage to 12-volt current from batteries. In a few settlements members are permitted to use 110-volt current from small inverters or generators for specified commercial use; however, they are not allowed to tap public utility lines. Apart from taboos on video games, Hutterites and Brethren do permit the use of computers. Although the Amish may not own personal computers, their more progressive communities permit limited use of computers for business purposes if they are owned by outsiders.[5]

In their acceptance of new technologies, Hutterites and Brethren are similar in many ways. Both permit cars, trucks, and the latest in agricultural technology. Both are comfortable with large enterprises. Neither shies away from computers or similar technologies simply because they are "high tech." Yet the relationship of the individual Hutterite to technological devices—the individual's sense of access, use, and discretion—is nothing like that of the individual Brethren. Hutterites may use a CB radio or a computer, but always with the clear understanding that it is colony property being used for colony purposes. Brethren can drive to the city to make a purchase and use their own personal computers without ever consulting another member of the church.

Hutterites could do none of these activities without consulting colony leaders. And when a computer is purchased, it is clear that it is a *colony* computer for colony purposes. Neither group shies away from technology per se, but Hutterites would never dream of granting the level of individual autonomy that Brethren do on such matters. Thus, although Hutterites and Brethren appear similar in their acceptance of technology at the group level, it is experienced quite differently at the individual level. When it comes to personal access and control, Hutterites are far closer to the Amish and Mennonites—who ban entire classes of technology—than to the more freewheeling Brethren.

Religious Organization. Differences also persist in religious polity and organization. The more loosely woven Brethren are more process-oriented in their polity and manner of decision making as shown in Table 7.4. Although all of the groups encourage congregational autonomy to some extent, the Brethren have a more pliable decision-making structure that reflects their more open and flexible ethos. The Brethren are the only group with a national Annual Meeting.[6] They welcome lay members to their Annual Meeting and emphasize the importance of making decisions by unanimous consent. This emphasis on national unity means that they have less congregational autonomy than other Old Order groups. Mennonites are somewhat similar because moral author-

TABLE 7.4 DIFFERENCES IN RELIGIOUS ORGANIZATION
AMONG THE FOUR GROUPS

	Hutterite	Amish	Mennonites	Brethren
Conference structure	No	Some[a]	Yes	No
Democratic process	Low	Low	Low	High
National meeting	No	No	No	Yes
Office of bishop	No	Yes	Yes	No
Ordination by lot	Yes	Yes	Yes	No
Process orientation	Low	Low	Low	High
Subaffiliations	Yes	Yes	Yes	No
Unanimous consent	Low	Medium	Medium	High

[a]Ministers and bishops in some regions meet periodically in the equivalent of a conference but ultimate authority lies in the congregation.

ity for them resides in the larger conference, not the congregation. Mennonite leaders meet in conference twice a year, but only ordained officials attend. This pattern is also followed by the Amish in a few areas of the country. Typically Hutterite and Amish officials gather as needed when special problems arise. For both Hutterites and Amish, moral authority ultimately rests in the local congregation.

Without formal subgroups, the Brethren are the most united body. The other groups are more diversified because they have several subaffiliations. Brethren diversity arises from a greater latitude of personal choice rather than from a variety of subaffiliations. And the scope of Brethren unity, although national, focuses on fewer issues that require majority consent. Only the Mennonites and Amish use the term *bishop* for their senior ordained officials. Hutterite and Brethren elders have considerable influence even though the term *bishop* is not used. Hutterites, Mennonites, and Amish use the casting of lots to select ordained leaders. This process provides a divine legitimation that helps to underscore the authority of leaders and broadens their span of influence. In a similar way the "voicing" of the congregation to select leaders bestows spiritual authority upon Brethren ministers.

Religious Practices. An important source of Old Order identity for all of these communities lies in their preservation of traditional ritual and symbol. These trademarks of Old Order life vary, of course, from community to community. In addition to prescribed attire for public settings, each group has explicit expectations for dress at ceremonial gatherings—

Sunday worship, weddings, and funerals. The dress code at these sacred occasions varies by subaffiliation and congregation within each group, but for the individual, the expectations for attire are always clear, albeit usually taken for granted.

The beard is a public symbol of religious affiliation for male members in all of the groups except the Mennonites. Women in all groups wear a head covering in public settings—in the case of the Hutterites, a special bandana—although the style of the covering varies considerably from group to group.

Table 7.5 displays the religious diversity among the groups on several key rituals. Except for the Brethren, all of the groups speak a Germanic dialect, not only for everyday life but also for worship.[7] Immersion baptism is a Brethren distinctive, as is the Love Feast. All of the groups practice footwashing and the holy kiss except the Hutterites. The shunning of wayward souls is practiced most conscientiously by the Amish, to a lesser extent by the Hutterites and Mennonites, and not at all in recent years by the Brethren.

The Amish rejection of meetinghouses for worship symbolizes their sharp break with prevailing religious practices. The stark meetinghouses of the other groups, with their plain architecture and unpretentious furnishings, signal humility and separation from "high" church edifices. Although the Brethren and Hutterites use electricity and modern heating systems in their meetinghouses, the architecture and furnishings remain plain and simple. The Mennonites, however, prefer the simplicity of old-fashioned structures untainted by technology.[8]

An Amish man attended an Old Order Mennonite service and then reflected on his observation in an Old Order newspaper. "So different, yet

TABLE 7.5 DIFFERENCES IN RELIGIOUS PRACTICE AMONG THE FOUR GROUPS

	Hutterites	Amish	Mennonites	Brethren
Footwashing	No	Yes	Yes	Yes
Germanic dialect	Yes	Yes	Yes	No
Holy Kiss	No	Yes	Yes	Yes
Immersion baptism	No	No	No	Yes
Love feast	No	No	No	Yes
Meetinghouses	Yes	No	Yes	Yes
Shunning	Some	Yes	Some	No

in many ways our thoughts and problems are the same. This Mennonite and Amish religion, the carriages are so different, but still 4 wheels and horse drawn. The simple meetinghouse with hat racks and the singing table where our worship service may be in shops, tobacco sheds, house or barn, chicken house or at times in stores or warehouses. With their 3 ministers per 600 to 800 souls, where we install 4 per 140 to 200 souls."[9]

His keen observation about the rates of ordained officials to souls, which includes children, is an important factor in social control. This may be one of the reasons that the Amish have less need than the Mennonites for a written *Ordnung*.

The Amish observer continued his comparison of Amish and Mennonite practices with these comments. "No doubt it started the same in the old country. Now today many differences and we have service every 2 weeks for 3 hours and a meal afterwards. Thus about 4–5 hours of fellowship, while the Mennonites have 2 hours of worship every Sunday, then after the service everybody visits a spell, then home for the mit tage, noon meal."

The diversity of practice has shaped the identity of each group and marks the borders between them. On some dimensions of difference displayed in Tables 7.1 through 7.5, the Hutterites and Brethren stand apart, while the Amish and Mennonites are closer together. The Mennonite and Amish overlap is reinforced by the fact that they often live in the same areas and sometimes share the same schools. They read the same Old Order newspapers and periodicals, and rely on the same Dordrecht Confession of Faith for their doctrinal base. All of these factors enhance their sense of religious kinship.

The groups do not fall on a neat, linear continuum. On some issues the Hutterites and Brethren are more alike, on others the Hutterites share more in common with the Amish than the Brethren, and so on. Indeed, each community has cleared its own path to heaven. In the following sections, we highlight the factors that have distinguished each group's story.

THE HUTTERITE ROAD

Commitments to communal property and colony life provide the fundamental source of Hutterite identity and distinguish them among Old Order groups. To retain such radical practices requires vigilance and careful social control. Their pattern of geographic isolation makes it easier for them to exercise the necessary control and to regulate interaction with outsiders. Moreover, living in an ethnic enclave diminishes the importance of distinctive dress in managing outside relations. Because all of life is immersed within the community, the Hutterites have fewer worries about controlling leisure behavior than most of the other groups.

In the context of communal living, technology is less of a threat because it is owned and supervised by the colony. Amish, Mennonites, and Brethren, lacking the benefits of communal ownership and surveillance, have more worries when technology slips into private hands. In a communal setting, the benefits of technology accrue to the colony and are less likely to disturb the egalitarian balance of power among members. By limiting the number of persons per colony, the Hutterites are able to keep social relationships on an informal scale despite the widespread use of technology.

The growing use of large farm machinery, however, reduces the need for human labor and may not provide adequate jobs for the number of people required for a robust colony. The expanding use of technology

Hutterites use gigantic self-propelled combines to harvest wheat on large prairie farms. *Source:* Ivan Glick

may be indirectly linked to the shrinking size of Hutterite families. While the labor of sixty to seventy persons was required in the past to maintain a viable colony, advanced mechanization could cut the requisite number in half, leaving a colony productive but feeble in terms of family structure and social life. Thus, while other groups worry that unbridled technology may build pyramids of individual power and unwanted ties to the outside world, the Hutterites face a different threat: vanishing jobs that may disrupt their centuries-old structure of colony life.

The range of cultural production is severely controlled in the Hutterite cocoon. Social isolation limits exposure to alternate ideas. All the conduits that would supply cultural resources for competing worldviews—conversation, transportation, print and electronic media—are carefully controlled. Internal deviance and external cultural contamination are greatly reduced by following prescribed ritual recipes. The Hutterites have in some ways reproduced the isolated world of a medieval monastery in the midst of the twenty-first-century.

Hutterites are not illiterate, but their world is effectively one of pre-literacy. Their religious worldview is largely medieval because the sacred sermons that are preached in every service were crafted by ancient leaders centuries ago. It is not that the Hutterites look so far back; it is that they blend the present into the past and the future. In a sense, the future folds back into the past and both are lived out in the continuous present.

Teaching and interpretation are highly controlled: individual study of Scripture and personal interpretations of the faith are discouraged. In the absence of new sermons, Hutterite history and lore provide the primary storehouse of cultural resources. Little space is necessary for individual expression, for the communal environment calls for common and repetitive action. In such a world, an embrace of individualism would wreak havoc with a social order where roles are carefully prescribed.

Dress codes and symbolic rituals serve to express community solidarity and stifle individual expression rather than build distinctions between the colonists and their non-Hutterite neighbors. With geographical separation there is less need for visible barriers. Cultural distinctives derive more from social isolation than from deliberate attempts to cultivate peculiar symbols. The social isolation also shapes their distinctive style of interaction. With weakly developed notions of individual needs and feelings, the popular norms of civility that build self-esteem are unnecessary. Individual agency is minimized. Individuals do not eat alone, go to town without permission, or even decide whether or not they will move when the colony splits. Individual Hutterites are virtually removed from external markets of every sort—labor, consumption, and religion. All of these have been kept at bay. The personal is expanded to the level of community, and the community detaches itself from the broader public.

More than the Amish and Mennonites, the Hutterites share with the Brethren a fairly sharp dichotomy between rational means of production and religious tradition. They have welcomed the most sophisticated technology for agricultural purposes, while still clinging to centuries-old religious rituals. Hutterites have no qualms about applying the powers of human reason to agricultural economics, but they refuse to rationalize religious practice. The cultural wall between rationalized modes of production and traditional ritual has held for the moment, but whether it will remain firm over the decades is, of course, uncertain.

THE MENNONITE ROAD

Unlike the Hutterites, the Mennonite protest against progress does not enjoy the benefits of geographic isolation and communal ownership. Living and mingling among worldlings, the Mennonites have found it necessary to stress separation from society in more specific and symbolic ways. They frequently speak about nonconformity to the world and articulate their apartness in their attire and everyday activities. They have bridled technology by forbidding the ownership of motor vehicles and by restricting some forms of farm technology. Unlike most Amish, the Mennonites do permit tractors in the field, so long as they are equipped with steel wheels. Their acceptance of electricity and private phones will, in time, likely lead to more appliances in Mennonite homes and more sophisticated tools in their shops.

Mennonite ordained officials meet twice a year in their church-wide conference. This gathering, as well as a written *Ordnung*, are important means of maintaining unity of belief and practice across the various settlements. The Ontario Conference meets apart from the Pennsylvania-based Groffdale Conference, but the two meetings serve similar functions. Although their attire appears less distinctive than the Amish, the Mennonites are actually more uniform in other practices because they have fewer subgroups and less congregational autonomy.

The preachers' table *(right)* and singers' table *(left)* in a Mennonite meeting-house. All of the groups use meetinghouses for Sunday services except the Amish, who meet in their homes. *Source:* Dennis Hughes

Despite their easy access to electricity and telephones, the Mennonites have been more reluctant to abandon farming than the Amish. In Lancaster County, Pennsylvania, where both groups face a severe shortage of land, the Mennonites have migrated in larger numbers to other states in order to remain on the farm. The Amish, on the other hand, have more readily forsaken their plows to establish small businesses. The use of the tractor encourages migration because Mennonites are able to farm hilly land that is more difficult for the Amish to farm. A more centralized conference structure with fewer bishops enables leaders to have greater influence over occupational directions. In the case of the Mennonites, the senior Mennonite bishop clearly favors farming. With more congregational autonomy and many bishops, the Amish find it more difficult to keep members on the farm. One Mennonite elder thinks that their uniform *Ordnung* makes it easier to start new settlements because "we have fewer church problems than the Amish." These factors may partially explain why Mennonites and Amish have responded differently to the scarcity of farmland in Lancaster County.

Thus, the Mennonite ability to control acculturation and maintain uniformity has been aided by their centralized conference, small number of bishops, and written *Ordnung*. Their use of the Germanic dialect, a strong commitment to farming, a cap on eighth-grade education, and the development of private schools have also helped them, at least for the moment, to remain on their peculiar path of piety.

THE AMISH ROAD

The marvel of the Amish lies in their ability to maintain a distinctive national identity in some two dozen states without the centralized structures of the Mennonites and Brethren or the residential segregation of the Hutterites. With more than 180,000 souls in more than 1,200 congregations, the Amish are the largest of the four groups. They have preserved a distinctive cultural face without a national structure or a common *Ordnung*. Like the Mennonites, they use the 1632 Dordrecht Confession of Faith for baptismal instruction, but they typically lack written authorities such as the *Ordnung* of the Mennonites or the minutes of the Brethren Annual Meeting.

One source of unity across the settlements is an annual directory of ministers that includes the hymns and Bible readings for each Sunday as well as for special days.[10] This enables congregations across the country to follow the same liturgical format and hear the same biblical readings. It is also customary in all congregations to sing the "Lob Lied" as the second hymn in the worship service. This traditional hymn of praise reminds members in every worship service that they are united in song with brothers and sisters across the land. These features provide a ritual continuity that unites Amish congregations across geography and beyond their differences of practice.

The various affiliations of Old Order Amish, from the ultraconservative Swartzentrubers to the more progressive communities, vary considerably on many details of practice—including acceptable forms of technology, the color of buggies, the number of suspender straps, and the style of head coverings for women, to name but a few. Despite their wide-rang-

An Amish farmer uses a modern hay baler but pulls it with horses.
Source: Dennis Hughes

ing diversity and congregational autonomy, certain practices persist across the groups: meeting in homes for worship, the use of horses for transportation and fieldwork, a taboo on telephones in homes, the rejection of 110-volt electricity from public utility lines, avoidance of higher education, the Pennsylvania German dialect, beards for men, head coverings for women, and various forms of plain attire.[11]

Despite their commitment to traditional practice, the Amish in many settlements have entered the broader marketplace to sell their products. This trend has increased in recent decades with the development of microenterprises and leads to considerable contact with outsiders in routine social and economic transactions. Although they sell products on external markets, their labor market is primarily ethnic. Rather than selling their labor to non-Amish, many Amish have set up their own cottage industries or they work for Amish entrepreneurs.[12] Unlike Hutterites, whose colony organizes their economic life, individual Amish people make many decisions about their livelihood within the guidelines of the church.

Yet the Amish clearly insulate themselves in some social domains: education, employment, use of public utilities, political involvement, and use of public media. So while contacts with outsiders are frequent, there are many limits. Separate schooling, marriage, language, modes of transportation, and ethnic employment filter outside influences and reinforce Amish visions of reality. Cultural borders, articulated by various symbols, focus on dress, technology, lifestyle, and rituals of worship. Distinctive dress clarifies identities and loyalties as the Amish interact with outsiders. With many border crossings, cultural identity could easily erode without the aid of visible reminders.

Strong bishops and small congregations help to enhance surveillance and minimize cultural backsliding. Unlike the Mennonites with their central conference structure and few bishops, the Amish have a loose federation of congregations each with its own bishop. (In some settlements two congregations may share one bishop.) This symbol of ecclesiastical authority in each congregation enhances social control because the bishop has frequent face-to-face contact with all of the members. The hundreds of bishops across the 250 settlements never meet together, but in some settlements they gather as special issues arise. The implicit threat of shunning is, of course, a powerful reminder of the location of cultural borders. The Amish have been able to preserve their basic markers of identity despite a diversity of practice in various settlements.

THE BRETHREN ROAD

In many ways the Brethren are conducting an Old Order experiment, because they cling to an Old Order identity in the midst of much social and cultural openness. They have remained Old Order without the aid of a special dialect. Their experience suggests that while a dialect may restrict external interaction and bolster Old Order identity, it is not necessarily essential.[13]

Another typical mark of Old Order life is a taboo on motor vehicles. Again, the Brethren have broken the mold. Their concession to cars may have weakened Brethren ties to the local community, but it has strengthened their ties to a national fellowship by encouraging visiting across the

The Brethren own and operate motor vehicles on a regular basis.
Source: Roanoke Times

brotherhood and attendance at Annual Meeting. The Brethren have also accepted the use of the camera, which suggests a more modern view of the self as well as a desire to remain connected to a geographically scattered fellowship.

On education, the Brethren also break rank. They have been slower to pull their offspring out of public schools and to build private schools of their own. Moreover, they are more willing to permit some members to pursue higher education. In recent years some Brethren parents, worried about the impact of public schools, have established private schools for their children. Other families have begun home-schooling, a fairly rare practice in the other groups.

The flexible style of Brethren decision making enables members to participate in the life of the church in ways that are impossible in the other groups. With fewer distinctive practices, the Brethren have in some ways spiritualized their Old Order identity by emphasizing the process and the spirit of working together in a loving manner. Their style of interpersonal relations seeks to embody a gentle spirit. They have cultivated a religious vocabulary that encourages a more elaborated description of religious reality. The Brethren find it easier than the other groups to use words to describe their theological commitments. In all of these ways, Old Order identity among the Brethren is more articulate, affective, and entwined with rituals and ordinances.

Although not enthusiastic about evangelistic missions, the Brethren have a more personal accent to their religious experience than the Hutterites, whose autonomous sense of self is less developed. Brethren speak of a transformation of the heart and place more emphasis on volition than on mere compliance, an emphasis that derives from their own Radical Pietist roots. Still, they are reluctant to go too far in emphasizing personal salvation, personal evangelism, revival meetings, and missions, all of which focus on the individual. While the tie between self and salvation is important, too much emphasis on self undermines communal understandings of salvation.

The outcome of the Brethren experiment is uncertain. Will English-speaking Brethren, touring the country in automobiles, attending public schools, and sitting at their computers, be able to preserve Old Order ways over the generations? That is a question that worries even their leaders.

As we have seen, despite their common convictions, differences abound among the groups. Each has found a different way to forge a peculiar identity in its particular social context. These Old Order communities are indeed taking different roads to the pearly gates, and each contingent is carrying a distinctive banner that has been woven by its unique cultural experience.

CHAPTER EIGHT

Preserving a Pilgrim People

The children are our most important crop.
—Amish farmer

THE SOCIAL CONSTRUCTION OF IDENTITY

How have these communities been able to maintain an Old Order identity in the midst of modern life? Our comparative analysis suggests that the answer does not rest on one or two simple factors. Each community continually reconstructs its own version of Old Order life in the context of its peculiar set of circumstances. Although the particulars vary, some common themes permeate all the groups.

A Cultural Fabric. Group identities are socially constructed over time from a multitude of social and cultural materials. The unique religious heritage of each group, for instance, shapes their identity in a profound and enduring manner. Relationships with other Old Order groups and with other Anabaptist churches also contribute. Patterns of conflict and cooperation with the larger society add their imprint as well. Furthermore, collective self-understandings are shaped by urbanization and technological advances. The press of urbanization and the high cost of land, for example, has eroded Amish ties with farming in some areas. The arrival of the car expanded Brethren spatial horizons, extending their connections with distant Brethren. Thus, the construction of group identities reflects a dynamic interaction between both internal and external social conditions.

Old Order identities are constructed over time by weaving together a variety of materials in a special way for each community. Some of the raw materials that have helped to shape these identities include: (1) historical legacies, (2) intergroup relations, and (3) symbolic meanings. Identity construction is a dynamic process of cultural negotiation in the face of ever-changing socioeconomic conditions. While it is true that all the groups have preserved an Old Order identity throughout the twentieth century, it is also true that their identities have been tailored in distinctive fashions.

Historical Lineage. The particular religious heritage of each community shapes its collective memory in profound ways. The birth pangs of each group—the reasons and conditions associated with its inception—form its collective self-understandings. These memories, captured in story, legend, and song are passed down over the generations.

The Hutterites, Mennonites, and Amish all experienced significant persecution in their early history in Europe. The stories of their martyrs, retold again and again in sermons, remain fresh in the collective memory. Old Orders still hear the clang of chains falling on prison floors and smell the smoke of martyrs burning alive. The Brethren, with fewer memories of persecution threaded into their heritage, carry less sectarian baggage. They are less suspicious of the outside world, and this different outlook may partially account for their greater flexibility in adapting to social change. However, they need to articulate their separation from the world more deliberately because they live so dangerously close to it. Hence, they appear more sectarian in other ways. In any event, the religious heritage of each Old Order community is important in the construction and maintenance of its identity.

The heritage of each group is entangled in the larger Anabaptist story as well. Old Orders define themselves in comparison to other Anabaptist groups. The Hutterites, for instance, know that they are the only Anabaptists who have practiced community of goods over the centuries. In their view, they are the only remnant within the fold with the courage to forsake private property for the sake of Christ. Thus, they carry the burden of preserving communal sharing within the Anabaptist family.

The Old German Baptist Brethren trace their roots to the three-way Brethren division of the 1880s. They were the remnant that tried to pre-

Mennonite children enjoy a game of tag during recess. Private schools play an important role in transmitting and preserving Old Order identities. *Source:* Keith Baum

serve the precious faith of their ancestors amidst a schism in the Brethren household. Thus even today they have an obligation—a righteous responsibility—to maintain and preserve historic Brethren ways. If they succumb to the pressures of change and drift into the wake of the more worldly Brethren, the historic patterns of Brethren faith may be lost forever. Then they will be no better than the group from which they separated, thus negating their very reason for being. Thus, Old Order Brethren identity is shaped by their relationships with mainstream Brethren denominations that provide a negative reference group for the Old Orders, who can wear the Old Order label as long as they lag behind other, more worldly Brethren.

Old Order Mennonites face a similar challenge. Not only must they distinguish themselves from the Amish, who often live nearby, but they must also remain apart from both mainstream Mennonites and the Old Order car-driving Mennonites from whom they parted. A group that breaks off from another Old Order group carries a double burden of tradition. When a new group becomes "Old Order" within an existing Old Order tradition, it must stay more Old Order than its Old Order parent in order to be faithful to its identity. How many burdens of conservatism a group carries depends on how many steps it is away from its initial Old Order beginnings. The conservative sentiment among the Old Order horse-and-buggy Mennonites runs deep because the legacy of their past endows them with a special responsibility to wear the conservative mantle. Indeed, this may be one of the reasons that their cultural mindset at times seems more provincial than that of many Amish.

The Amish, on the other hand, carry a lighter burden to cling to conservatism. They, of course, were conservers at the time of their origin in 1693, when they branched off from the Swiss Mennonites in Europe. The Old Order label was affixed to the Amish, however, when other progressive-minded Amish affiliated with Mennonite groups in the 1860s and 1870s. Thus in North America, the Old Order Amish view themselves as the trunk of the Amish tree, firmly rooted in tradition, not as a new conservative splinter group. Their Old Order identity was reinforced again in the twentieth century as Beachy Amish and New Order Amish groups splintered off in progressive directions. In relation to mainstream Mennonites, who acculturated rapidly in the twentieth century, the Amish could easily remain Old Order by lagging behind the Mennonites at a comfortable distance. There are also ultraconservative clusters of Amish groups, such as the Swartzentruber and Nebraska clans, that carry a heavy conservative burden because they are, indeed, "Old Orders" within the Old Order Amish family. Thus, the location of a group in Old Order social space is always relative as it fluctuates in a dynamic field of crisscrossing relationships.

The Amish departure from the Mennonite flock took place more than three hundred years ago in Europe. By contrast, the team Mennonites separated from Old Order car-driving Mennonites in the twentieth century, within the memory of elderly members still living in the 1990s. Thus, unlike Old Order Mennonites, who carry a double or in some cases a triple burden of conservatism, the Amish, on average, are more self-confident and open to change. The Amish can carry the Old Order flag with ease as long as they trail a bit behind the New Order Amish and the more progressive Mennonites that have accepted cars, televisions, divorce, political involvement, and higher education.[1] In sum, the historical context that gave rise to each group is formative in shaping its identity.

Intergroup Relations. Relationships with other Old Order groups are etched into Old Order identities. Managing intergroup relations involves maintaining the proper distance vis-à-vis these other bodies and finding appropriate symbols to mark the fences. The acceptance of a practice by a progressive group may preclude it from ever being accepted by a conservative group without a serious loss of face. Progressive movements, by defining inappropriate behavior, serve as negative reference groups for Old Orders. When a particular practice becomes the mark of distinction between two Old Order groups at the time of a schism, its symbolic significance looms large. If the use of cars, the size of bonnets, or the color of carriages, mark differences at a division, such markers often become permanent dyes in the fabric of each group's identity.

Although the markers clarify boundaries for insiders, they often baffle outsiders. The long flowing beards of both Brethren and Amish sometimes encourage confusion in public settings. The Brethren use of the car, however, quickly distinguishes them. The Hutterites are rarely confused with other Old Orders because they live in different geographical areas. However, confusion often arises between Amish and Mennonites, who frequently live side by side. In Lancaster County the color of carriages—Mennonite buggies are black, and Amish buggies are gray—clarifies tribal identity. In the Elkhart-Lagrange area of Indiana, the style of carriage, rather than its color, distinguishes Amish and Mennonite flocks. Regardless of where they live, Amish men wear beards and Mennonite men are clean-shaven. Mennonite youth often ride bicycles, which are off-limits in some Amish communities.

These distinctive practices help insiders and outsiders alike to remember who is affiliated with whom. The symbols that etch the lines of identity vary from settlement to settlement among the various groups. Although many of these markers appear trivial and sometimes downright silly to outsiders, they are important signs of belonging inside the fold.

Symbolic Meanings. Our comparative analysis underlines the distinction between the *practical* utility of a practice and its *symbolic* significance. Consider, for example the practical and symbolic aspects of several practices. The use of gas lanterns means the average Amish family goes to bed early. Meeting in homes for worship brings all the members of Amish districts into each others' homes about once a year. Even though these two practices appear to be preeminently practical, when Amish people *identify themselves* as people "who don't use electricity and who don't have meetinghouses," the practices become highly symbolic.

Brethren gather for fellowship after a Sunday morning service.
Source: Roanoke Times

The absence of television in Old Order homes not only signals separation from the world but also means that homes are relatively quiet and that members are more likely to read or play table games together. Brethren ownership of cars spreads their social relationships over a wide geographical area. The absence of Sunday school places a greater burden on Brethren parents to educate their young. Such customs make a real difference in Old Order life but also become symbolic threads in their robes of identity.

Horses also illustrate the blend of symbolic and substantive threads. The use of horses for fieldwork makes a material difference in Amish life. Plowing with them takes longer. Moreover, it is difficult to plow at night or on hilly land and rocky soil. Horses compact the soil less than tractors; they also require more human labor and limit the acreage of family farms. Horses cost considerably less than tractors and provide manure for fertilizer. In all of these ways horse-farming makes a practical difference in Amish life.

But horses are also symbols, important icons of Amish identity. Insiders and outsiders alike can easily identify an Amish farm. In the first half of the twentieth century as American farmers welcomed tractors, the Amish spurned them. The horse soon became a symbolic weapon in the

Amish war against progress—the very essence of Amish identity. To be an Amish farmer meant that one farmed with horses. Even in the few Amish settlements that permit tractors in the field, horse-and-buggy transportation remains central to Amish identity. So over the years, the horse has not only been harnessed with a practical role, but it has been saddled with symbolic importance as well.

The same object embodies very different meanings in different contexts, however. For Hutterites and Brethren the tractor is a simple tool of production. In Amish eyes, however, it stands for worldliness; it is an implement that might lead to the car and to the demise of Amish society. The fact that Hutterites, Mennonites, and Brethren use tractors for fieldwork indicates that horses are not necessary to maintain an Old Order identity. Indeed, the Amish might use tractors for fieldwork and, like their Mennonite cousins, still preserve Old Order ways. But to abandon the horse now, after hitching so much of their collective identity to it, would be a frontal assault on Amish identity. The centrality of the horse to Amish identity creates powerful pressures to keep it plodding across Amish fields.

Indeed, the horse is important to Amish identity despite the experience of other groups. The Hutterites can readily accept tractors and motor vehicles because they are communally owned and controlled. The Brethren had few worries about the tractor because they were already driving cars before tractors arrived on the scene. The Mennonites gradually accepted the tractor and were able to help control its use by a common *Ordnung*, which most Amish lack.

Moreover, Mennonite fears of the car run very deep, because it was a prime reason for their separation from car-driving Mennonites in the 1920s and '30s. Mennonite acceptance of the car today would mean an enormous cultural loss of face, and thus fear of the car is strong. The car taboo is so central to Mennonite identity that the use of tractors will unlikely lead to using cars. Thus, tractors are simply a lesser threat to the Mennonites than to the Amish. Because the car was not tied to Amish beginnings, their resistance to it is weaker. Consequently, using horses in the field provides a buffer of sorts that keeps the Amish a step or so away from the car. In short, the horse and the car have quite different meanings and play different roles in the symbolic universe of each group.

Many practices that carry real consequences—social, economic, and material—grow in their symbolic significance as they become enmeshed in a group's identity. And over the years their symbolic meaning may begin to overshadow, or at least equal, their original purpose. Some practices grow in symbolic significance, while others decline. Some customs are primarily symbolic and make little practical difference in daily life. The Brethren practice of baptism by immersion carries little material significance except that Brethren baptisms are typically held outdoors; however, the symbolic significance packed into this particular ritual is enormous for the Brethren. Discarding immersion baptism would destroy a key pillar of Brethren identity, whereas the mode of baptism used by the other groups is much more marginal to their religious identity.

The width, length, and color of the strings on head coverings typically grow in symbolic importance as groups acculturate. The style of covering strings for women and the style of hats and the width of their brims for men signify compliance with the *Ordnung*. The color and pattern of clothing and the presence or absence of beards also pack symbolic freight. These signals make little practical difference, but they are not inconsequential. As religious symbols they stir strong emotions, draw group boundaries, and provide traces of sin and salvation.

PRACTICING THE HABITS OF TRADITION

For Old Orders, habit looms large. In fact, Old Order routines are perpetuated as much out of habit as out of design. They often struggle for words when outsiders press for a rationale for familiar things, however peculiar, that have been woven into their daily routines. "It has always been done this way," is a common answer. There is a moral burden to follow tradition, a burden that even moderns carry, albeit to a lesser extent.

The Logic of Illogical Habits. In many cases there is little if any rationale for a particular habit—the size of a hat or color of a dress. One group's boundaries focus on technology, while another's center on sacred ritual. One places greater emphasis on personal appearance, while another monitors social interaction. The puzzles of restriction sometimes defy rational explanation, for their logic is more historical than systematic, more cultural than doctrinal. Take Amish buggies, for instance. There is no principle or rationale that explains why they must be yellow in one region and black in another. But once the color is established, often in the context of schism, there are compelling reasons to keep it.

A Mennonite carriage was adapted for a disabled member who uses a wheelchair. The back door opens to form a ramp for the wheel chair. *Source:* Dennis Hughes

How might yellow-buggied Amish account for why one of their members painted his buggy black? It might be a sign of rebellion or a testing of church authority and discipline. Perhaps the black-buggied member wants to assert his individuality. Why is he tampering with a color that was good enough for his parents and his grandparents? Does he simply need some attention? In Amish eyes, each of these possibilities is cause for alarm. There is hardly an honorable reason why a loyal member would even think of painting a yellow buggy black. At stake is "our" tribe's way of doing things. To challenge established routine is not the Amish way, especially on a conspicuous matter that would stir confusion both within and without the Amish world.

So while outsiders might ask: Why do they dress that way? or Why do they permit this while rejecting that? Old Orders rarely think about such things. Why, indeed, do Brethren drive expensive cars and yet remove a simple radio? Why do Mennonites hire a taxi when they may not own cars? And why do some Amish permit telephones in a shop but never in their homes? Why indeed?

Old Orders have different questions for outsiders. Why do they go shopping when they have nothing in particular to buy? Why do they *drive* to a health club in order to *walk* on a machine? Why do they eat so *much* fat-free food if they are really trying to lose weight? And why do they shower in the morning before getting dirty?

Whether one is Old Order or middle American, what seems normal to insiders is puzzling to outsiders. In both cases, insiders gloss over "inconsistencies" that outsiders might question. "That's just the way we do it" is a common response of the natives in any cultural system. We rarely contemplate why we do what we do until someone presses the issue.

Recent work in the social sciences suggests that human behavior is indeed less purposive and value-driven than many have assumed. Pierre Bourdieu, for instance, writes of an intangible *habitus*—an unconscious disposition to act in certain ways based on prior experiences—that guides human behavior.[2] *Habitus* is not a type of knowledge that can be neatly expressed. Like the language we speak, it is something we do almost automatically. And even though the actions may have a structure or pattern, it is not one that we consciously decipher before acting them out. Informed by the legacy of our social relationships, our actions are transposable and adaptable to new situations. Typically, it is only *after* our routines are challenged that we reflect on their meaning and try to formulate reasonable accounts of them.

Considered in this light, abstract principles of humility and nonconformity that Old Orders can cite are as much *post hoc* rationales supplied on demand to justify routine activities as they are values that guide Old Order behavior. Do Old Orders dress plainly in order to express a commitment to humility and nonconformity, or do they invoke these time-honored words in order to make sense of their own habit of dressing plainly? Perhaps some of both is true, yet recent cognitive theory suggests there may be more of the latter than was once thought.

Related to this understanding of human behavior is Giddens's distinction between practical and discursive consciousness.[3] *Practical consciousness* is the realm of Bourdieu's *habitus*, the routines we "know" but cannot express, the patterns we enact without understanding. *Discursive consciousness*, on the other hand, is the realm of intentional plans and systematic reflection. To the extent that Old Order activities flow by habit alone, they pertain to the practical domain; to the extent that they are understood to express certain values or achieve certain ends, they are discursive. To further complicate matters, what is discursive for leaders may remain unreflective or practical for others. And what is practical at a certain point in time may become discursive once challenged, when people are compelled to explain their behavior.

In short, if tradition has any bearing on the reality of everyday life, it means that the differences between Old Order groups, as well as their differences with the cultural mainstream, are mostly matters of habit—enacted on a daily basis without conscious contemplation. Even though these habits may be linked to overarching themes that are repeated in sermons and expressed in conversations, systematic rationales are often lacking. Much of what outsiders perceive as perplexing about Old Order life is actually automatic. If you ask Amish children why they dress the way they do, they are likely to simply say, "Because that's just the way we dress." Some adults could supply a more elaborate answer, but most would have to pause before doing so in the same manner that modern men pause when asked why they wear ties—which, of course, reminds us that patterns of habit shape the lives, not just of Old Orders, but of everyone.

A Hutterite youth choir. Youth learn Old Order habits by participating in all aspects of their community. *Source:* Jan Gleysteen

After reflection, Old Orders might comment on the importance of simplicity, separation from the world, or humility, but these are legitimating accounts that are only invoked after the question is posed. Before donning their clothes each morning, members do not actually think, "I'm going to embody humility today," any more than we moderns ponder principles of entertainment before turning on our television, or of hygiene before brushing our teeth. The ordinary things we repeat day after day are not that well thought out. In a word, tradition's residence is at the intersection of habit and deliberate action. For most Old Orders this is a broad intersection, and even for many moderns it is much broader than they would like to think.

Historical Puzzles of Change. Rather than always reflecting moral principles, technological puzzles are often tied to historical happenstance. Each group lives under the long shadow of its own heritage, and at times the best explanation of apparent inconsistency is historical accumulation.

Consider the use of lawnmowers in some Amish communities. A power lawnmower is opposed by the church at a historical moment for a certain set of reasons, but a weedeater slips through years later when completely different arguments frame the discussion. Had both tools appeared at the same time, both might have been approved or rejected; but the subsequent blessing on the weedeater is insufficient to overturn a long-established ban on the lawnmower.[4] Tradition carries its own impressive weight. Unbewildered, Old Order members are likely to view the approval of one and rejection of the other as a reasonable balance at the moment—they neither reject progress out of hand nor grab every new gadget that comes along. Each decision must be reviewed in the context of the moment. Indeed, the riddles that baffle outsiders typically appear logical and sensible within the corridors of Old Order life.

Each group's configuration of prohibitions and permissions is so historically grounded, in fact, that one would have to reimagine history to picture it otherwise. Had the first personal computers offered realistic sound and image capabilities, the Brethren might have rejected them outright forever. As it happened, however, the early ones were more like typewriters with long memories and thus were classified as productive tools. Decades earlier, the more technologically primitive tape recorder was spurned because it was too much like a phonograph, it singled out individuals for special attention, and it provided entertainment. When answering machines appeared, though scarcely entertaining, they were assessed in light of the existing ban on tape recorders. Had answering machines appeared before the tape recorder, they might have been classified as practical tools and more easily accepted. Perhaps the tape recorder might have been accepted on the premise that "we already use answering machines, so what's the difference?" Thus the historical sequence and the immediate social context shape what to Old Order minds is a rational response to new technology.

In eastern Pennsylvania the Amish rejection of private telephones and high-wire electricity congealed partly in response to the formation of a progressive subgroup. As the progressives welcomed innovations, the Old Order identity became pegged to their absence. It was not only a traditional response, but an expedient one as well. As they eyed the progressives moving into the mainstream, the Amish saw telephones, electricity, and cars all bundled together. If they accepted one, they would be hard-pressed to deny the others. Having staked their identity on certain restrictions, the Amish found difficulty discerning which restriction was the kingpin that kept the whole structure intact. Was it electricity, the car, or the telephone that would speed things up and usher worldly influences into the home? The safest thing was to go slow and concede on small things—batteries, telephones at the end of the lane, taxis hired for special purposes—rather than to give away the store by plugging into public utility lines, or trading in horsepower for large mechanical tractors.

Each group draws a line in the cultural sand, and once drawn, it impacts future decisions. Identity gets intertwined with specific prohibitions and staked on certain rejections. Thus, the accumulation of previous decisions within each community partially explains the diversity and logic of their practice. Despite the continuity in Old Order life, each decade yields new practices, challenges, and lines of reasoning that feed the decision-making process. No decision to accept a new practice stands on its own. Each is part of a chronological chain, inextricably linked to the decisions that came before and those that might follow. Even though the Old Order label leads us to assume their patterns are old, each generation, in a sense, reconstructs its Old Order identity anew for its own time and place.

Each group struggles to maintain Old Order patterns while adapting to many pressures for social change. Strategies to preserve the integrity of their community include determining critical thresholds, balancing threats, and negotiating change. These strategies reflect the dynamic tensions within each community as it tries to preserve its identity in the face of modern life.

Determining Critical Thresholds. The rate of social change is regulated to some extent by establishing critical thresholds. The impact of a given technology like the car is neither foreordained nor automatic. Yet the acceptance of a new technology forces Old Order communities to place constraints in areas that were formerly self-limiting. Particular decisions determine thresholds that open or close the doors to a host of other decisions. There is little need to ban car radios if cars are not permitted in the first place. And there is little need to outlaw television where there are no electrical outlets. But when the Amish use inverters to produce homemade 110-volt electricity from batteries in order to operate cash registers and copy machines, the taboo on television suddenly becomes relevant and in need of fortification, lest televisions are also plugged into inverters.

Threshold decisions are tied to long-term consequences. "How," Old Orders ask, "will the acceptance of one thing lead to another? How will it change our life in the long run?" As one Amish bishop noted, "The car is not such a bad thing in itself; it's what it brings along with it." Electricity, cars, language, dress, education, and social relations are critical thresholds that, if passed, lead inevitably to other changes. The implications of various benchmarks fluctuate from group to group.

Telephones, cars, and computers expand the possibilities not only for contacting outsiders but also for keeping in touch with insiders who live at a distance. It is hard to imagine the coast-to-coast web of relations among the Brethren without telephones and vans to sustain it. The opportunities for Mennonites and Amish to interact with distant brothers and sisters is much more restricted. Even though they hire vans or use public transportation to travel out of state, they typically remain grounded in the local settlement. Brethren, on the other hand, are much more invested and united in their long-distance connections.

Hutterites are another matter altogether. Having rejected separate dwellings in favor of colony life, and private property in favor of communal ownership, they have little reason to restrict transportation technologies. Cars and trucks pose little threat if members cannot own them. Similarly, telephones, CB radios, and computers are rendered harmless when operated at the community's discretion and under its supervision. Communal ownership enables Hutterites to achieve levels of control similar to those of the Mennonites and Amish without suppressing technology. Hutterites may thus reap whatever benefits a technology offers the colony without taking the risks that come with individual ownership.

In short, cars, radios, and computers carry a different meaning and set a different threshold for Hutterites than for Amish, Mennonites, or Brethren. For the Amish, they represent activities that could quickly spin out of control. For Hutterites, on the other hand, they can more easily be controlled for specific purposes without worrisome side effects.

Yet the reverse is also true; in some ways the Brethren have to be on their technological guard much more than the Hutterites. Because Brethren endorse private property, as do the Mennonites and Amish, they sometimes must ban an item outright if they seek to restrict it. And even though they have never snubbed technology as much as the Mennonites or Amish do, the Brethren have consistently resisted its allure in one area: entertainment and mass media. As powerful as computers may be, they can at least be justified as productive tools. But a simple AM radio, apart from occasional weather reports and news, represents nothing more than pure—or in Brethren minds, tainted—entertainment.

Despite their educational value, Old Orders would say the same for tape recorders, VCRs, video equipment, and most of all, television. All Old Order groups stand in solidarity against these tools of entertainment that cannot be controlled and that in time would subvert treasured values and church authority. Moreover, their use would radically alter pastimes, including family interaction and fellowship. Simply stated, Sunday afternoons of visiting and fellowship would soon give way to football and Bud Lite commercials. Holiness would succumb to Hollywood, something all four groups are determined to avoid.

For these reasons the Brethren prohibit audio and video images of all types, whether transmitted via computer, cassette, compact disc, or television. Moreover, technologies that even Hutterites can exploit for productive advantage—CB radios, answering machines, and multimedia computers—are problematic for Brethren because of their potential for

Brethren teens are exposed to outside values and friendships in public high schools. *Source: Roanoke Times*

misuse. Personal prohibitions on tape recorders are difficult to justify in homes with answering machines, as are taboos on radios in homes with CBs and bans on television in the presence of multimedia computers. In each case, the reasons for rejecting the former raise serious questions about the latter, so Brethren must craft awkward guidelines—computers *without soundcards* can be purchased *for productive purposes only*—in order to sustain their general openness to new technologies while holding worldly entertainment at bay. Both the Mennonites and Amish, who have not crossed the computer threshold, and the Hutterites, who use computers in a communal context, have fewer distinctions to explain.

The technological differences between Old Order groups are only loosely tied to their moral appraisal of particular products. The Amish, for example, do not use electric lights, yet they are not morally offended by those who do. Similarly, Mennonites do not own cars, yet they are not morally opposed to riding in them. The product itself does not give offense, and most Old Orders make no assumption that theirs is the only way, nor do they think that God smiles whenever someone turns off a light or wrecks a car. However, were an *Amish* person to install electric lights, or a *Mennonite* to buy a car, it would cause a stir—not because of moral repugnance at the technology itself, but because it violates the community's moral order. The offender has crossed a behavioral frontier; the product has penetrated a sacred domain.

To say it another way, technologies carry culturally assigned meanings, and they belong in certain social spaces and not in others. Border crossings confuse longstanding assumptions about the boundaries between Old Order and worldly culture, raise questions about longstanding habits, and beg for justification of both the habit and the violation. It is this blurring of everyday scripts and routines that invites moral censure. The Amish who would shun one of their own for installing electricity would never say that a Mennonite neighbor who lights her home with electricity is dimming her prospects of eternal life, or that a Brethren brother is driving his car down the road to perdition. To the extent that Old Order groups differ in their moral appraisal of specific technologies, those appraisals end at the boundary of each fellowship. In other words, the thresholds of significance shift from group to group—what is a threshold for one is not for another.

Balancing Threats. Old Order communities adapt to social change by balancing competing threats. A comparative analysis helps to assess the role that a particular practice plays in preserving a group's identity. Without the benefit of comparison, it is easy to overplay the importance of a peculiar habit—the use of dialect, horse-drawn transportation, or lanterns. If considered alone in the context of one group, a practice may appear unduly significant. A comparative perspective shows how each group's sociocultural system balances the relative importance of a host of intersecting forces.

One group may accent a particular practice in order to compensate for the absence of another. Without a larger conference structure, for example, it becomes important for the Amish to have a bishop in each congregation. Among Brethren, the importance of attending the national Annual Meeting made it more acceptable to allow cars. Residential segregation permits the Hutterites to be more relaxed about regulating leisure. Moreover, with communal ownership they can readily accept almost any form of productive technology with little fear. The Mennonites, with their uniform *Ordnung* across several states, can more easily control the use of electricity in their homes.

Each group in its own manner tries to balance the impinging factors in ways that will preserve and enhance its own identity. Consequently, the same practice, such as using tractors in the field, may play a quite different role in one group than in another. To say it another way, a given practice—using electricity—cannot be taken at face value but must be interpreted in the context of a group's *total* social system. In one group a new form of technology may be a serious threat, but in another group the same device may appear rather benign. This process of cultural compensation, carried out informally over the decades, enables each group to adjust and readjust the lines of propriety within a dynamic social matrix. Each group creates its identity by using its own recipe of cultural ingredients. Although some of the ingredients are similar, their relative role and influence varies from group to group, depending on the particular recipe.

Negotiating Change. All of the communities are involved in a dynamic process of negotiating change. Such negotiations often strike cultural compromises between economic forces on the one hand, and traditional patterns on the other. The lure of convenience and efficiency may threaten traditional customs and rituals that provide a primal source of identity. Consequently, the communities must draw and redraw the lines of cultural propriety in ways that permit greater convenience without completely obliterating Old Order ways. These cultural compromises, so to speak, blend new and old, high technology with persistent tradition, in unusual ways that may look laughable to outsiders.

The Hutterites were willing to accept public education, but only if the schools were placed on the colony so elders could scrutinize their operations and students would be immune from outside peers. Telephones were accepted into some Hutterite colonies with the proviso that lay members would only use them for internal communication. Colony leaders, of course, could use them for business contacts and communication with other colonies. Vans and trucks were gradually accepted by the Hutterites, but typically not cars, and of course all vehicles had to be owned by the colony. Modern technology was acceptable in the communal kitchens of the Hutterites, but automatic dishwashers came slowly in some colonies because leaders feared they would create too much leisure for women.

The trail of social change in these communities is littered with compromise. The Mennonites in Canada were willing to place rubber tires on their tractors but with certain limitations: the size of the tractor and its use on highways. Private telephones in homes were also acceptable with restrictions—they must be black, one per home, and without answering machines. Among the Groffdale Conference Mennonites, electricity and telephones were reluctantly permitted in the homes of lay members for many years but not in the homes of ministers until recently. Rubber on carriage wheels gradually came into use but not among ordained leaders who were expected to hold the banner of conservatism high. Groffdale Mennonites could use their tractors in the field but only if they had steel wheels.

The Amish have negotiated their way through turbulent rapids of social change by making distinctions between the *use* and *ownership* of certain types of technology. Motor vehicles may be hired for certain purposes but not owned or driven. In some settlements electricity from

An Amish father and son in a phone booth adjacent to their shop. Telephones are forbidden in Amish homes but permitted in or near shops in some settlements. *Source:* Dennis Hughes

public utility lines may be used in rented buildings—barns and retail stores—but not in those owned by the Amish. Contractors may use electric power tools at public construction sites but not install electricity in their own home. Likewise, members may use public telephones but not install telephones in their homes.

The perplexing puzzles of social change in Amish life are many.[5] Tractors may be used at the barn but not taken to the field in many communities. Modern machinery may be used in the field as long as it rolls on steel wheels and is pulled by horses. Telephones may be placed at the end of a lane, outside a shed, or in a place of business, but not in a private home. Moreover, 12-volt electricity from batteries is permitted in private homes but not standard electricity tapped from public lines. Modern lathes and drill presses are used in some Amish shops if they are powered by air or hydraulic power.

The rise of small industries in many Amish communities was also a compromise between farm and factory. The Amish agreed to abandon their plows but not to enter large urban industries; instead, they created their own miniature factories where they could continue to control the terms and conditions of their work. They would work in "factories" but only in small ones that were Amish owned and controlled.[6]

The Brethren now permit their members to rent a VCR for one day but strictly for business. They have increasingly made a distinction between casual dress and plain dress in some congregations. Plain dress must be worn to church, but casual dress may be worn in other settings, thus enabling Brethren to more easily blend into the crowd. These negotiated patterns represent critical thresholds that will likely lead to even more change.

All of these cultural compromises, negotiated informally over the decades, enable Old Order communities to adapt to social changes without conceding their identities. These social bargains blend convenience and tradition in ways that baffle outsiders but that enable pilgrim peoples to preserve their distinctive ways in the face of rapid social change.

The Texture of Old Order Identity

Despite their reconstruction over the years, the social garments of Old Order identity share many features. First, they are *thick*. The layers of identity in each group have been reinforced by historical experiences that have enhanced their durability. Some groups have more layers of social clothing than others. Without communal living, a special dialect, and horse-drawn transportation, the Brethren wear lighter raiment. The many layers of Amish identity are bolstered by the use of dialect, distinctive clothing, horse-drawn transportation, and private schools.

The threads of identity are also *tangible.* They are not relegated to abstract words, vague memories, ethnic holidays, and mere decorative art. As we have seen, symbolic meanings and customs thrive, but in the Old Order world the markers of identity also carry a utilitarian cast. From wearing beards to driving horses, from prayer coverings to private schools, these robes of ethnicity shape the very character of everyday life. Old Order identity is rooted in the practical structures and habits that literally regulate the pace and organization of daily life.

These garments are also *public.* Unlike some ethnic identities, these are not stored in private closets and only worn for public celebrations of ethnicity. Nor are they undergarments, reserved for intimate family rites. These are public cloaks of ethnicity that remind neighbor and stranger alike of one's primary social allegiance. Driving in carriages, farming with horses, using steel-wheeled tractors, and living in communal apartments all publicly declare identity, loyalty, and affiliation. Collective nametags of sorts, these signs of ethnicity leave no room for ambiguity. These Old Order labels mark the boundaries of membership and thereby enable members to know who they are and to whom they belong.

Public visibility in one way or another reinforces Old Order identities and creates expectations for behavior. Brethren men, for example, have been expected to wear long, flowing beards and women to wear pointed triangular capes over their dresses. Mennonites are expected to meet in plain meetinghouses, Hutterites to live in colonies, and Amish to use horse-drawn carriages. Tourism, especially among the Amish, has created expectations for behavior, clarified group boundaries, and reinforced collective self-confidence. One Amishman confided, "We must be doing something right if so many people come to see us." Public expectations for Old Order practice underscore traditional identities and exert pressure to uphold them even in the face of change.

Finally, these earthly outfits carry heavenly meanings. These are *sacred* symbols. The distinctive practices that lace each community become, in time, symbols of righteous living. To discard these emblems, to handle them carelessly, to mock them, is not a mere breach of communal trust but is an act of defiance against God Almighty. Faithful pilgrims on the backroad to heaven must be clad in the raiment of righteousness, a raiment that declares their heavenly citizenship and prepares them for the portals of heaven.

Chapter Nine

Ironies of a Postmodern Journey

A favorite Amish pastime is drinking buttermilk keggers.
—Playboy Magazine

The Old Order Protest

The four groups in our study developed their identities in the late nineteenth century as a protest against modernity. In many ways the social expressions of modernity were a "new order" of things that provided a catalyst for Old Order reactions. A century later, what some have labeled "postmodern" influences have undermined the certainty and credibility of the modern project. Thus the Old Orders find themselves in a rather different world today. How will they fare in a fuzzier postmodern setting? In this final chapter, we reflect on some of the ironies of an Old Order journey in the context of contemporary culture.

The celebrated Age of Enlightenment signaled, in many ways, the beginning of the modern era. The Enlightenment promised to shatter the traditions that had shackled the human spirit for many centuries. Human reason, technology, and the hope of democracy promised freedom from the bondage of provincial habits as well as liberation from the oppressions of autocracy, racism, and patriarchy, to name a few. A disenchanted world would be a brighter one. Progress, moving forward and upward with efficiency, became the mantra of the new age. The Enlightenment promised greater happiness to those who would chart their course without the social burdens of a fettered past. A liberated self, freed from religious and social restrictions, free to make independent choices, would be a more satisfied and fulfilled one.

By the early twentieth century, industrialization fueled by the assumptions of modernity, was indeed expanding social choices. More recently the array of choices has exploded with endless possibilities of food, clothing, entertainment, lifestyle, and even religious faith. The touting of individual rights, championing of technical wizardry, and chucking of tradition were viewed by moderns as mileposts on the road to progress.

As others rushed forward, the Old Orders not only hesitated, but they had deep doubts about the modern project altogether. Proclaiming themselves pilgrims on another road, they doubted that technological progress and personal freedom would really garner greater happiness. In fact, they saw the speed and commotion about them as the handiwork of fallen angels. At its deepest level, their protest was aimed at the spirit of progress itself.

Although their protest was deep, it certainly was not complete. Along the way Old Order groups have tapped some rather sophisticated technology—chemical fertilizers, insecticides, and artificial insemination, for example. They use modern medicines and enjoy many conveniences of modern life. Physicians, dentists, optometrists, accountants, bankers, and lawyers regularly serve Old Order communities. Although they sample these modern fruits, Old Orders are skeptical of the branches that sustain them—the spirit of progress that champions personal rights and human control. In their eyes, this spirit will ultimately lead to perdition. The spirit of progress, to Old Order thinking, feeds the carnal culture of the world, a culture they seek to avoid.

The Old Order critique of progress has focused on three areas. First, they question the power of human reason as a basis for knowledge. The claims of tradition and the Bible ring truer to them than those of science and higher education. Second, they doubt that personal autonomy brings greater freedom or happiness. Rather, they argue that only within the web of stable communities will individuals find security and satisfaction. Finally, they dispute the claim of the multicultural canon that all values and beliefs are equally valid. Such tolerance, they believe, denies the very possibility of truth. As devoted sectarians, they believe that their precious heritage can only be preserved if they separate themselves from the acidic influences of moral relativity.

Some Hutterite colonies operate businesses that manufacture and sell products to the public. This colony is located in Minnesota. *Source:* Jan Gleysteen

A tripod of commitments binds Old Order groups together and sets them apart from the cultural mainstream. The legs of this tripod—ancient authorities, communal constraints, and righteous separation—clash with the pillars of modern culture. These antimodern assumptions unlock the essence of Old Order views.

Ancient Authorities

At the heart of Old Order culture lies a profound respect for the wisdom of traditional ways. As the label implies, *Old Orders* are cautious about change and often doubt that new ways are better than old ones. This does not mean that they refuse to change; they are simply confident that innovation will not nourish the human spirit or lead to eternal life. They are sure that faster cars, more computers, more consumption, greater convenience, and longer vacations will not lead to inner peace. Old Orders doubt that every new digital image and scientific discovery will usher in greater levels of satisfaction. From their view on the backroad, faster looks frenetic, bigger seems burdensome, and novel often appears naive or unnecessary. In short, they are skeptics who question many of the assumptions that moderns accept without blinking.

Old Orders trust tradition in several ways. First, they are literal believers. They believe in a real heaven and a hot hell. Their God has not been explained away by modern science or thinned by systematic theology. Sin and salvation remain unstrained by the filters of psychological and philosophical critique. To their way of thinking, the Bible is more trustworthy than scientific research. They accept the direct word of Scripture and have little interest in scholarly renderings of holy writ. These believers live under a sacred canopy that covers their community and shields them from the wiles of the devil. Few stains of secularization tarnish the luster of their faith.

Second, Old Orders respect the authority of human wisdom handed across the generations. The word of an elder carries more respect than the memo of an expert. They have as much confidence in a proverb about the weather as in the latest satellite forecast. Many will sip herbal tea before consulting a doctor. Problems are discussed among friends rather than taken to therapists. A year of practical apprenticeship, in their eyes, is more valuable than four years of a liberal arts education. Indeed, in all of these ways Old Orders view the wisdom of experience, distilled over the ages, as more trustworthy than the latest research findings. All four groups use some of the fruits of progress, of course, but none of them believe that science will save the world.

Third, they find value in continuing to do things the way they have "always" been done, upholding repetition for repetition's sake. When Brethren eat the same food at Love Feast time after time, it is not because there is something sacred in the apple butter. Rather the apple butter connects them to their parents, grandparents, and great-grandparents. The repetition extends the bonds of fellowship across the generations. Thus the question is not so much "Couldn't we do otherwise?" as "Why shouldn't we continue?" Why change if the old still works? In the same way that moderns take pride at purchasing the latest convenience or knowing the latest information, Old Orders take pride in doing things the same old way. They prefer the time-proven patterns of the past.

All of this shows that Old Orders experience time itself quite differently. Unlike moderns, who impose financial planning schemes upon the future while measuring today's successes against yesterday's goals, Old Orders hold a less linear view. While it would be misleading to say that they only live for today, Old Orders view the present as a time to contribute to the community, to be faithful to ancient truths, and to labor and wait on the Lord. In general, Old Order time is more expansive and less expensive than that of moderns. It cycles round and round like the seasons and rains of their rural existence. Time cannot be managed, for it is the Lord's; thus one can never be sure of the next page on the divine calendar.

COMMUNAL RESTRAINTS

In their most sweeping departure from modern life, Old Orders do not consider the individual the supreme agent of moral authority. They refuse to entrust matters of eternal significance to the whims and deceptions of individual conscience. They rarely talk of individual rights, preferring to speak of duty or submission. While they value personal spirituality, they are suspicious of overly subjective experience and unique interpretations of Scripture. Individualized thinking, in a word, is dangerous.

If the individual is not sovereign, then who holds the compass of moral direction? In all four groups it is the church—the faith community—that governs the moral life of the individual. But unlike modern religion, which is often confined to specific hours and activities, the moral authority of Old Order faith covers *all* dimensions of life. From dress to technology, from leisure to vocation, the church exercises authority over individual choice. While it does not dictate the specific outcomes, it sets the boundaries for choices.

Old Orders believe that the church holds the keys to the gates of heaven. Citing chapter 18 of Matthew's gospel, they believe that what is "bound or loosed" on earth is "bound or loosed" in heaven. Roughly

Amish families sometimes shop at large retail malls. *Source:* Keith Baum

translated, this means that the church has not only the authority, but indeed the obligation, to open and close heaven's gate—to set specific guidelines for baptism and standards for faithfulness. Transgression brings excommunication and judgment, yet the judgment is viewed differently from group to group. When the Amish excommunicate, they turn the person "over to Satan" (1 Cor. 5:5). When Brethren do it, they turn him or her over to God, believing that the church may disown but that God will render final judgment (1 Cor. 5:13). In both cases, Old Orders are not afraid to say no, not afraid to set explicit boundaries of faithfulness.

Even leaders are subject to communal authority. The Hutterites insist that their ministers read age-old sermons to prevent errors from seeping into the faith. In the other communities, preachers may interpret the Scripture but always within a communal context, because after the sermon, other ministers give "testimony" to its truth. Young men cannot choose a ministerial vocation; they must wait for a call from the community. And when it comes, it is a lifelong commitment. Once installed, ministers are subject to clear lines of seniority and deference in exercising their functions. Brethren even deny their leaders the power to discipline, insisting that they, like all members, are subject to the congregation. In these and other ways, communal restraints remove individuals from the pedestal of moral authority.

In so many ways, the church stands between the powers of heaven and the individual heart. As an external mediator, it guides individuals along the paths of righteousness. A communal priest of sorts, the congregation—and especially its leaders—embody and articulate the will of God on earth. Obedience to the *Ordnung* of the church is an outward sign that one has yielded to the will of God. Hence, *Gelassenheit* is mediated through the community: as one yields and gives in to the community, one submits to the will of God. To disobey the counsel of the church is to defy Almighty God. Each community in its own way asks members to surrender self, swallow arrogance, and relinquish rights—not merely for the sake of conformity, but because this is the ultimate act of righteousness that God requires of faithful followers.

Old Order members define themselves in terms of their sense of continuity with *their* social world—the family and congregational networks around them. When personal identity flows from these structures, it does not need to be constructed around a self that has to search for its own distinctive expression. Old Order youth do not need to spend several years of their life traveling around the globe trying to "find" themselves. By their late teens Old Order youth, for the most part, have a clear sense of personal and social identity; they are ready to settle down and be baptized, and to fully assume the roles of adulthood.[1]

Baptism is a serious moment. More than a polite ritual, baptism is a vow to submit to God through the agency of church authority. It symbolizes citizenship in a separate kingdom with its own laws. It is a pledge of allegiance to the *Ordnung,* a promise to heed the voice of the church. In a manner of speaking, it is a choice to relinquish choices. All four groups uphold the integrity of adult baptism. Thus in their view, it would be better not to join than to be baptized in a cavalier fashion and later stray from the flock. Baptism carries both lifelong and eternal consequences. Those who break their baptismal vow without remorse are subject to excommunication, and in some of the groups to shunning.

Unlike some religious traditions that celebrate diversity, Old Orders plead for similarity. They celebrate unity and like-mindedness within their membership. Members are admonished to give up and give in for the peace of the community. To join an Old Order community is to embrace an ethic of restraint: to see the value in limits, to know the joy of surrender.

RIGHTEOUS SEPARATION

Taking seriously the Lord's command to "come out from among them, and be ye separate" and to "touch not the unclean thing,"[2] Old Orders draw clear lines of distinction from the world. But more than horizontal lines, they create vertical ladders, so to speak, that enable them to claim higher ground in murky moral terrain. In a real sense, Old Orders strive to be both different and more righteous—to elevate themselves in a world apart, to become "a city set on a hill" (Matt. 5:14).

To maintain such distinctions requires vigilance and a willingness to establish rungs of demarcation on ladders of morality. The upward climb is difficult, but oft-repeated scriptures—"Be not conformed to this world," "Ye cannot serve God and mammon," "Be not unequally yoked with unbelievers"—remind them of the dangers of falling. The Hutterite separation, with its segregated colonies, is of course clear-cut; but even they must monitor their boundaries. Embracing biblical images, Old Order groups know, that although they are not *of* the world, they are *in* it and affected by it. Their overriding task is to be a salt that retains its flavor, to remain in the world without being overwhelmed by it.

In Old Order eyes "the world" is the dominant social system, with all its values, vices, and gadgets, that surrounds and seduces the faith community. Members know that Scripture admonishes them to "love not the world, neither the things that are in the world," and that many so-called Christians seem to care more about the things of the world than God's "plain commands." Moreover, Old Orders know they must draw lines of distinction if they hope to survive as a people and have a heritage to pass on to their children.

The currents of culture are always changing. In the modern era they used to brim with powerful, competing truths, each of them claiming a channel to the divine. Now, in the postmodern setting, they swirl with half-truths or guesses—true for only a person or a moment, and thus hardly "true" at all. In such a milieu, Old Order claims that *something* or *anything* is pure or righteous irks postmoderns, who raise eyebrows at all such pretensions. To claim to be different is tolerable, for the multicultural ethos welcomes variety. Indeed, Americans are more than happy to place Old Orders alongside African Americans, Koreans, Muslims, and Native Americans and celebrate their part in the colorful human mosaic. For Old Orders to claim righteousness, however, is a very different matter.

To go even farther, as Old Orders do, and call the world a "carnal" kingdom that may tumble one day into an inglorious pit, defies contemporary codes of civility. From the world's perspective, there are appropriate and inappropriate ways to be "different." Horizontal *fences* may draw praise, but *ladders* of righteousness draw scorn. Old Orders draw their boundaries both ways, overlaying their fences with ladders. They are not only different, like Hispanics or Koreans, but they also seek to be righteous. One reason moderns may view them with delight is that from a distance outsiders see only the fences. From the Old Order view, however, worldlings have not made the commitments that permit them to follow such standards. Worldlings are different, *and* they fall short. At issue is both identity and propriety.

In sum, the Old Order protest rests on a trilogy of commitments—acceptance of ancient authorities, communal restraints, and righteous separation. These themes blazon the backroad to heaven, marking its detour from the boulevard called Progress.

Against Modernity

The Old Order protest was a boycott of modernity—that intellectual and social expression of the Enlightenment that was coming into full bloom in the late nineteenth century. If Old Order identities crystallized as a protest against the modern world of the late nineteenth century, what will be their fate in a *post*modern setting? The foundational identities of these groups were forged as the industrial expressions of modernity were making their mark. Many other Anabaptist groups welcomed the promise of industrialization, albeit with some reluctance, and gradually cast their lot with modernity. The Old Orders, clinging to preindustrial modes of thought and social organization, drew a line in the sand and grounded their very identity on a protest of the modern project.

As traditionalist communities, they were not persuaded that reason alone would generate satisfactory answers for a good life; they heeded instead the wisdom of tribal lore. These stubborn farmers doubted that scientific progress was progress at all; indeed, they found religious explanations more plausible and satisfying. Even today very little science is taught in their schools. The very idea that the self was the primary social reality they found preposterous and virtually idolatrous—a conviction that led to their taboo on photographs. A photographic image of an individual, extracted from its social setting, was in their minds the equivalent of creating an idol. So strident was their sentiment against individual photographs that some cited the Ten Commandment's prohibition against "graven images" as a proof text.

The advent of the car and the telephone also stirred controversies in Old Order communities that brought other taboos as well. The car was a symbol of modernity par excellence—automatic mobility, independence, individualism, power, a product of a highly centralized and specialized assembly line. Indeed, the assembly line, with its standardization and efficient productivity, provided a motif for modernity itself. The automobile would obliterate geographical boundaries, expand social horizons, and free individuals from local constraints. For progressives, the automobile was a striking achievement of the forces of modernity. Old Orders thought otherwise. In their minds, the car promised to unravel and fragment their tight-knit ethnic communities. In sum, for Old Orders, modernity was the Great Separator that threatened to pull their corporate life asunder.[3]

The introduction of the telephone in the first decade of the twentieth century offered instant communication and vast possibilities for connecting people in faraway places. In modern eyes it was a stunning achievement; to Old Orders it opened the door of communication with strangers. Moreover, it promised to undermine the patterns of face-to-face communication that integrated their oral-based communities. When television arrived in midcentury, it posed an even greater threat: it would deliver the values and images of a foreign, decadent culture directly into the sitting rooms of rural homes. Without hesitation, all the Old Order groups slapped a firm taboo on television that continues even today.

In all of these ways, the Old Order communities defined their very existence as over against the modern project. They were sectarians to the core, setting themselves against the modern enterprise, which these groups simply called "the world." Using religious and biblical imagery to sanction their stance, they sought to separate themselves from the world that was being created by modernity. They could only preserve themselves by separating from the Great Separator that threatened to fragment their communities. In many ways Old Order history can be summarized as an attempt to hold the powerful forces of modernity at bay.

The proponents of progress, including many of their fellow Anabaptists, derided Old Order communities as backward, primitive, and lagging behind the times. Some progressives viewed them as hopelessly naive, unwilling to face up to the realities of the modern world and join the bandwagon of progress. The Old Orders, who rejected cars, telephones, and televisions—the ubiquitous symbols of progress—as well as individualism, higher education, and scientific achievement, sometimes became objects of scorn in the first half of the century. Even some fellow Anabaptists mocked the conservers for their narrow-minded traditionalism.[4] These stubborn traditionalists, many thought, would surely fade into oblivion as modernity marched forward on the shoulders of the twentieth century. A curious thing happened, however, near the end of the century. Modernity ran out of steam.

POSTMODERN REALITIES

The emergence of postmodern thought in the last half of the twentieth century offered a fresh critique of the modern project. Ironically, postmodernists now joined with Old Orders in scrapping the claims of modernity, albeit with rather different types of doubts. Doubts about the meaning of progress, universal claims of truth, and grand philosophical narratives began to fill the air. Modern truths seemed to implode or, as some have written, modernity was collapsing under its own weight. With modernity groaning under the critique of postmodern thought, the downside of modernity—fragmentation, alienation, loneliness, and nihilism—came into sharper focus.

Three metaphors help to capture the social realities that distinguish traditional, modern, and postmodern societies. If *home* is the metaphor for the Old Order world, *factory* conveys many of the assumptions that underlie modernity—efficiency, progress, order, clarity. *Theater* is perhaps the best symbol of the postmodern world, where in the end all that

Brethren often eat fast food when they travel. *Source: Roanoke Times*

appears to be real may only be illusion. Central to the Old Order discourse with modernity were distinctions between sacred and secular, unity and variety, steadfastness and progress, community and self, faith and reason. Postmodern realities transcend many if not all of these distinctions, because the essence of postmodernism is the blurring of clear categories and sharp distinctions. In the modern world, the lines and distinctions were sharp and clear; in the postmodern setting, everything is fuzzy and shifting. Postmodern sensitivities are ironic because both modern *and* traditional truths are partially embraced, which is to say they are not really embraced as truths at all.

Both Old Orders and moderns see a traditional-progressive dichotomy, but they have different moral views of the two poles. The Old Orders understand a truth revealed, moderns a truth unfolding and yet to be discovered. For the former, the self becomes rooted in a metaphysical home; for the latter, as Robert Bellah puts it, one must leave home.[5] Postmodernity sees no such dichotomy. Truth is reduced to spectacle; it is anything that can be experienced and enjoyed. The postmodern self is not rooted in a metaphysical home and does not leave home; instead home is everywhere and nowhere. The song "Nowhere Man," by John Lennon and Paul McCartney captures this fuzziness so well that it could be the first entry in a postmodern hymnbook: "He's a real nowhere man, / living in his nowhere land, / making all his nowhere plans for nobody. / Doesn't have a point of view, / knows not where he's going to. / Isn't he a bit like you and me?"

After decades of battle against the known temptations of modernity, the Amish and other Old Order groups found themselves in the midst of a less assured and less combative world. Indeed, despite their old-fashioned ways, they had survived the press of industrialization. Contrary to the predictions of some social prognosticators, these tradition-bent communities were not merely surviving but actually thriving. The twentieth century, surprisingly, had turned out to be their moment in the sun, not their demise. In the midst of high technology, and despite their rejection of cars, computers, televisions, and higher education, these groups were booming. In short, the Old Orders had won the battle with modernity.

The larger world was also beginning to pay more attention. The enemy was showing respect. While mainstream Mennonites were busy sending missionaries to "foreign fields" around the world, international visitors, ironically, began coming to see the natives at home—Amish and Old Order Mennonites working in their fields. Indeed, tourists by the millions began coming not only to stare, but to discover something of their own past and explore the sense of wholeness that seemed to permeate these exceptional communities.[6] And in another ironic twist of history, the automobile that the Old Orders had forbidden in order to keep the world at bay was now bringing moderns by the thousands to Old Order homesteads. Plain people, whose ancestors centuries earlier had been killed for their religious beliefs, were now becoming objects of public curiosity and admiration.

The reasons for the growing curiosity about the Amish and other Old

An Amish quilt and fabric shop. Electric lights are permitted because the facility is rented. *Source:* Dennis Hughes

Order groups are varied. Many visitors are driven by sheer curiosity. Others, troubled by the stresses of modern life, are attracted to the wholeness that seems to grace Old Order communities. Many find in the Amish a genuine connection to their imagined American past. Millions of on-lookers are charmed by a people who have had the stubborn courage to temper the forces of modernity. While moderns in the mid-twentieth century pitied the Amish because they were backward and naive, post-moderns now suspect that the Amish might be happier than themselves. In their opposition to modernity, postmodern enthusiasts affirm the Amish, buy their goods, and flatter them, even though they never take them seriously as the embodiment of ultimate truth. They are mostly interested in Old Orders because they are cute and quaint and are able to create handcrafted knickknacks.

Meanwhile, the Old Order communities have been undergoing a rehabilitation among their fellow Anabaptists. Some mainstream Mennonites and Brethren themselves have been having doubts about the modern project. Like other Americans, their rates of divorce, family instability, and trips to the therapist rose during the last half of the twentieth century. They too have questioned some of the assumptions that led them from sectarian backwaters to the main street of American society. Perhaps their religious kin in the Amish and other Old Order communities had some secrets to the good life that the progressives had lost in their heated pursuit of progress. Mainstream Anabaptists, in short, are making fewer jokes about their Old Order cousins. Old Order communities, in other words, have gained a new sense of respect within the Anabaptist fold as well as in the broader society.[7]

The new position of Old Order communities in the postmodern context is more than a little ironic. If modernity itself is losing its cultural viability, if what Old Orders have set themselves against from their historical beginnings is fraying, how can they assure themselves of a sufficient reason for being? What will they protest if the "enemy" is gone or always changing form? Postmodernity, even in the best-case scenario, is too ambiguous to provide a cogent target for protest. Will Old Orders be lost if they have won the battle with modernity? Can they learn to shadowbox? What sorts of battles will they need to wage in the postmodern context? How can they protest something so fluid as postmodernity, especially when it celebrates them? Will the struggles of the twenty-first century be different from those of the late nineteenth century?

Several examples illustrate the difference between the modern and postmodern challenge for these communities. The camera, car, and telephone represent in many ways the values and patterns of the modern era. By contrast, videotape, televised commercials, and the worldwide web reflect the virtual and changing realities of postmodern times. For Old Order communities, as we have seen, individual photographs were taboo because they called undue attention to the self. The reality captured by the camera, although decontextualized by studio props, gave the appearance, nonetheless, of a reliable image of a fixed reality. Videotape, by contrast, can fast forward and replay images; while computers can blend, merge, and edit them, creating entirely new images from multiple sources—can add an ear here or there, shrink an arm, morph two persons into one, or even add your face to someone else's body. The shifting realities of digital video images symbolize the fluid and simulated nature of postmodernity. If modernity was a stationary spotlight that focused our attention upon objects of importance, postmodernity is a lava lamp that mesmerizes us with its constantly changing form.

THE POSTMODERN CHALLENGE

Henry Ford and Bill Gates represent, perhaps, the different realities of modern and postmodern worlds. In Old Order eyes, the car threatened to pull apart their communities by providing automatic mobility that would entice members away from home. And although they have made some concessions to the use of hired vehicles, the Hutterites, Mennonites, and Amish still forbid the private ownership of automobiles. Computers and the World Wide Web, symbolic of the entanglements of postmodern expression, are more difficult to cope with than cars. One Mennonite bishop described the dilemma by saying, "It is difficult for the church to know where to draw the line with computers, because there is a computer chip in handheld calculators, which the church approves." Yet, he wondered, "How are those chips different from the chips in computers with monitors, which the church forbids?" Computers can be used quietly at home. Indeed, some Old Order business people find them very useful for commercial purposes. Hutterites and Brethren routinely use computers for their business enterprises, but the Hutterites keep them under communal surveillance. Given the growing importance of the complicated World Wide Web, Old Order communities wonder how to draw meaningful lines of separation without becoming hopelessly entangled in a worldly octopus. Computers are indeed a more complicated and unpredictable challenge than automobiles because they can virtually bring the entire world into Old Order homes.

A recent issue of *Wired* magazine featured a story on the Amish struggle with cell phones.[8] This device is another example of the shifting sand of postmodern realities. For nearly a century the Amish steadfastly forbid the installation of phones in their homes.[9] Public phones could be used for emergencies, and in some communities families shared a phone in an outdoor shanty to make necessary outgoing calls. With the rise of small businesses, telephones have been permitted in outbuildings and shops in many settlements across the country. In several more progressive Amish settlements, cell phones have sparked some controversy. They can be hidden, carried, and stored with ease, making it difficult for the church to control them. Individuals can easily tuck them in a pocket, use them on the sly, and yet appear to be within the moral boundaries of the church. The cell phone controversy is but another example of the amorphous nature of the postmodern challenge for Old Order communities.

With modernity's universalizing and unifying themes under strain, postmodernity endorses pastiche, particularity, and the integrity of local stories. Meaning is now found in the tribal stories of particular peoples, not in universal themes or the metanarratives that span all times. In this cultural context, the particularity of Old Order truths gains a new legitimacy. To be sure, Old Order beliefs would never be embraced by the world at large, but Old Orders have never wanted to evangelize the world anyway. To them missionary and evangelistic efforts are just another expression of the arrogant attitude of modernity that sought to impose a privileged set of ideas on others. In the more tolerant climes of postmodernity, Old Order beliefs can stand out and be counted for whatever they are without incurring scorn. Amish, Mennonites, and the like are no longer cultural relics of bygone years, but they are now seen as interesting expressions of cultural diversity that minimally, at least, deserve some respect. No longer forced to battle universal truth claims about reason, progress, and other byproducts of the Enlightenment, Old Orders now have a larger and more legitimate space in which to live with integrity.

In some ways, postmoderns have finally caught up with the Old Orders, who were suspicious of progress, reason, and the self even before it became fashionable. By some ironic twist of history, Old Orders were ahead of the times in their critique of modernity. But make no mistake, the Old Orders are not postmodernists, even though they bask in its tolerance and share some of its critique of modernity. In many ways, they repudiate the basic themes of the postmodern mantra—relativity, consumerism, lack of coherence, and the pleasures of spectacle. And as we have argued, they do listen to ancient authorities—and religious ones at that. They contend for communal constraints and erect walls of righteous separation, all of which defy postmodern sensitivities. So while they might join postmoderns in a critique of modernity, they surely are not postmodern.

A Postmodern Commodity

A special danger lurks beneath the surface of postmodern times for Old Order people—a more sinister one than the lack of a clear target of protest or the temptation to bask in the glow of public acclaim. The new challenge is the threat of commodification—the possibility that Old Order people and their symbols will simply become an object of mass consumption. Increasingly, as David Weaver-Zercher has shown, their images are being traded on a large and hungry culture market.[10] Ironically, while these groups have mostly bucked the tidal wave of consumerism, their own symbols and images now risk becoming objects of consumption—commodities that are bought and sold as well as used to promote other products.

Rather than arguing against the Old Orders or calling them archaic, postmoderns welcome their look, their difference, their novelty. The postmodern world smiles at them and befriends them but does not take them any more seriously than any other truth in a multicultural world filled with many cultural truths. "Amish we luv ya" is the postmodern refrain that rings from the speakers of novelty shops across the nation.

The Amish have experienced this acclaim more than any of the groups.[11] Their name and images are used to sell everything from fashionable clothing in *Vogue* magazine to an Amish brand of computer software.[12] Amish images are traded on the popular culture market from Late Night talk shows to *Glamour* magazine. And as shown in Table 9.1, even David Letterman offered "advice" to Amish parents, who were certainly

TABLE 9.1 DAVID LETTERMAN'S TOP TEN SIGNS YOUR AMISH TEEN
IS IN TROUBLE

---

10. Sometimes stays in bed til after 6 A.M.
9. In his sock drawer, you find pictures of women without bonnets.
8. Shows up at barn raisings in full "Kiss" makeup.
7. When you criticize him, he yells, "Thou suck!"
6. His name is Jebediah, but he goes by "Jeb Daddy."
5. Defiantly says, "If I had a radio, I'd listen to rap."
4. You come upon his secret stash of colorful socks.
3. Uses slang expression: "Talk to the hand, cause the beard ain't listening."
2. Was recently pulled over for "driving under the influence of cottage cheese."
1. He's wearing his big black hat backwards.

Source: Late Night Show Top Ten Archive, Top Ten List for 24 June 1998.

not watching, after two Amish youth were arrested for selling drugs. The Amish label will sell virtually any product. A search on the worldwide web shows thousands of sites hawking products with an Amish image of one sort or another. From television commercials to tourist destinations, Amish sells. Ironically, some of the media and products sold with an Amish label are decidedly non-Amish—television commercials and computer software, to name but two of the obvious. The Amish themselves rarely tag their products with an Amish label, but outsiders have seized the opportunity with gusto.

If the Amish are a harbinger of how Old Order groups will fare in the postmodern context, this commodification of a people and their culture is worrisome. Gigantic commercial enterprises generate millions of dollars on the Amish label. Postmoderns flatter and celebrate the Amish by buying their goods, but such attention is disarming and seductive. It is one thing for a group to define itself against a known adversary—modernity—but quite another to craft its own identity with integrity in the midst of growing commercial applause. Commercial acclaim for Amish products is not particularly new, but the scope and intensity of interest as well as the Amish response have accelerated.

And this is the troubling question: Will the commercial hype and glitz create expectations and dependencies that in their own way will begin to alter Old Order identities? Will Old Orders begin to think of themselves in the images created by the market place—as merely the makers of buggies, trinkets, and quilts? Moreover, this new symbiotic relationship may create an economic dependence that will not only make them captive to producing what the market demands, but also perpetuate their cultural practices, not from conviction, but because the market expects it and their very survival demands it. In the irony of ironies, these sectarian separatists now may be staking their very survival on a love affair with a world that they were taught to despise. This is perhaps their ultimate challenge in the contemporary setting. And if they succumb to it, the Old Orders will have sold their souls for a pot of postmodern porridge.

Enchantment and Torment

Why do we want to see the words "Old Order" up in lights? Why do we make them stars? They are, of course, different, but mere difference is not enough. Is it their courage to buck the tide of progress that wins our admiration? Are we fascinated by their sense of place, their strength of identity, their apparent security, and even their sense of confidence? We admire their ability to fashion a humane system that ranks high on human satisfaction. In the midst of a frantic and fragmented world, the Old Order sense of wholeness lures and inspires us. They seem to have discovered an alternate way to fill the longings of the human heart. But why, ironically, are we charmed by a people who repudiate many of the values that most of us cherish—individualism, inclusivity, tolerance, choice, and diversity? Are Old Orders merely cultural roadkill on the highway of progress, or do they offer viable prototypes for postmodern living?

If we take them seriously, if we go beyond the captivating nostalgia, Old Orders and their ways are troublesome, even offensive. We are troubled by folks who limit education, restrict occupations, curb personal freedom, and stifle personal achievement and artistic expression. Their pleas for obedience—for yielding to community—appear oppressive, sexist, and suffocating by any stretch of contemporary standards. The provincial uniformity of Old Order culture irritates our penchant for diversity and pluralism. After all, a well-rounded, well-traveled, easy-going cosmopolitan is the idol of postmodern culture. The intolerance and rigidity of Old Order life surely squelches the human spirit and cultivates a myopic worldview. Indeed, it squanders enormous human potential. Consider the hundreds of *potential* pilots, physicians, nurses, lawyers, and engineers who plow the fields, build the homes, and pull the weeds in Old Order gardens.

The conformity of Old Order pilgrims also nags us. Fidelity to tradition—conforming to church regulations, driving identical carriages, dressing alike—cultivates a bland, boring, even robotic uniformity. Such habits nurture a herd mentality that hampers human dignity by promoting what appears to be thoughtless ritualism. Are these folks merely puppets of their culture, controlled by the strings of religious tradition? The Old Order disdain for critical thinking and scientific exploration troubles even those with postmodern inclinations. Surely it would be a dismal world if everyone joined an Old Order group and shunned science, higher education, open inquiry, computer technology, artistic creativity, and global communication.

Nevertheless, Old Orders torment the postmodern soul. Their communal constraints have crafted a secure cultural home without the aid of higher education. The unemployed and uninsured are missing here. Widows and orphans, the destitute and disabled, are encompassed within the bonds of community. A spontaneous, humane social security springs into action in the face of fire, disability, sickness, senility, and death. Drug abuse, alcoholism, and poverty are rare. Youth are occasionally arrested for disturbing the peace or driving under the influence, but violent crime is virtually nil. Divorce is unheard of, and the elderly grow old within a caring circle of family and friends. Suicide and mental illness rates dip below national norms. As in any society there are unhappy marriages, cantankerous personalities, family feuds, and sporadic reports of sexual abuse.[13] But all things considered, the quality of Old Order life seems remarkable by contemporary standards.

Youthful teachers master the craft of teaching without the benefit of college, let alone high school. The eight-grade Mennonite and Amish private schools produce entrepreneurs who are able to develop and manage thriving businesses. Unlike much contemporary work, which is often fraught with alienation, Old Order work pulses with meaning, human dignity, and a delight in artisanship. Parents deliver and raise their babies without the aid of self-help books. Seminars on stress management, time management, and assertiveness training are unheard of in these communities. Immediate and extended families provide a network of care throughout the life cycle.

Moreover, Old Order groups seem to function almost effortlessly— without consultants, strategic plans, or long-term economic forecasts. The more politicians declare war on poverty, ignorance, assault weapons, and drugs, the more things appear to go awry. Highly publicized accounts of Amish drug use notwithstanding, Old Orders seem firmly in charge of their destiny.

Most troubling of all to outsiders is the fear that, despite our smorgasbord of high-tech gadgets, abundant leisure, and heroic efforts to control things, the Old Orders might actually live more satisfied—even happier—lives than the rest of us. A recent ABC television program on happiness featured a segment on happiness in the Amish community.[14] Despite all our comfort and convenience, the possibility that these folks are happier haunts, indeed, torments the postmodern soul. Perhaps that is why we are so intrigued by Old Order ways.

Old Order pilgrims trouble us because they unravel our assumptions

Canadian Mennonites on a backroad to heaven. *Source:* Carl Hiebert

about bigness, progress, diversity, education, freedom, individual dignity, and tradition. They propose that tolerance and individualism may have to yield if they spoil the virtues of an orderly community. The upside-down values of Old Order life esteem tradition more than change, lift communal goals above personal ones, acclaim work over consumption, and place personal sacrifice above pleasure. They question if "newer," "bigger," "faster," and "more powerful" necessarily mean "better." The wisdom afloat in their cultural reservoir suggests that some things are best removed from individual choice, that firm limits and clear boundaries may best preserve human dignity over the generations. It *is* possible, the Old Orders argue, to tame technology, to control the size of things, to bridle bureaucracy, and to hold things to a humane scale. Moreover, they contend that living with modest humility in a well-ordered and bounded community is indeed the highest calling—the supreme virtue.

NEAR THE OUTSKIRTS OF HEAVEN

By the end of their journey, Old Orders hope to reach the outskirts of heaven, with the pearly gates in sight. Their backroad journey may appear virtuous at times, but make no mistake: Old Order virtues come with a price—one that few outsiders are willing to pay. These communal outcomes require sacrifice: giving up assertive individualism. They require forgoing individual preference in dress, transportation, and education. They require accepting restrictions on convenience, friendship, marriage, mobility, and occupational choice. They require striking a delicate balance between communal restraint and personal freedom. Moreover, they require avoiding consumerism, commercial leisure, and mass media. These outcomes pivot on a religious worldview. In short, such outcomes require the embrace of a different world—a world where the welfare of the community supersedes personal freedom, a world that by most benchmarks is provincial and restrictive.

The personal costs of Old Order ways are high, but the benefits—identity, meaning, and belonging—are surely precious commodities in the midst of social fragmentation. The satisfactions bequeathed by traditional ways may compensate somewhat for all the necessary sacrifice. Indeed, first-time visitors to Old Order communities are surprised by the latitude of personal freedom within the fences of Old Order life—surprised by the dignity afforded individuals within the limits of constraint. Thus, in the larger scheme of things, the habits that appear to hamper the human spirit may indeed free it.

Old Orders contend that the backroad to heaven requires living in stable communities that restrain individualism and limit choice—communities that offer guidance from their storehouse of collective wisdom. Such communities, they argue, provide identity, security, meaning—and, for the most part, happiness. And while others may agree that some self-sacrifice, sharing, and suffering is noble, even necessary for the common good, the pilgrims on the backroad to heaven contend that such virtues cannot be left to the whims of personal preference but must be shaped by fellow travelers and inspired by a holy vision.

Notes

PREFACE

1. The intensity of the media interest in this story is underscored by the fact that more than fifty news agencies contacted Donald B. Kraybill as they scrambled to cover the story. This event likely received more media attention than any other episode in Amish history.

2. Labi (1998) "Amiss Among the Amish," *Time,* 29 June 1998. Remnick (1998) "Bad Seeds," *New Yorker,* 20 July 1998, 28–33.

3. Putnam's (1995) widely influential article on bowling alone argues that there has been a decline of civic engagement in American life. His recent book develops the argument in greater detail (Putnam 2000).

4. We have included various Brethren groups under the rubric of Anabaptist-affiliated even though they did not have a direct organic connection to Anabaptism historically. They were, however, strongly influenced by Anabaptist ideas, and there has been considerable cross-fertilization over the years.

5. These estimates include Hutterite, Mennonite, Amish, and Brethren groups of all stripes in the United States. Three of the groups in our study (Hutterites, Amish, and Mennonites) have members living in both the United States and Canada. Our broad numerical estimates of Anabaptist populations in the United States excludes Canadian members. However, in discussions of the membership of each group in our study, we do include Canadian members. Thus, unless otherwise specified, when we discuss Hutterites, for example, we are referring to Hutterites in the United States and Canada.

CHAPTER 1. THE OLD ROAD TO HEAVEN

1. For introductions to Anabaptist history and thought, consult Dyck (1993), Loewen and Nolt (1996), Snyder (1995), and Weaver (1987). Selected Anabaptist primary sources appear in English in Klaassen (1981). *The Brethren Encyclope-*

dia (1983–84) and *The Mennonite Encyclopedia* (1955–59, 1990) include a wide variety of articles related to the Anabaptist movement, its subsequent history, current expressions, and present-day groups.

2. Although it is not customary to label Hutterites as Old Order, we have included them in our study despite the fact that they do not explicitly call themselves Old Order. Their view of moral authority, their worldview, and their self-understanding fit our understanding of the meaning of Old Order. Most telling is their use of sermons written in the sixteenth century. Moreover, their Old Order identity crystallized in the 1870s and 1880s when two-thirds of the Hutterite immigrants dropped their communal understandings and eventually joined various Mennonite groups. The story of the noncommunal prairie people, or *Prairieleut*, is told by R. Janzen (1999). Thus Hutterite self-identity was forming in North America in the 1800s, about the same time as that of the other Old Order groups.

3. An example of this is "Damned: Emma's Choice," a lengthy story of a shunned Amish woman that appeared in the *Philadelphia Inquirer Magazine*, 30 January 1994. For other stories of ex-Amish who have left the community under duress, see Garrett (1998).

4. Kraybill (2001), Nolt (1992a), and Scott (1996) have charted the rapid growth of many of the Old Order communities.

5. We are grateful to Steven M. Nolt for several rounds of critical discussion that helped us to clarify our definition of Old Order groups. In a personal communication dated 2 August 1999, he suggested that scholarly definitions of Old Order groups could be roughly sorted into three types: historical/religious, technology usage, and worldview. Our emphasis on the source and nature of moral authority approximates in some ways the worldview approach, but our accent on moral authority is more focused and fundamental than the worldview approach. The historical approach has many shortcomings because groups that embody Old Order traits as we define them may not use the Old Order label. Others who at a particular historical moment were clearly Old Order may over time lose their Old Order understandings about the nature of moral authority even though they still wear the label. In addition, some Amish groups only use the "Old Order" label if they are located near "New Order" groups. The Old Order label is of little use if they are not living close to more progressive groups.

A definition that hinges primarily on technology deals with only a surface expression of the deeper issue of moral authority. Thus, we contend that a particular understanding of moral authority is *the* defining characteristic of Old Order communities, but such understandings come in many degrees. Although it is tempting, we think it is not wise to define Old Order groups by a single criterion related to a specific practice such as horse-and-buggy transportation, the use of a dialect, or a particular ritual. Although all of these factors may be important in shaping an Old Order identity, the deeper issue is the nature of moral authority, not a particular practice. We expand our definitional discussion of the meaning of Old Order in Chapters 6 and 8 and in the beginning of Chapter 9.

The social base of Old Order communities may, in the long run, shape their identity. Is a particular type of social base—a rural or agrarian one, for example—necessary to maintain an Old Order identity? To say it another way, it may only be possible to sustain a traditional understanding of moral authority in the context of a face-to-face geographical agrarian community. If this is the case, nonfarm occupations may, in time, become a key marker of the shift away from an Old Order identity. Perhaps occupation itself is not literally so much the key issue as is the maintenance of a face-to-face community in a rural context.

CHAPTER 2. THE HUTTERITES

1. Introductions to Hutterite history are provided by Gross (1998), Harrison (1997), J. Hostetler (1997), and Packull (1995). *The Chronicle of the Hutterian Brethren*, Vol. 1 (1987) and Vol. 2 (1998) contains some 1,600 pages of primary source documents. John Hofer (1988), a Hutterite minister, has written a recent interpretation of the Hutterite story that is used in some of their schools.

2. The story of the noncommunal prairie people or *Prairieleut* is told by Janzen (1999) and is also found in the compilation titled *History of the Hutterite Mennonites* (1974).

3. In the early 1990s a painful division within the Schmiedleut resulted in two Schmiedleut branches known as the Wipf and Kleinsasser groups. The more progressive Kleinsasser faction had affiliated for several years with another communal group known as the Society of Brothers, or Bruderhof. The Society of Brothers has five colonies, or bruderhofs, located in New York and Pennsylvania. Two are based in England and one in Australia. Their headquarters are in Rifton, New York, at the Woodcrest community. The Society of Brothers, founded in 1920 by Eberhard Arnold in Germany, has had various relationships with the more traditional Hutterites over the years. The Bruderhof established a relationship in the 1930s that dissolved in the 1950s. A formal relationship was established in 1974 and included some intermarriage. The strongest ties were with Schmiedleut colonies, but formal relationships between the Hutterites and the Bruderhof dissolved once again in the 1990s. Jeschke (1994) provides a helpful overview and chronology of the complicated and often acrimonious disputes that strained the relationship between the Society of Brothers and the Hutterites and caused division within the Schmiedleut group itself.

The division within the Schmiedleut occurred gradually in the mid-1990s and reflected some trends that had begun years before. About sixty of the Schmiedleut colonies affiliate with an elder named Jacob Kleinsasser. Most of these colonies are in Manitoba, Canada, and are known as the Kleinsasser group, and sometimes the Oilers, because of some supposed oil investments. Their formal name is the Schmiedleut Conference of the Hutterian Brethren.

The other faction, known informally as the Gibbs group, or Gibbleut, is named for an attorney, Donald Gibb, who provided legal advice in the division. This group of about 110 colonies, which calls itself the Schmiedleut Committee Group, has numerous colonies in both the United States and Canada.

This division within the Schmiedleut has been very painful, acrimonious, and complicated. It has not been a "clean" break because some of the members of a Gibb colony may personally align themselves with the Kleinsasser group and vice versa. Other members remain somewhat neutral despite the affiliation of their particular colony. Hostile feelings have become so strong in some cases that factions have sued each other in courts of law, breaking the historic Anabaptist taboo on litigation.

4. Personal correspondence to Donald B. Kraybill from Robert Rhodes dated 13 September 1999. Rhodes is a nonethnic Hutterite who joined a Schmiedleut colony in Minnesota.

5. Unless otherwise noted, the observations reported in this chapter were made during visits by Donald B. Kraybill to ten Schmiedleut colonies in South Dakota in July 1992, and in Manitoba in November 1992 and May 1994. Unless cited otherwise, the quoted remarks in this chapter were made by Hutterites in these colonies during the field research. We thank Mr. Orlando Goering, who was especially helpful in gathering and tabulating demographic data on sixteen colonies in South Dakota. He also provided information on defectors and on other aspects of colony life.

6. P. Hofer (1973:24) and others use this biblical image to describe the colony. The metaphor of the ark was also used by the Catholic Church in medieval times to describe the church.

7. The Hutterisch dialect has Austrian roots, specifically Carinthian and Tyrolean, but also Russian elements and increasingly some English. The archaic form of High German used in sermons and taught in the German schools of the colonies is quite different from modern German. Elements of Hutterisch enter into many sermons as well.

8. The use of computers varies considerably. In more progressive colonies, computers are used for business and personal purposes. Some colonies have Web pages. One colony in Manitoba has a site that describes the Hutterian Church at www.hutterianbrethren.com. Some colonies use satellite-linked weather and market news sources as well.

9. Ehrenpreis (1978:62, 35–36) was written in 1650.

10. Riedemann's (1970:89) *Confession of Faith* was originally published in 1545. John J. Friesen (1999) has recently completed a new translation of Riedemann's confession.

11. Waldner (1990:5).

12. Waldner (1990:3).

13. Ehrenpreis (1978:45).

14. The quotes in this paraphrase are from Ehrenpreis (1978:10–25).

15. Ehrenpreis (1978:15).

16. Cited in Hostetler and Huntington (1996:64).

17. The practice of strapping is no longer universal. Some Schmiedleut colonies have abolished corporal punishment in their schools, but it is still used in many colonies.

18. Hostetler and Huntington (1996:67).

19. Ehrenpreis (1978) introduces these ideas in a long epistle he wrote in 1650 on "Brotherly Community: The Highest Command of Love." The quote comes from Ehrenpreis (1978:64–65).

20. *The Chronicle of the Hutterian Brethren,* Vol. 1 (1987).

21. Hofer (1973:29).

22. Peter Hofer (1973:34–35) cites 1 John 5:19 as well as other biblical passages that underscore separation from the world.

23. Hostetler (1997:153).

24. Hostetler (1997:126–33) provides an extensive account of Hutterite tribulations during World War I.

25. We are indebted to William Janzen (1990) for an excellent study of church-state relations that compares the Mennonite, Hutterite, and Doukhobor experience in Canada. Much of the material in this section reflects Janzen's analysis of Hutterite conflicts with Canadian governments.

26. An arsonist ignited a fire on 8 March 1998 at a new colony (Camrose) near Shelby, Montana, that caused around $100,000 in damage. This was the third act of vandalism aimed at new property bought by the Hutterites, and authorities suspect that it was set by outsiders who were resentful of the Hutterite expansion.

27. Janzen (1990:78).

28. In a few cases some colonies have established their own private schools. Although infrequent, this is more common in the United States than in Canada.

29. In one colony in the United States, the corporate income is divided equally among all families and individual taxes are paid accordingly with returns filed for each family. Corporate and property taxes are paid as would be the case with any other corporation or farm. The steward and a hired accountant file all the tax forms rather than individual families.

30. One Hutterite described the colony as a small enclosed porch (*forhofgangle*) outside of heaven.

31. Among some Schmiedleut colonies, English translations of Hutterite sermons are increasing. Although no colonies use English exclusively, "translated

Hutterite sermons are quietly growing in popularity, especially as knowledge of the archaic German falters, along with the ability of some elders to teach it" according to one informant.

32. Hofer (1973:31–32).

33. This quotation is reported by Hostetler and Huntington (1996:125).

34. Huntington (1992 and 1996) provides an overview of some of the technological changes afoot in Hutterite society.

35. Huntington (1995 and 1996) offers an excellent overview of gender roles, particularly the role of women in colony life.

36. Hostetler and Huntington (1996:66).

37. In a four-page paper used for training of German teachers, minister Samuel Kleinsasser (1994:1) describes the purpose and goal of the German school.

38. This story of symbolic change was provided by Steven M. Nolt.

39. Hostetler and Huntington (1996:75).

40. There is considerable networking among Hutterite English teachers from all the *leut*, especially in far Western Canada and Montana. These annual gatherings typically attract mostly outside teachers, but occasionally some Hutterite educators participate in them as well.

41. In some colonies the tradition patterns of education are changing. Some of the more progressive colonies among the Schmiedleut, and to a lesser extent among the Dariusleut, encourage their youth to finish high school in the English school. A few Hutterites are even receiving some college training. These changes have been prompted by the increased use of technology as well as by the interest of a few colonies in training Hutterite teachers and nurses. In Manitoba a teacher education program is offered to Hutterite teachers through Brandon University. These innovations are rarely found among the Lehrerleut.

42. Some Hutterites will greet outsiders with a handshake, but not in every colony. A handshake is also used as a sign of spiritual fellowship among both men and women in Hutterite circles. In earlier days the "holy kiss" practiced by the other three groups was used by some Hutterites. According to one informant, ministers would greet each other with a kiss. The practice has fallen away, at least among the Schmiedleut.

43. For an insightful discussion of the male and female subcultures in Hutterite colonies see Hostetler and Huntington (1996:35–39). Huntington (1992, 1995, 1996) provides penetrating insights into gender roles and the female subculture of colony life.

44. Cited in Hostetler and Huntington (1996:36).

45. The tabulation of names was based on data from the *Hutterite Telephone and Address Book* (2000), which lists the name of the minister and manager for each colony.

46. These estimates are based on data from 16 Schmiedleut colonies in South Dakota numbering 1,853 persons. The data were gathered and tabulated in 1993 by Orlando Goering for the preparation of this chapter.

47. The exact number of Hutterites is not known, but the number of colonies in 1999 was 425. The average number of persons in a colony varies with the age of the colony, but on the average ranges from 90 to 100 persons; thus, the total number of Hutterites likely ranges from 39,000 to 43,000.

48. Some seekers come to the communities but leave after a time and rarely join. According to one informant, probably less than a dozen outsiders have joined in the last ten years.

49. A Hutterite colony, Palmgrove, in Nigeria is affiliated with the Kleinsasser group of Schmiedleut colonies. This effort represents a growing interest in mission outreach by some of the more progressive colonies.

50. Many current observers of Hutterite life have noted the decline of family size: Boldt (1989), Boldt and Roberts (1980), Driedger (1995), Huntington (1992), Peter (1987), Stephenson (1991).

51. Professor Claudia Konker made this observation in a telephone conversation with Donald B. Kraybill on 1 April 1996.

52. Gertrude Huntington reported this comment from a colonist in a phone conversation with Donald B. Kraybill, 28 March 1996.

53. The colony gun, usually under the control of the field boss or cattleman, is used for killing injured cattle or varmints. Occasionally a colonist may be tempted to keep a gun on the sly in order to kill animals for pelts to sell for personal gain. This, of course, is taboo and subject to formal sanctions.

54. The Hutterites would not call the practice of shunning a ritual of shaming, but from a sociological perspective, the shunning sometimes serves that function.

55. Shunning between colonies occurred among the Schmiedleut in the early 1990s when a schism, related to relationships with the Society of Brothers, divided them into two factions. Jeschke (1994) provides a helpful analysis of this dispute as well as a good discussion of the process of exclusion in Hutterite life.

56. Goering (1993), Hartse (1993, 1994, 1995), J. Hostetler (1997:273–83), and Peter et al. (1982) provide extensive discussions of the reasons and patterns of defection.

57. For example, in the spring of 1998, several Hutterite men were charged in a provincial court in Alberta with sex offenses ranging from incest to fondling. Judge Gordon Clozza urged Hutterite leaders to establish a sex education program for their youth. This story was reported in *Mennonite Weekly Review,* 9 July 1998.

58. Professor Ed Boldt noted these reasons in personal conversations with

Donald B. Kraybill on 1 November 1992. Professor Claudia Konker confirmed them in a telephone conversation with Donald B. Kraybill on 1 April 1996.

59. These comments were made by defectors in interviews conducted by Orlando Goering and summarized in correspondence to Donald B. Kraybill on 2 March 1993.

60. Ibid.

61. In a mid-twentieth-century study of Hutterite life, Eaton (1952:338) called their process of social change "controlled acculturation." In this process, "one culture accepts a practice from another culture, but integrates the new practice into its own existing value system."

CHAPTER 3. THE MENNONITES

1. Some Mennonites of Swiss and South German origin migrated from Pennsylvania to Ontario, Canada, beginning in 1786. The Old Order Mennonites in Ontario trace their roots to this stream of migration.

2. The data sources for this chapter include participant observation and extended interviews by Donald B. Kraybill in Old Order Mennonite communities in Indiana, Virginia, Pennsylvania, and Ontario between 1992 and 1997. Unless otherwise identified, the quotations in this chapter come from conversations in those interviews. In addition to the interviews, a questionnaire was sent to a bishop in each of the settlements to obtain basic information about churches, schools, and current practices. We are grateful to Florence Horning, who gathered many of the primary and secondary data sources and corresponded with many Old Order leaders. Her knowledge of Old Order ways was extremely helpful in all aspects of the project. Tom Elliot provided helpful assistance and access to the Old Order Mennonite community in Indiana. We thank Allen Hoover for his estimates of the population and membership of the Groffdale Conference. Numerous persons provided helpful counsel; among them are Levi Frey, Isaac Horst, James P. Hurd, Amos B. Hoover, and Allen Hoover. Their insights and assistance have greatly improved the accuracy of our text.

3. The first groups formed in Indiana and Ohio in 1872; the last one in York County, Pennsylvania, in 1913. Compared with the burgeoning literature on the Old Order Amish, the Old Order Mennonites have received little attention. Scott (1996) provides an excellent introduction to the many varieties of Old Order and conservative Mennonite groups living in the United Sates and Canada. There are few basic sociological studies or full length histories of Old Order Mennonites. Hoover, Miller, and Freeman (1978) offer a good overview of Old Order Mennonite history from an Old Order Mennonite perspective. The best historical introduction to the Old Order Mennonites and Amish in nineteenth-century America is chapter 8, "Keeping the Old Order," in Schlabach (1988:201–29). Cronk's (1977) study of *Gelassenheit* in Old Order Mennonite and Amish com-

munities provides an excellent analysis of Old Order ritual. *The Mennonite Encyclopedia* offers overview essays on the Old Order Mennonites (4:47–49 and 5:654–55). Lloyd Weiler (1995) wrote an overview of the history of the Old Order Mennonites from an Old Order perspective. Lee (1995) recently completed a sociological study of the Weaverland Conference an Old Order Mennonite automobile group in New York state. Scott discusses Mennonite attire (1986) and a wedding and baptism (1988).

The most prolific Old Order Mennonite writer in Ontario is Isaac Horst. His numerous booklets on Mennonite ways and beliefs appear in the bibliography. His most important description of Old Order practices in Ontario is *Separate and Peculiar* (1983a). In recent years many of Horst's essays have been published in the *Mennonite Reporter,* a newspaper that serves many Mennonite groups in Canada, and in *Family Life,* an Amish publication. A helpful sociological analysis of Old Order Mennonite society is found in two essays by John F. Peters (1987, 1994). In the first study, Peters (1987) discusses socialization practices; the 1994 essay analyzes Old Order Mennonite economics. Mary Ann Horst (1992) provides a popular introduction to her Old Order Mennonite heritage in Ontario. J. Winfield Fretz (1989) includes the Old Order Mennonites in his sociological study of the Mennonite groups in the Waterloo, Ontario, area. For his master's thesis, Brubacher (1984) studied patterns of social interaction among Old Order Canadian Mennonites.

4. An earlier Old Order division, led by Jacob Stauffer in Lancaster County, Pennsylvania, in 1845, resulted in a small group of conservative "Stauffer" or "Pike" Mennonites. This chapter focuses on the Old Order groups that emerged after 1872.

5. An excellent collection of primary source materials on the formation of Old Order views was compiled by Amos Hoover (1982). In an insightful essay, Beulah Stauffer Hostetler (1992) compares the formation of several Old Order groups between 1850 and 1900. Martin and Martin (1985) have compiled a book that traces the life and genealogy of Bishop Jonas Martin, one of the major leaders of the Old Order movement. The 1893–1993 centennial of the Old Order division in Lancaster County brought several historical reflections on the Old Orders. For example, see Benowitz (1993) and Weiler (1993).

6. Schlabach (1988:201–03) as well as Loewen and Nolt (1996:186–88) see the formation of Old Order identities as an alternative renewal movement.

7. Horst (1989:9).

8. The pulpit controversy was surely not the cause of the Old Order schism in the Lancaster, Pennsylvania, area, but it did inflame the dissatisfaction that led to the division. The pulpit incident is described by Martin and Martin (1985:38–40) and in many other sources as well.

9. The factors leading to these divisions are complicated, but in every case the

more progressive faction eventually began using cars. The division in Ontario in 1939 led to the formation of the Markham-Waterloo group of Mennonites, who adopted the automobile and today are associated with the Weaverland Conference of Pennsylvania.

10. Although often dubbed "blackbumper Mennonites," their official name is the Weaverland Conference Mennonite Church. They are also frequently called "Horning Mennonites" after the name of their first bishop, Moses Horning. Today members no longer must paint their bumpers black, but the cars themselves are expected to be black. Ministers, however, are still expected to have black bumpers.

11. The largest group of team Mennonites formed in Lancaster County, Pennsylvania, in 1927. Their official name is the Groffdale Conference. They are also known locally as the "Wenger" Mennonites because Joseph Wenger, a conservative leader, became their first bishop after the 1927 division. He was ordained bishop in the fall of 1927 by Bishop John Martin of Indiana. Historically, the team group in Ontario was sometimes known as the Woolwich Mennonites because of the area in which they originated. Their legal name is the Old Order Mennonite Society of British North America. They are known to their neighbors and the public as simply "Old Order Mennonites."

12. The English language had already been accepted by all the Mennonite groups in Virginia before the Old Order division occurred in 1901.

13. James P. Hurd (1999:21) makes this estimate. For a historical sketch of the settlement in Missouri, see Shirk (1998). In 1970 five families began this settlement. Today it is home to more than 170 families.

14. This estimate was calculated by James P. Hurd (1999:55) in his study of the Martindale district in Lancaster County where 79 of 177 people migrated to other states.

15. Meetinghouses in Ontario have a number of distinctions. They have no anteroom or minister's room. In contrast to Groffdale meetinghouses, the Canadian ones have a slightly raised pulpit and do not have a singer's table.

16. For an overview of these small independent groups, see Scott (1996).

17. These calculations are based on family information provided by directories of the Groffdale Conference, *Directory* (1992) and *Directory* (1997).

18. Almost all the men in Old Order communities marry. Because men are more likely to leave the community prior to baptism and because natural birth ratios favor women, Old Order communities tend to have sizeable numbers of unmarried women but few bachelors. See Meyers (1994a) for a discussion of this issue in the Amish communities of Indiana.

19. Three documents provide important primary sources for insights into the moral order of Old Order Mennonite communities: (1) *Confession* (1996) contains both the eighteen articles of the Dordrecht Confession of Faith written in

1632 and procedures for important ceremonies in Old Order congregations—ordinations, communions, marriages, and funerals. *Confession* (1996) is based on a translation of Benjamin Eby's 1841 Church Regulations and has been revised several times by various Old Order Mennonite groups. The Weaverland Conference produced a revised edition in English in 1996 that, according to one Old Order Mennonite historian, reflects the ritual procedures of most Old Order Mennonite groups. (2) The "Groffdale Conference Ordnung" is a twelve-page document in German that describes the expectations for members of the conference in the early 1990s. An English translation by Amos Hoover was an important primary source for this chapter. Florence Horning and Hedda Durnbaugh also assisted in the translation. The "Groffdale Conference Ordnung" (unpublished and undated) was first written in the mid-1970s to promote uniformity when new settlements were being established in other counties of Pennsylvania and in other states. Prior to that time, the *Ordnung* was unwritten. (3) An untitled *Ordnung* from the team Mennonites in Ontario reflects their practices in the early 1990s. This two-page Ontario document, translated into English (possibly by Isaac R. Horst), spells out their expectations for membership.

20. Horst (1979:69).

21. Groffdale Conference Ordnung, unpublished and undated. Quotations from the *Ordnung* throughout this chapter are from this document.

22. These behaviors are all explicitly mentioned in the Groffdale Conference Ordnung.

23. Although specific patterns of attire are expected by members, dress standards have not been an explicit test of membership in the Groffdale Conference. For a detailed description of Old Order Mennonite dress practices, consult Scott (1986).

24. The Ontario Mennonites require dresses to be "no more than nine inches above the floor." The Canadians also discourage wearing dark-framed glasses, preferring metal rims instead.

25. For a recent translation of the Dordrecht Confession of Faith, see Irvin B. Horst (1988). This confession of faith is used by most of the Old Order Mennonite and Old Order Amish churches. Instruction classes prior to baptism typically are based on the eighteen articles of faith as recorded in *Confession* (1996).

26. I. R. Horst (1989).

27. These figures are cited in Brubacher's (1984:118, 120) study of twenty-one family heads in the Mount Forest Mennonite community in Ontario. They are likely high because this is a newer community surrounded by outsiders.

28. The German words that shape Old Order views are *wehrlos* (defenseless) and *wehrlosigkeit* (defenselessness), typically known as "nonresistance" in English.

29. Informal comments by Isaac R. Horst to Donald B. Kraybill.

30. For a helpful analysis of socialization in the Ontario Mennonite community, see the sociological essay by Peters (1987).

31. James P. Hurd (1999:60) calculated this percentage based on the decision of 197 children who were under the age of 15 in the Martindale District (Lancaster County) in 1968.

32. These estimates are based on tabulations of membership figures in the *Directory* (1992) and the *Directory* (1993), which suggests that retention among the Groffdale Conference is 81 percent, while in the Ontario Conference it is about 75 percent. Some Mennonite informants estimate retention rates of 90 percent and higher in their congregations. Isaac R. Horst (1991) estimates that 90 percent of the Canadian youth join the church. A few leave the church after baptism.

33. Our estimate of the distribution of these surnames is based on the listings in *Directory* (1992) and *Directory* (1993).

34. M. A. Horst (1992:19–21).

35. The quotes from these two paragraphs come from Isaac R. Horst (1990).

36. John F. Peters (1987, 2000) provides an excellent sociological description of socialization and family life cycle stages among the Old Order Ontario Mennonites.

37. Mennonite parochial schools in Canada were founded in 1966. A five-man committee serves as an advisory board that sets policies for all the schools. A three-member local board hires the teachers for each school.

38. This landmark legal case, *Wisconsin v. Yoder*, is discussed by Keim (1975) and Meyers (1993). Source materials related to the conflict between public school officials and the plain community in Pennsylvania have been compiled by Lapp (1991).

39. This is an estimate of the number of schools operated by the Groffdale and the related Mennonite conferences in Virginia and Canada. It is based on information provided by informants and written responses from leaders in various communities. The *Blackboard Bulletin* reports a total of 220 Old Order Mennonite schools, but some of these are operated by other conservative Mennonite groups such as Weaverland Conference or independent team groups ("School" 1995).

40. Dewalt and Troxell (1989) provide a careful ethnographic description of a one-room Old Order Mennonite school in southeastern Pennsylvania.

41. These are shortened versions of the three questions. The complete questions are available in *Confession* (1996:49–50). In Ontario the baptism typically follows the Sunday morning sermon. The Groffdale Conference usually baptizes at the preparatory service on the Saturday preceding communion.

42. The baptismal practices may vary somewhat from region to region. The ones described here are typical in the Canadian churches as outlined by Isaac R.

Horst (1979:32–34; 1991). *Confession* (1996:47–88) also outlines the prescribed procedures.

43. For extended descriptions of Mennonite weddings, see J. D. Hoover (1990), I. R. Horst (1979), Hurd (1999), and Scott (1988:36–38).

44. I. R. Horst (1993:29).

45. For an excellent discussion of Old Order Mennonite gender roles and family life cycle stages in Ontario, see John Peters (2000).

46. John Peters (1994:156–59) provides a detailed discussion of the work of Old Order Mennonite women in Ontario.

47. Various Old Order Mennonite rituals are described in *Confession* (1996) and by Isaac R. Horst (1983a) and Scott (1988, 1996).

48. In Ontario the ministers are all present when the service begins, and one of the ministers announces the first hymn, which opens the service. The text is read before the opening sermon, and the benediction comes after the last hymn in Ontario. *Confession* (1996) provides the order of service followed by many Old Order groups in the United States. See also Scott (1988:91 and 1996:38).

49. Old Order Mennonite documents typically use the spelling "counsel" rather "council" when they refer to their counsel meetings and counsel room.

50. In Ontario the conference is held on a Friday. The next day, Saturday, the bishops convene to discuss the results of the conference and write down any decisions, which are then read in the congregations after the communion service.

51. The Groffdale Conference meets on the Friday preceding Good Friday and on the first Friday in October. The Ontario Conference meets on Friday following Good Friday and on the first Friday in September.

52. The procedure for an ordination service is spelled out in *Confession* (1996:63–72). The following description is based on the personal observations of Donald B. Kraybill at an ordination service in Lancaster County, Pennsylvania, on 12 December 1995.

53. The only exceptions to the taboo on air travel in Ontario is the use of an ambulance helicopter for medical emergencies.

54. Hurd (1999:55) studied the occupational patterns in the Martindale district (Lancaster County) and found that 75 percent of the men were farmers.

55. The most detailed analysis of Old Order Mennonite work and economics was conducted by John Peters (1994). His study of Ontario Mennonites found that 38 percent of Mennonites over 24 years of age were involved in some type of nonfarm work. Many of these were also involved in farming.

56. Ed Klimuska (1993) describes the different responses to the decline of farmland in Lancaster County in a series of six articles titled "Old Order Lancaster County," which appeared in the *Lancaster New Era* and were subsequently published as a tabloid reprint.

57. Dress practices, electricity, and telephones were never a test of member-

ship in the Groffdale Conference. Traditional patterns of attire and the rejection of electricity and telephones were the norm for many years, although they were not specifically mentioned in the *Ordnung* as an official cause for excommunication.

CHAPTER FOUR: THE AMISH

1. *Witness* was photographed on site in Lancaster County, Pennsylvania, in the summer of 1984 and released in the spring of 1985. The "plain clothing" modeled with Amish props appeared in the August 1993 issue of *Vogue*. The *Glamour* story appeared in the August 1999 issue. David Luthy (1994c) explores the ironies and excesses surrounding the marketing of the Amish in the Amish magazine *Family Life*. In a fascinating study, David Weaver-Zercher (2001) analyzes the domestication of the Amish in public consciousness.

2. For a good general introduction to Amish history, consult Nolt (1992b). Roth (1993) has recently translated the letters surrounding the Amish division of 1693 and reviewed the issues involved in the group's formation. John A. Hostetler (1993) provides a general introduction to Amish life and culture, and Kraybill (2001) traces social changes in the twentieth century in the Lancaster Amish settlement.

3. About a century later, several New Order Amish congregations formed between 1960 and 1975. The New Order Amish developed as some Amish sought more personal Bible study, stricter moral standards for their youth, and more conveniences. The New Order Amish represent less than 10 percent of the total Amish family. New Order Amish groups generally have more liberal and varied practices related to telephones in the home, electricity from public utilities, and the use of farm equipment. They often have Sunday schools and organized activities for their youth. The story of the formation of the New Order Amish congregations in Holmes County, Ohio, is told by Kline and Beachy (1998).

4. Paton Yoder (1991) chronicles the issues that provoked controversy in the Amish communities in the last half of the nineteenth century and subsequent formation of the Old Order groups. See also chapters 8 and 9 of Nolt (1992b) and the work of Beulah Stauffer Hostetler (1992:5–25) for a comparative analysis of Old Order origins.

5. A listing of all the Amish settlements in North America by state and province was compiled by Luthy (1994a and 1997). This enumeration includes the founding date and number of congregations in the settlement.

6. This estimate is based on the assumption that church districts average about 150 persons (children and adults). The number may be slightly higher in the older settlements such as those in Lancaster County, Pennsylvania, and Holmes County, Ohio, and somewhat lower in the smaller and newer settlements. Thus 150 is a reasonable estimate for all settlements. At the beginning of 2000 there

were more than 1,200 church districts in North America, yielding an estimated population of 180,000. These estimates are derived from several sources: Raber (2000), Luthy (1997), amd Amish informants.

7. This is the number of settlements that were established and still in existence at the end of 1992. About eighteen additional settlements were founded but failed during these two decades. Luthy's (1994a) tabulation of the new settlements is described in detail in an article on "Amish Migration, 1972–1992."

8. The observations reported in this chapter are based on field work and interviews conducted by Donald B. Kraybill in numerous Amish settlements in several states between 1989 and 1999.

9. In a few settlements, for example, Kalona, Iowa, and Kokomo, Indiana, tractors are permitted in Old Order Amish fields. The vast majority of Old Order Amish settlements prohibit the use of tractors for fieldwork, but some of them allow the use of tractors at the barn to operate high-power equipment.

10. There are a few exceptions to these broad generalizations in some communities and affiliations, but for the most part they apply to the bulk of Old Order Amish communities in North America. For example, one Old Order Amish congregation in Somerset County, Pennsylvania, has a meetinghouse, but this is a rare exception.

11. This advice was given by the bishops of the Lancaster (Pa.) settlement in 1996.

12. The patterns of shunning vary considerably from settlement to settlement and are enforced quite differently by various families.

13. The history and work of the National Amish Steering Committee is described by Olshan (1993 and 1994).

14. Olshan and Schmidt (1994) discuss the conundrums of gender roles in Amish society in the context of feminist theory.

15. For an analytical discussion of the role of women in Amish Society, see Olshan and Schmidt (1994). Louise Stoltzfus (1994, 1998) offers many insights into the lives and wisdom of Amish women. For examples of repression, see Garrett (1998), as well as the stories of Amish women in "Damned: Emma's Choice," a lengthy story of a shunned Amish woman that appeared in the *Philadelphia Inquirer Magazine*, 30 January 1994, and "Escaping Amish Repression: One Woman's Story" in *Glamour*, August 1999.

16. The full text of the Supreme Court's decision, as well as several essays discussing the case, are available in Keim (1975).

17. These figures are reported in the November 1999 issue of the *Blackboard Bulletin*'s "School Directory for 1999–2000" (1999:7–22). Meyers (1993) and Huntington (1994) provide historical overviews of the rise of Amish schools and the various conflicts with the state. Hostetler and Huntington (1992) describe the cultural ethos and curriculum of Amish schools.

18. The only exception to this are the instruction classes for candidates prior to baptism.

19. Hostetler and Huntington (1992:93-97).

20. The wedding practices described in this chapter are typical of the Lancaster County, Pennsylvania, settlement and are based on participant observation by Donald B. Kraybill. As Stephen Scott (1988) shows, the practices vary from settlement to settlement. He provides a detailed description of a wedding ceremony.

21. This is typical fare in the Lancaster, Pennsylvania, community. The menu varies from settlement to settlement. See Scott (1988) for menus in various settlements.

22. These figures are provided by Meyers (1994b) in a detailed study of the shifting occupational patterns in the Elkhart-Lagrange settlement.

23. The 1977 data were provided by the Sanitary Engineering Department of Geauga County, Ohio, and summarized in a memo to Uria R. Byler dated 3 August 1977. A copy of the memo is located in the Heritage Historical Library, Aylmer, Ontario. Peter Gail reports the current number in various occupations in this settlement in an article in the April 1994 issue of the *Plain Communities Business Exchange.*

24. These numbers, derived from the settlement directories, are reported by Kreps, Kreps, and Donnermeyer (1992:14). A tabulation of the occupational data in the 1988 *Directory* for the Holmes County area of Ohio, broken down by affiliation, showed the following number of farmers in three of the larger groups: Andy Weaver group, 46 percent; Old Order group, 36 percent; and New Order group, 35 percent. Kraybill (1994b) provides a detailed discussion of the occupational shifts in this settlement.

25. In a sample of ten church districts, Kraybill (2001) found that 45 percent were involved in agriculture. The proportion who are farming varies considerably from district to district, depending on their location in Lancaster County. In some church districts the number of farmers dips as low as 10 percent. In districts in the southern end of the county the number of farmers may climb as high as 90 percent.

26. The dramatic rise of these microenterprises in Lancaster's Amish community is described in detail in a full-length book by Kraybill and Nolt (1995).

27. The impact and long-term consequence of these enterprises on Amish society is discussed more fully in Olshan (1994) and Kraybill and Nolt (1994, 1995).

28. For an in-depth discussion of the Amish view of the state, see Paton Yoder (1993).

29. A series of essays edited by Kraybill (1993) describes the conflicts between the Amish and the state over these and other issues.

30. In the Amish community near Shipshewana, Indiana, some Amish factory

workers are beginning to receive Social Security benefits upon their retirement. This significant departure from the traditional Amish boycott of Social Security is creating lively discussion.

31. The formation, history, and work of the National Amish Steering Committee is told by Olshan (1993).

32. On the role that outsiders often play in assisting the Amish in legal matters, see Kidder (1993).

33. Keim (1993) traces the experience of Amish conscientious objectors in the American context from the Revolutionary War up to the present.

34. For a history of the Amish struggle with the state over education, see Meyers (1993) and Huntington (1994).

35. These included *Wisconsin v. Yoder* (1972), *United States v. Lee* (1982), and *Minnesota v. Hershberger* (1990). The court ruled in favor of the Amish in the first case and against them in the second case, which involved Social Security payments by an Amish employer. The third case, regarding the use of slow-moving-vehicle signs, was returned to the Minnesota supreme court. All of these cases are described in detail in Kraybill (1993).

36. For more extended discussions of social change in Amish communities, consult Kraybill (2001), and Kraybill and Olshan (1994).

37. Some observers estimate that about one hundred people from non-Amish backgrounds are members of either Old Order or New Order Amish congregations.

38. This pattern appears to be growing in the Lancaster settlement, based on reports of family physicians who relate to the Amish and from Amish informants themselves.

39. Some 81 percent of adult children affiliate with the church in the Elkhart-Lagrange settlement in northern Indiana. The Lancaster settlement retains more than 90 percent of its youth. In a recent article, Meyers (1994a) reports his findings from an in-depth analysis of defection patterns in the Elkhart-Lagrange settlement. He found retention rates ranging from 68 to 92 percent between 1920 and 1969. The estimate of 81 percent for the Elkhart-Lagrange settlement is based on data compiled in the *Indiana Amish Directory, Lagrange and Elkhart Counties, (Directory,* 1988a). The estimates for the Lancaster, Pennsylvania, settlement are based on a study of ten church districts conducted in 2000, as well as on numerous personal interviews (Kraybill 2001:14). In the Holmes County area of Ohio, the retention rates vary by affiliation. In the large Old Order group, about 85 percent of the youth join the church. The more conservative "Andy Weaver" people hold about 95 percent of their youth. On the other hand, the more progressive New Order community only attracts about 57 percent of its offspring. The retention data for the Holmes County settlement were derived from the *Ohio Amish Directory of Holmes County and Vicinity (Directory,* 1988b). Data

were gathered on all of the New Order Congregations and on all of the districts affiliated with the Andy Weaver group. A sample of one-third of the Old Order districts was used to generate the estimates for the Old Order group. For a comparative study of these groups and the factors influencing their retention patterns, see Kraybill (1994b). Generally speaking, the more conservative affiliations typically have higher retention rates. More progressive New Order groups permit more personal freedom and individualistic expressions of religious faith. Such openness makes it easier for youth to leave and move up the "Anabaptist escalator" by joining a more progressive Beachy Amish or Mennonite group.

40. The most thorough study of Amish youth to date has been conducted by Stevick (2000). His research into many settlements describes the struggles of Amish youth and the process by which they eventually choose to join or leave the church.

CHAPTER FIVE: THE BRETHREN

1. Benedict (1967:3–4). Even early in their development, the Brethren thought of themselves as *altung brüdern* (old Brethren), reflecting their goal of preserving the patterns and witness of the primitive (apostolic) church.

2. The primary source of information for this chapter is a series of direct observations and interviews with Old German Baptist Brethren conducted by Carl F. Bowman over a seven-year period during the 1990s. Personal interviews were conducted with Brethren from Kansas, California, Indiana, Ohio, Virginia, and Pennsylvania, many of these during Annual Meetings held in Ohio and Virginia. Old German Baptist Brethren in both states were gracious enough to invite the interviewer into their homes and religious services. Background information on the emergence of the Schwarzenau Brethren and their migration and development in America may be obtained from the following published sources: Bowman (1995); Durnbaugh (1984, 1992, 1997); Stoffer (1989); Willoughby (1999). A comprehensive record of Old German Baptist Brethren rulings and decisions is available in *Minutes* (1981). Proceedings from later years are printed separately for each year.

3. This pejorative assessment came from J. S. Flory (1932:79), president emeritus of Bridgewater College (Va.).

4. Membership data are from *The Old German Baptist Brethren Church, Directory of Officials* (2000). The estimate of total community size is based upon a ratio of 3.3 community participants per member, derived from the adjusted ratio of family members to church members in one Virginia congregation. The ratio was calibrated downward to adjust for adult married children who, though members of the family, are no longer members of the church member's household. (Before the adjustment, the ratio was 4.9 family members per church member.)

5. Membership in 1950 was less than four thousand; by the year 2000 it had exceeded six thousand. Several separations from the Old German Baptist Brethren church during the twentieth century have had a limited impact upon the size of the membership. Existing groups that have separated from the Old German Baptist Brethren include the Old Brethren (organized in 1913); Old Order German Baptist Church (organized in 1921); and Old Brethren German Baptist Church (organized in 1939). The long-term status of a group of Wisconsin Brethren who have recently withdrawn from the Old German Baptist Brethren is still uncertain.

6. Technically, Brethren are not to cooperate in obtaining a divorce. If a partner divorces them without their cooperation, then they are not held accountable. In such situations they may not remarry so long as the former partner is living.

7. Old German Baptist Brethren Hymn Book, hymn 299. Hymn quotations that follow are from this hymnal.

8. Yet Brethren never would have organized in the first place if inner awakenings were all that mattered. The founders were unhappy with the potpourri of practices endorsed by their fellow Pietists as well as their neglect of outward ordinances. Alexander Mack Sr., leader of the first Brethren, wrote that the true spirit of Christ would never guide believers into a confusion of separate voices but only into consistency, both among themselves and with the original apostles. Disheartened with what they considered a disregard for clear scriptural commands, Mack and his followers rebaptized themselves into a new fellowship based on the New Testament and modeled after the primitive church. They sought to obey Christ in all things.

9. The baptismal scriptures guiding the service are John 3:5, Mark 16:16, and Matthew 28:19.

10. 1848 Annual Meeting Minutes, Article 3.

11. The difference between the handling of "private" sins and "gross" sins is also explained. The latter are reported directly to the church.

12. See Romans 6:16, 1 Corinthians 16:20, 2 Corinthians 13:12, and 1 Thessalonians 5:26. In 1 Peter 5:14, Peter also admonished Christians to "greet one another with a kiss of charity."

13. Annual Meeting Minutes, 1974, 4.

14. The Community of True Inspiration (later known as the Amana Community) and the Moravian Church are groups from similar German Pietist roots that practice a "love feast." The Methodists, influenced by Moravians, also practiced a love feast historically, although all of these love feasts differ from the form adopted by Brethren.

15. The Brethren talk of "feetwashing" rather than "footwashing" as is the customary usage among Mennonites and Amish. The literature of Brethren and

Mennonites consistently records this distinction of spelling. Hence, to be consistent we use "feetwashing" in this chapter, but "footwashing" in the other chapters of the book.

16. Culp (1976:111–114).

17. The details in this paragraph, as well as other parts of this description of the love feast draw heavily from Fred Benedict's (1967) account of the Brethren Love Feast.

18. Benedict (1967:9).

19. At a recent dinner gathering of Old German Baptist Brethren, an outsider asked, "What was going on before the preaching when the ministers were turning to one another and commenting quietly?" The host joked that the ministers were saying, "I want to be the one to speak!" "No, me—you got to preach last time." "No, you always dominate. Let me go first." After everyone had a good laugh, the brother responded with a more serious explanation.

20. In this as in other practices, Brethren follow Scripture as their tradition illumines it. In this case they point to 1 Corinthians 11:34—"If any man hunger, let him eat at home; that ye come not together unto condemnation."

21. Benedict (1967:19).

22. Benedict (1967:23–24).

23. In addition to personal interviews and observation of two Annual Meetings by Carl F. Bowman, the following sources were also helpful in constructing this account: Miller (1973); Scott (1988); and "1993 Annual Meeting," a press release prepared by the Old German Baptist Brethren for the 1993 Annual Meeting held near Eldorado, Ohio.

24. There are about twenty-five committees involved in planning and managing the Annual Meetings. The supply figures pertain to the 1993 Annual Meeting.

25. In the words of Elder Henry Kurtz (1867), "[E]very Yearly Meeting was a solemn act of renewing our covenant, into which each one of us had entered, when we made a public confession of our faith. . . . This covenant is renewed in every communion we attend, and, as to the whole body of the church, was renewed at every Annual Meeting by the articles agreed on, signed and sealed under the most solemn sanction of the divine presence, which had been sought by the most humble prayer of all the faithful, and by the influence of the Holy Spirit had again become united and 'joined together in the same mind, and in the same judgment,'—and by celebrating a lovefeast."

26. Both quotes are from Benedict (1992:95).

27. Annual Meeting Minutes, 1992, Article 2.

28. While only men have a "voice" in the decisions of Annual Meeting, women are voiced in the decisions of local districts.

29. Regarding "voting," see the Annual Meeting minutes for 1976, article 4;

1979, article 8; and 1986, article 5. Concerning disruptions, see the statements of Standing Committee to the 1967 and 1977 Annual Meetings. See also Lester Fisher's (1976:130–35) account on Annual Meeting. The fact that sisters are denied the liberty to speak during Annual Meeting debate has sparked little controversy. In local districts they may speak when a voice is taken. Regarding women's participation, a 1967 Standing Committee statement asserted that "sisters are not given the liberty to speak upon subjects before the Meeting." Marcus Miller's (1973:90–91) nuanced rendering of the Old German Baptist decision-making process expressly rejects characterizing it as a "vote." While Stephen Scott's (1988:77) description of the Annual Meeting glosses over this particular by describing the foreman as calling "for a voice vote," this was probably an accurate rendering of what he observed. During the 1970s and 1980s, there was a great deal of procedural confusion among the German Baptists themselves regarding decision by majority vote. Since that time, unanimous consent has been solidly reaffirmed as the method for reaching decisions.

30. During the mid-1970s, for instance, some Brethren cared more about pushing their own agendas and winning "votes" than preserving unity. Among the Annual Meeting disruptions were the following: the slighting of committee responses to queries, younger Brethren asserting themselves while the elderly remained silent, giving harsh and inflammatory speeches, shouting when a voice was taken in order to win, and refusing to submit when the will of the body was clear. Brethren had to be reminded repeatedly that Annual Meeting's purpose was unity, not personal agendas. Despite the fact that a 1976 request to settle outcomes by a show of hands was rejected, a 1986 query suggests that majority rule was indeed employed to reach difficult decisions during the early 1980s. Since that time, the procedure of unanimous consent has been more consistently applied, though its implementation remains a challenge.

31. See Annual Meeting Minutes for 1925, article 1; 1943, article 2; 1946, article 2; 1975, article 4.

32. See Annual Meeting Minutes for 1977, article 4; 1978, article 3; and 1994, article 5.

33. Annual Meeting Minutes, 1988, article 3.

34. Annual Meeting Minutes, 1992, article 1.

35. Annual Meeting Minutes, 1994, article 3. This decision maintained the stipulation that "if a computer is used for entertainment purposes, the user should fall into the hands of the Church." In 1993 some Brethren discovered that they had unwittingly become software pirates. "Many of our members have become involved in this practice unaware that it is illegal." Annual Meeting counseled that all members should learn the conditions of their license agreements and abide by them (Annual Meeting Minutes, 1993, article 3).

36. See Annual Meeting Minutes for 1941, article 2 and 1953, article 1.

37. See Annual Meeting Minutes for 1957, article 1 and 1959, article 5. See also the Labor Relations Committee reports to the 1956–59 Annual Meetings.

38. Annual Meeting Minutes for 1961, article 2.

39. Annual Meeting Minutes for 1990, article 11. See also article 2 on participation in *Open Doors*.

40. Annual Meeting Minutes for 1994, article 10.

41. *The Brethren's Reasons* is a doctrinal statement outlining the Old German Baptists' motives for separating from the main body of Brethren. It offers this description of their order of dress: "*Resolved . . .* that we strictly adhere to a plain and decent uniformity of dress as soldiers of King Immanuel; that the brethren wear a plain, round-breasted coat with standing collar, hat, overcoat, and everything else to correspond. A plain way of wearing the hair and beard—no fashionable mustaches and no roached or shingled hair. The sisters also to wear a plain, modest dress and bonnet, also a plain white cap in time of worship or on going abroad; in short, that the brethren and sisters let their light shine as a light on a 'candlestick,' and not part or wholly under the 'bushel,' but to show the world that we try to possess what we profess." (Annual Meeting Minutes 1981, Appendix, 39).

42. See the Annual Meeting Minutes, 1921, 4; 1949, 2 and 5; 1953, 4; 1963, 1; 1965, 2 and 4; 1971, 2; 1976, 1; 1990, 5; and 1991, 4.

43. *Doctrinal Treatise: Old German Baptist Brethren* (Covington, Ohio: The Vindicator, 1980), 48.

44. Annual Meeting Minutes, 1950, 3.

45. These excerpts from Annual Meeting Minutes of the 1990s are illustrative of recent differences regarding the exercise of church authority and discipline.

Chapter Six: Common Convictions

1. At baptism, Brethren candidates pledge to follow the instruction of Matthew 18 and agree to hear and obey the authority of the church rather than the specific rules of the *Ordnung*.

2. The Brethren also shunned excommunicated members in earlier years, but they have not practiced shunning in recent decades.

3. Cronk (1977, 1981) has done the seminal work on the significance of *Gelassenheit* in Old Order communities. The actual word *Gelassenheit* appears most frequently in the early Hutterite literature. The word itself is rarely found in the literature or vocabulary of the other groups, but its conceptual meaning is widespread among all four groups. Kraybill (2001) used it to interpret Amish culture in his study of the Lancaster, Pennsylvania, settlement. See also Klaassen (1991).

4. In the words of one martyr, Michael Sattler, "Christians are fully yielded

and have placed their trust in their Father in heaven without any outward or worldly arms" (J. H. Yoder 1973:23). Such self-abandonment for the sake of God's kingdom was the very heart of *Gelassenheit.*

5. "Demut ist die schönste Tugne" appears in *Unpartheyisches Gesangbuch,* p. 149. English translation by Amos B. Hoover.

6. These phrases come from Scripture passages in Roman 12:2, 1 John 2:15, 2 Corinthians 6:17–18, and 2 Corinthians 6:14 respectively. Other passages that are sometimes cited as well include John 17:14–15, James 1:27, 1 Peter 2:9, James 4:4, and Titus 2:14.

7. The exceptions to this are some Brethren and Amish entrepreneurs whose business involvements place them in bureaucratic settings. Those who work as day laborers in factories also experience the culture of bureaucracy. But within the community, bureaucracy is missing.

8. In more progressive Amish communities, some Amish business people have joined partnerships and corporations controlled by non-Amish. Sometimes controlling interest is given to trustworthy outsiders so that the company is free from church restrictions on the ownership of telephones, computers, and motor vehicles. Likewise in the more progressive Amish communities, some members hold commercial insurance policies, albeit discreetly.

9. Cronk (1977, 1981) provides a probing discussion of work as a ritual of *Gelassenheit* in Old Order communities.

10. For an engaging treatment of the significance of dress in modern culture, see the recent work of Rubinstein (1995).

11. This restriction is one of several publication guidelines that appears in *Die Botschaft,* a widely circulated newspaper published in Lancaster, Pennsylvania, and read by Old Order Amish and Mennonites across North America.

12. The most conservative Amish groups rarely use telephones except for emergencies. In an interesting study, Umble (1996) traces Old Order resistance to the telephone in eastern Pennsylvania.

13. Scott (1988) describes a variety of rituals—weddings, baptisms, ordinations, funerals, and worship services—in Old Order communities across North America.

14. Although each Brethren congregation observes only one Love Feast a year, many Brethren also attend the Love Feasts of other congregations and hence participate in several of these rituals each year.

15. While Old Order ritual is most pronounced in the area of worship, it also flourishes in the smaller routines of life, such as having guests to dinner. There is no manual for proper dining, yet it flows the same way time after time. The Old Orders invariably get it right. Among Brethren, Mennonites, and Amish, the hosts sit at one end of the table with the guests arranged by seniority along the sides and the younger adults or children at the other end. At the start of the

meal in a Mennonite home, the foods are placed on the table including the dessert (cake and/or fruit), which typically sits at the end opposite the hosts. The male host leads in prayer (or asks a visiting minister to do so), then the hostess takes charge. First she directs that the bread be passed, then the butter, then the home-made jam or apple butter, then the main dishes, all in the same direction. Rather than requesting food to be passed when they are ready for seconds, guests wait. The hostess monitors the situation and sends everything around in the same or-derly sequence when the time is right. Eventually she instructs someone to pass the dessert, which all have been eyeing. Throughout the meal conversation is punctuated by comfortable moments of silence. The oldest take the lead in con-versation; younger persons wait until spoken to. After the meal men move to the living room, and women remain to clean up the dishes. Taking advantage of the absent males, they visit freely while completing their tasks. Afterward, they re-join the men in the living room.

16. These characteristics of religious ritual are not necessarily distinctive to Old Order Anabaptist groups. Similar ritual patterns and themes, albeit with dif-ferent symbols and meaning, are found in some Protestant as well as some Catholic churches.

17. This was the view reported in "Disciplining and Reconciling," a paper approved by the Church of the Brethren Conference in 1976.

18. These comments on the reflexivity of modernity are based on Giddens' (1990:37–40) discussion of the concept.

19. The Brethren also describe themselves as "primitive Christians," believ-ers who seek to emulate the "primitive" apostolic church as described in the book of Acts.

Chapter Seven: Four Roads to Heaven

1. We are indebted to Boldt (1978) for the notion of structural tightness in his analysis of the Hutterites.

2. For a history of Amish conflicts with the state, see Kraybill (1993).

3. Consult Olshan (1994) for an extended discussion of this point.

4. In the more progressive Amish communities, some families use their car-riages primarily on Sunday and on other holidays. Business owners and some families are highly dependent on hired motor vehicles (with drivers) for daily transportation beyond their immediate community.

5. All the groups frown on owning and using cameras except the Brethren, who dropped the taboo in 1977.

6. The Groffdale Mennonite Conference, which meets in the fall and spring, in some ways approximates the Brethren Annual Meeting, but the Mennonite gathering does not involve lay members. It only lasts for a day and does not focus on fellowship and worship as does the Brethren Annual Meeting.

7. The Old German Baptist Brethren formed in 1881 after English had been adopted by the main body of German Baptist Brethren. Thus, like the Old Order Mennonites of Virginia, the Brethren had dropped the Germanic dialect before the Old Order group was formed.

8. Electricity has been installed in a few Mennonite meetinghouses to operate fans for ventilation or furnaces, but not to operate lights.

9. Amishman Samuel Stoltzfus writing in *Die Botschaft*, 29 July 1998, 25.

10. The specified Scripture readings for each Sunday as well as a directory of ministers and congregational districts are printed annually in *The New American Almanac* published by Ben J. Raber in Baltic, Ohio.

11. There are a few minor variations in these practices among the Old Order Amish. In several settlements tractors are used in the field. Among New Order Amish groups these practices vary considerably and tend to be less traditional.

12. In some settlements in Ohio and Indiana, the practice of working in larger factories that are operated by outsiders is an exception to the pattern of working within Amish-owned businesses. See Meyers (1994b) for a discussion of Amish employment in large factories in the Elkhart-Lagrange settlement of Indiana.

13. The English-speaking Old Order Mennonites of Virginia confirm this observation as well.

Chapter Eight: Preserving a Pilgrim People

1. This does not mean that New Order groups have to be present to maintain Old Order Amish identities, but it does mean that group boundaries and identities are reinforced when both affiliations live within close proximity.

2. Bourdieu (1977:72) defines *habitus* as "systems of durable, transposable dispositions" that, shaped by socialization, influence actors to respond in habitual ways and yet with freedom to improvise in particular situations. Swartz (1997) clarifies and summarizes the concept of *habitus* as, "a set of deeply internalized master dispositions that generate action. They point toward a theory of action that is practical rather than discursive, prereflective rather than conscious, embodied as well as cognitive, durable though adaptive, reproductive though generative and inventive, and the product of particular social conditions though transposable to others." *Gelassenheit* in many ways is a master disposition, a *habitus* of Old Order life. For helpful interpretations of Bourdieu, see Calhoun, LiPuma, and Postone (1993); Lemert (1997); and Swartz (1997).

3. Giddens 1990.

4. For a discussion of the process of social change and the factors that regulate the inclusion and rejection of items in the *Ordnung* of Amish communities, see Kraybill (2001 and 1994a).

5. For extended discussions of the perplexing puzzles created by social change in Amish society, see Kraybill (2001, 1994a, and 1998a).

6. The story and possible consequences of this far-reaching occupational transformation in Amish society is told by Kraybill and Nolt (1995).

Chapter Nine: Ironies of a Postmodern Journey

Epigraph: In July 1999 *Playboy* Magazine listed the following five "favorite Amish summer pastimes": (1) Drinking molasses till you heave, (2) Blowing past Dairy Queen on a bitchin' Clydesdale, (3) Sleeping till six A.M., (4) Driving to Reading and kicking some Mennonite butt, (5) Drinking buttermilk keggers. These were likely adopted from David Letterman's "Top Ten Amish Spring Break Activities," published by Letterman (1991). *Playboy*'s interest in the Amish reflects the popular consumption of Amish images in the contemporary culture market. David Letterman also offered "Top Ten Signs Your Amish Teen is in Trouble" on his *Late Show* on 24 June 1998, following the national publicity on the arrests of two Amish boys for trafficking in cocaine in Lancaster County.

1. See Stevick (2000) for an in-depth study of the social world of Amish youth.

2. These phrases come from 2 Corinthians 6:17.

3. Kraybill (1994c: 32–33) provides an elaboration of this key point that the social forces of modernity—specialization, discontinuity, mobility, and individualism—threatened to fragment the solidarity of close knit Old Order communities. It was in this sense that modernity, alias "the world" was perceived as a Great Separator.

4. Jokes and stories in the more progressive Mennonite communities, for example, sometimes belittled the perceived provincialism and naiveté of the Amish.

5. Bellah et al. (1985:56–62) makes this argument in *Habits of the Heart*.

6. The history of "Amish" tourism is told by Luthy (1994b).

7. David Weaver-Zercher, in personal communication dated 29 August 1999, notes that if other Anabaptists are showing more respect for the Amish it may not necessarily result from a disenchantment with modernity. Another explanation may be that when mainstream Anabaptists were closer to, but moving away from, traditional practices, they may have found it psychologically necessary to ridicule what they were leaving. That may no longer be the case as they become more socially distant.

8. The article, "Look Who's Talking," written by Howard Rheingold, appeared in the January 1999 issue of *Wired* magazine.

9. Umble (1996) charts the history of the controversy over telephones in Old Order Amish and Mennonite committees.

10. The most creative and significant study of this topic has been completed by David Weaver-Zercher (1997, 1999, 2001). He explores the discovery and domestication of the Old Order Amish and shows how non-Amish interpreters present and interpret representations of the Amish to the larger public. Representations—symbols and images—of the Amish are bought and sold, in essence

traded in the public culture market. From food and crafts to films and software, from advertising images in *Vogue* to jokes by late night comedians, Amish images are traded in the culture market. Luthy (1994c) also provides an interesting history of various products that have been used to market the Amish.

11. The Amish have clearly received the most public notoriety on the culture market in the twentieth century. However, in recent years more attention has been given to the Hutterites, as exemplified by cookbooks, a color photography book (S. Hofer 1998) and other products distributed by Hofer Publishers, a firm operated by Samuel Hofer, an ex-Hutterite. Two recent photographic presentations of the Old Order Mennonites in Canada (Kenna 1995 and Hiebert 1998) suggest a growing interest by the culture market in Old Order Mennonite images. The Brethren enjoyed a multipage spread with many color photographs in a feature story in the *Roanoke Times* (Roanoke, Va.) that ran for three days, 8–10 November 1998. Titled "The German Baptist: A Simple Way of Life," the series was written by Holly Roberson with photographs by Kelly Hahn Johnson. Many of the photographs appear in this book.

12. See the August 1993 issue of *Vogue* magazine.

13. There are clearly some occasions of sexual abuse in Old Order communities. No systematic research has been conducted on the topic, so it is difficult to identify rates or trends or make accurate comparisons with other groups. Counselors in local areas that provide services to Old Order people occasionally provide anecdotal evidence of abuse. In 1997 ABC television's *20/20* program featured a sensationalized interpretation of sexual abuse and domestic breakup in an Ohio Amish family and essentially argued that "the Amish are just like the rest of us." In 1998 sexual abuse perpetuated by several men in a Hutterite colony in Alberta received media attention.

14. This hour-long program on the roots of happiness that included a short segment on the Amish was aired by ABC on 15 April 1996.

Selected References

This listing of selected references includes references cited by the authors in the notes as well as other select works related to the four groups. Bibliographic information for some sources—interviews, newsletters, local newspapers—not appearing in this list are provided in the notes.

Baer, Hans A.
  1976 "The Effect of Technological Innovation on Hutterite Culture." *Plains Anthropologist* 21 (72):187–98.
Beiler, Joseph F.
  1982 "Ordnung." *Mennonite Quarterly Review* 56 (October): 482.
Bellah, R. N., R. Madsen, W. M. Sullivan, A. Swindler, and S. M. Tipton.
  1985 *Habits of the Heart: Individualism and Commitment in American Life.* Berkeley: University of California Press.
Benedict, Fred W.
  1967 "A Brief Account of the Origin and a Description of the Brethren Love Feast." Pendleton, Ind.: Old Brotherhood Publishers.
  1992 "The Old Order Brethren in Transition." In *Brethren in Transition,* edited by Emmert F. Bittinger. Camden, Maine: Penobscot Press.
Bennett, John W.
  1967 *Hutterite Brethren.* Stanford, Calif.: Stanford University Press.
Benowitz, Jean-Paul
  1993 "The Old Order Mennonite Division of 1893: An Interpretation." *Pennsylvania Mennonite Heritage* 16 (October): 14–17.
Blackboard Bulletin
  1957– Aylmer, Ont.: Pathway Publishers. Monthly periodical published for Old Order Amish and Mennonite teachers.

Boldt, Edward D.

  1978 "Structural Tightness, Autonomy, and Observability: An Analysis of
       Hutterite Conformity and Orderliness." *Canadian Journal of Sociol-
       ogy* 3(3): 349–63.

  1983 "The Recent Development of a Unique Population: The Hutterites of
       North America." *Prairie Forum* 8(2): 235–40.

  1989 "The Hutterites: Current Developments and Future Prospects." In
       Multiculturalism and Intergroup Relations, edited by James S. Frieder.
       New York: Greenwood Press.

Boldt, Edward D., and Lance W. Roberts

  1980 "The Decline of Hutterite Population Growth: Causes and Conse-
       quences—A Comment." *Canadian Ethnic Studies* 12(3): 111–17.

Bourdieu, Pierre

  1977 *Outline of a Theory of Practice.* Cambridge: University of Cambridge
       Press.

Bowman, Carl F.

  1995 *Brethren Society: The Cultural Transformation of a Peculiar People.*
       Baltimore: Johns Hopkins University Press.

The Brethren Encyclopedia

  1983-84 Vols. 1–3. Philadelphia: Brethren Encyclopedia, Inc.

Brubacher, Paul H.

  1984 "Dimensions of Social Interaction Between Old Order Mennonites
       and Non-Mennonites in the Mount Forest Area." Master's thesis, Uni-
       versity of Guelph.

Burkholder, L. J.

  1986 *A Brief History of the Mennonites in Ontario.* Altoona, Manitoba:
       Friesen Printers.

Calhoun, Craig, Edward LiPuma, and Moishe Postone

  1993 *Bourdieu: Critical Perspectives.* Chicago: University of Chicago Press.

Chronicle of the Hutterian Brethren.

  1987 Vol. 1. Edited and translated by the Hutterite Brethren. Rifton, N.Y.:
       Plough Publishing House.

  1998 Vol. 2. Edited and translated by the Hutterite Brethren. Crystal Spring
       Colony: St. Agathe, Manitoba.

Church of the Brethren Yearbook

  2000 Elgin, Ill.: Brethren Press.

*Confession of Faith of the Mennonites: Church Forms and Guidelines of the
Weaverland Conference*

  1996 Weaverland Conference: Lancaster, Pa.

Cronk, Sandra L.

  1977 "Gelassenheit: The Rites of the Redemptive Process in Old Order

Amish and Old Order Mennonite Communities." Ph.D. diss., University of Chicago.

    1981 "Gelassenheit: The Rites of the Redemptive Process in Old Order Amish and Old Order Mennonite Communities." *Mennonite Quarterly Review* 55(1): 544.

Culp, Lynn E.

    1976 "Solemn Promises." *The Vindicator* 107 (April):111–14.

Decker, John Sr.

    n.d. *What Is to Be Gained or Lost.* Olivet, S.Dak.: Wolf Creek Hutterian Brethren.

Dewalt, Mark W., and Bonnie K. Troxell

    1989 "Old Order Mennonite One-Room School: A Case Study." *Anthropology and Education Quarterly* 20:308–25.

Directory of the Families of the Old Order Mennonite Church in Ontario.

    1993 Heidelberg, Ont.: Edwin Weber.

Directory of the Groffdale Conference Mennonite Churches.

    1992 2d ed. Kutztown, Pa.: Laura N. Shirk.

    1997 3d ed. Kutztown, Pa.: Laura N. Shirk.

Directory of the Indiana Amish of Lagrange and Elkhart Counties

    1988a Middlebury, Ind.: Jerry E. Miller.

Directory of the Lancaster County Amish

    1996 Vols. 1 and 2. Gordonville, Pa.: Pequea Publishers.

Directory of Officials of the Old German Baptist Brethren

    2000 Covington, Ohio: Miami Valley Press.

Directory of the Ohio Amish of Holmes County and Vicinity

    1988b Millersburg, Ohio: Ohio Amish Directory, Inc.

Directory of the Weaverland Conference Mennonite Churches

    1995 Womelsdorf, Pa.: Ruth Ann Wise.

Doctrinal Treatise: Old German Baptist Brethren

    1980 Covington, Ohio: The Vindicator.

Dorsten, Linda

    1992 "Direct and Indirect Effects on Infant Mortality in a Traditional Religious-Ethnic Population." Paper presented at the North Central Sociological Association Annual Meetings, 26 April, Ft. Wayne, Indiana.

Driedger, Leo

    1995 "The Hutterites." In *The Peoples of Canada: An Encyclopedia for the Country.* Toronto: University of Toronto Press.

Durnbaugh, Donald F.

    1984 *Meet the Brethren.* Elgin, Ill.: Brethren Press.

    1992 *Brethren Beginnings: The Origin of the Church of the Brethren in Early Eighteenth-Century Europe.* Philadelphia: Brethren Encyclopedia.

1997 *Fruit of the Vine: A History of the Brethren 1708–1995.* Elgin, Ill.: Brethren Press.

Dyck, Cornelius J.

1993 *An Introduction to Mennonite History: A Popular History of the Anabaptists and the Mennonites.* 3d ed. Scottdale, Pa.: Herald Press.

1985 "The Suffering Church in Anabaptism." *Mennonite Quarterly Review* 59 (January): 523.

Eaton, Joseph W.

1952 "Controlled Acculturation: A Survival Technique of the Hutterites." *American Sociological Review* 17:331–40.

Ehrenpreis, Andreas

1978 *Brotherly Community the Highest Command of Love.* Rifton, N.Y.: Plough Publishing House.

Fisher, Lester

1976 "Annual Meeting: The Spirit of Unity." *The Vindicator* 107 (May):130–35.

Flint, David

1975 *The Hutterites: A Study in Prejudice.* Toronto: Oxford University Press.

Flory, J. S.

1932 *Flashlights From History: A Brief Study in Social Development.* Elgin, Ill: Brethren Publishing House.

Fretz, J. Winfield

1989 *The Waterloo Mennonites.* Waterloo, Ont.: Wilfred Laurier University Press.

Friedmann, Robert

1961 *Hutterite Studies.* Goshen, Ind.: Mennonite Historical Society.

Friesen, John J.

1999 Ed. and trans. *Peter Riedemann's Hutterite Confession of Faith.* Scottdale, Pa.: Herald Press.

Friesen, John W.

1977 *People, Culture, and Learning.* Calgary, Alberta: Detselig Enterprises Limited.

Garrett, Ottie A.

1998 *True Stories of the X-Amish.* Horse Cave, Ky.: New Leben.

Giddens, Anthony

1990 *The Consequences of Modernity.* Stanford, Calif.: Stanford University Press.

Goering, Orlando J.

1993 "Leaving the Colony." Paper presented to the 20th Annual Communal Studies Association, New Harmony, Ind., 14–17 October.

Groffdale Conference Calendar of Meetings.
    1999 Lancaster, Pa.: Groffdale Conference.
Gross, Leonard
    1998 *The Golden Years of the Hutterites,* rev. ed. Kitchener, Ont.: Pandora
        Press.
Harrison, Wes
    1997 *Andreas Ehrenpreis and Hutterite Faith and Practice.* Scottdale, Pa.:
        Herald Press.
Hartse, Caroline Marie
    1993 "On The Colony: Social and Religious Change Among Contemporary
        Hutterites." Ph.D. diss., University of New Mexico.
    1994 "The Emotional Acculturation of Hutterite Defectors." *Journal of
        Anthropological Research* 50: 69–85
    1995 "Social and Religious Change Among Contemporary Hutterites." *Folk*
        36: 109–30.
Hiebert, Carl
    1998 *Us Little People: Mennonite Children.* Toronto: Boston Mills Press.
History of the Hutterite Mennonites.
    1974 Freeman, S.Dak.: Hutterite Mennonite Centennial.
Hofer, John
    1988 *The History of the Hutterites,* rev. ed. Altona, Man.: D. W. Friesen &
        Sons.
Hofer, Peter
    1973 *The Hutterian Brethren and Their Beliefs.* Starbuck, Man.: The Hut-
        terian Brethren of Manitoba.
Hofer, Samuel
    1991 *Born Hutterite.* Saskatoon, Sask.: Hofer Publishing.
    1998 *The Hutterites: Lives and Images of a Communal People.* Saskatoon,
        Sask.: Hofer Publishers.
Holzach, Michael
    1993 *The Forgotten People.* Translated by Steven Goertz. Sioux Falls, S.Dak.:
        Ex Machina.
Hoover, Amos B.
    1982 Comp. *The Jonas Martin Era 1875–1925.* Denver, Pa.: Muddy Creek
        Farm Library.
Hoover, Amos B., David L. Miller, and Leonard Freeman
    1978 "The Old Order Mennonites." In *Mennonite World Handbook.* Carol
        Stream, Ill.: Mennonite World Conference.
Hoover, John David
    1990 "An Old Order Mennonite Wedding Ceremony in Pennsylvania."
        Pennsylvania Mennonite Heritage, 13 July, p. 1.

Horst, Irvin B.

    1988 Ed. and trans. *Mennonite Confession of Faith*. Lancaster, Pa.: Lancaster Mennonite Historical Society. Adopted by the Mennonites in Dordrecht, Holland, 1 April 1632.

Horst, Isaac R.

    1979 *Up the Conestoga*. Mount Forest, Ont.: Isaac R. Horst.

    1983a *Separate and Peculiar*. Mount Forest, Ont.: Isaac R. Horst.

    1983b *Thou Art Peter*. Mount Forest, Ont.: Isaac R. Horst.

    1985 *Why, Grossdaudy?* Mount Forest, Ont.: Isaac R. Horst.

    1989 "Introducing the Old Order Mennonites." *Mennonite Reporter*, 9 January.

    1990 "Our Deprived Children." *Family Life* (April).

    1991 "Old Order Youth Prepare to Join the Church." *Mennonite Reporter*, 18 February.

    1993 "The Role of Women." *Family Life* (November).

    2000 *A Separate People*. Scottdale, Pa.: Herald Press.

Horst, Mary Ann

    1992 *My Old Order Mennonite Heritage*. Kitchener, Ont.: Pennsylvania Dutch Crafts and Local Books.

Hostetler, Beulah Stauffer

    1992 "The Formation of the Old Orders." *Mennonite Quarterly Review* 66 (1): 5–25.

Hostetler, John A.

    1965 *Education and Marginality in the Communal Society of the Hutterites*. Final Research Report. University Park, Pa.: Pennsylvania State University.

    1993 *Amish Society*, 4th ed. Baltimore: Johns Hopkins University Press.

    1997 *Hutterite Society*, 2d ed. Baltimore: Johns Hopkins University Press.

Hostetler, John A., and Gertrude E. Huntington

    1992 *Amish Children: Education in the Family, School, and Community*, 2d ed. Fort Worth, Tex.: Harcourt Brace Jovanovich.

    1996 *The Hutterites in North America*, 3d ed. Philadelphia: Holt, Rinehart and Winston.

Hostetler, John A., Leonard Gross, and Elizabeth Bender

    1975 *Selected Hutterian Documents in Translation: 1542–1654*. Unpublished compilation. Philadelphia: Communal Studies Center, Temple University.

Hostetter, C. Nelson

    1997 Comp. *Anabaptist-Mennonites Nationwide USA*. Morgantown, Pa.: Masthof Press.

Huntington, Gertrude Enders

    1992 "Recent Developments Among the Hutterites." Paper presented at the Nineteenth Annual Communal Studies Conference, Navoo, Illinois, October.

    1994 "Persistence and Change in Amish Education." In *The Amish Struggle with Modernity,* ed. Donald B. Kraybill and Marc A. Olshan. Hanover: University Press of New England.

    1995 "A Separate Culture: Hutterite Women Within the Colony." Paper presented at Millersville University, Millersville, Pennsylvania, June 10.

    1996 "Age, Gender, and Influence in Hutterite Colonies." *Communities* 90 (Spring): 24–27.

Hurd, James P.

    1999 "Keeping Faith: The Groffdale Horse-and-Buggy Mennonites." Unpublished manuscript.

Hutter, Jakob

    1979 *Brotherly Faithfulness.* Rifton, N.Y.: Plough Publishing House.

Hutterite Roots.

    1985 Freeman, S.Dak.: Hutterite Mennonite Centennial.

Hutterite Telephone and Address Book

    2000 Cranford, Alberta: J. Wipt.

Janzen, Rod A.

    1999 *The Prairie People: Forgotten Anabaptists.* Hanover: University Press of New England.

Janzen, William

    1990 *Limits on Liberty.* Toronto: University of Toronto Press.

Jeschke, Marlin

    1994 "The Church Discipline Case Among the Hutterites of Manitoba." Paper presented to Mennonite Historical Society, 24 May, Goshen, Indiana.

Juhnke, James C.

    1989 *Vision, Doctrine, War.* Vol. 3 of *The Mennonite Experience in America.* Scottdale, Pa.: Herald Press.

Keim, Albert N.

    1975 Ed. *Compulsory Education and the Amish: The Right Not to Be Modern.* Boston: Beacon Press.

    1993 "Military Service and Conscription." In *The Amish and the State,* ed. Donald B. Kraybill. Baltimore: Johns Hopkins University Press.

Kenna, Kathleen

    1995 *A People Apart.* Boston: Houghton Mifflin.

Kidder, Robert L.

    1993 "The Role of Outsiders." In *The Amish and the State,* ed. Donald B. Kraybill. Baltimore: Johns Hopkins University Press.

Klaassen, Walter

    1981 Ed. *Anabaptism in Outline: Selected Primary Sources.* Scottdale, Pa.: Herald Press.

    1991 "Gelassenheit and Creation." *Conrad Grebel Review* 7:23–35.

Kleinsasser, Samuel

    1994 "The Purpose and Goal of the German School." Unpublished paper.

Klimuska, Ed

    1993 "Old Order Lancaster County." Tabloid reprint of a series of six articles. Lancaster, Pa.: *Lancaster New Era.*

Kline, Edward A., and Monroe L. Beachy

    1998 "History and Dynamics of the New Order Amish of Holmes County, Ohio." *Old Order Notes* (Fall-Winter): 7–20.

Kraybill, Donald B.

    1993 Ed. *The Amish and the State.* Baltimore: Johns Hopkins University Press.

    1994a "War Against Progress: Coping with Social Change." In *The Amish Struggle with Modernity,* ed. Donald B. Kraybill and Marc A. Olshan. Hanover: University Press of New England.

    1994b "Plotting Social Change Across Four Affiliations." In *The Amish Struggle with Modernity,* ed. Donald B. Kraybill and Marc A. Olshan. Hanover: University Press of New England.

    1994c "The Amish Encounter with Modernity." In *The Amish Struggle with Modernity,* ed. Donald B. Kraybill and Marc A. Olshan. Hanover: University Press of New England.

    1998a *The Puzzles of Amish Life,* rev. ed. Intercourse, Pa: Good Books.

    1998b "Plain Reservations: Amish and Mennonite Views of Media and Computers." *Journal of Mass Media Ethics* 13(2): 98–110.

    2001 *The Riddle of Amish Culture,* 2d ed. Baltimore: Johns Hopkins University Press.

Kraybill, Donald B., and Steven M. Nolt

    1994 "The Rise of Microenterprises." In *The Amish Struggle with Modernity,* ed. Donald B. Kraybill and Marc A. Olshan. Hanover: University Press of New England.

    1995 *Amish Enterprise: From Plows to Profits.* Baltimore: Johns Hopkins University Press.

Kraybill, Donald B., and Marc A. Olshan

    1994 Ed. *The Amish Struggle with Modernity.* Hanover, N.H.: University Press of New England.

Kreps, George M., Martha W. Kreps, and Joseph Donnermeyer

1992 "The Shifting Occupational Roles of the Amish in Ohio." Paper presented at fifty-fifth annual meeting of the Rural Sociological Society, Pennsylvania State University.

Kurtz, Henry

1867 *The Brethren's Encyclopedia Containing the United Counsels and Conclusions of the Brethren at Their Annual Meetings.* Columbiana, Ohio: Henry Kurtz.

Labi, Nadya

1998 "Amiss Among the Amish." *Time,* 29 June.

Lapp, Christ S.

1991 *Pennsylvania School History, 1690–1990.* Elverson, Pa.: Mennonite Family History.

Lambach, Ruth Baer

1993 "Colony Girl: A Hutterite Childhood." In *Women in Spiritual Communitarian Societies in the United States,* ed. Wendy E. Chmielewski. Syracuse: Syracuse University Press.

Lee, Daniel Blair

1995 "Black Hats and White Bonnets: Religious Ritual and Belief Among Weaverland Conference Mennonites." Ph.D. diss., Syracuse University.

Lemert, Charles C.

1997 *Social Things: An Introduction to the Sociological Life.* Lanham, Md.: Rowman and Littlefield.

Lipset, Seymour Martin

1996 *American Exceptionalism: A Double-Edged Sword.* New York: W. W. Norton.

Loewen, Harry, and Steven M. Nolt

1996 *Through Fire and Water: An Overview of Mennonite History.* Scottdale, Pa.: Herald Press.

Luthy, David

1992 "Amish Settlements Across America: 1991." *Family Life* 25 (April): 19–24.

1994a "Amish Migration Patterns: 1972–1992." In *The Amish Struggle with Modernity,* ed. Donald B. Kraybill and Marc A. Olshan. Hanover: University Press of New England.

1994b "The Origin and Growth of Amish Tourism." In *The Amish Struggle with Modernity,* ed. Donald B. Kraybill and Marc A. Olshan. Hanover, N.H.: University Press of New England.

1994c "Marketing the Amish." *Family Life* 27 (January): 20–23.

1997 "Amish Settlements Across America: 1996." *Family Life* 30 (May): 20–24.

Martin, Raymond S., and Elizabeth S. Martin

    1985 *Bishop Jonas H. Martin.* Baltimore: Gateway Press.

Mennonite Church Information 2000

    2000 Harrisonburg, Va.: Christian Light Publications.

Mennonite Directory 2000

    2000 Scottdale, Pa.: Herald Press.

Mennonite Encyclopedia: A Comprehensive Reference Work on the Anabaptist-Mennonite Movement

    1955–59 Vols. 1–4. Hillsboro, Kans.: Mennonite Brethren Publishing House; Newton, Kans.: Mennonite Publication Office; Scottdale, Pa.: Mennonite Publishing House.

    1990 Vol. 5. Scottdale, Pa.: Herald Press.

Meyers, Thomas J.

    1993 "Education and Schooling." In *The Amish and the State,* ed. Donald B. Kraybill. Baltimore: Johns Hopkins University Press.

    1994a "The Old Order Amish: To Remain in the Faith or to Leave." *Mennonite Quarterly Review* 68(3): 378–95.

    1994b "Lunch Pails and Factories." In *The Amish Struggle with Modernity,* ed. Donald B. Kraybill and Marc A. Olshan. Hanover, N.H.: University Press of New England.

Miller, Marcus

    1973 *Roots by the River. The History, Doctrine, and Practice of the Old German Baptist Brethren in Miami County, Ohio.* Piqua, Ohio: Hammer Graphics.

Minutes of the Annual Meetings of the Old German Baptist Brethren from 1778 to 1955 and Appendix.

    1981 Winona Lake, Ind.: BMH Printing.

Nolt, Steven M.

    1992a "The Mennonite Eclipse." *Festival Quarterly* 19 (Summer): 8–12.

    1992b *A History of the Amish.* Intercourse, Pa.: Good Books.

    1999 "Plain People and the Refinement of America." *Mennonite Historical Bulletin* 60 (October): 1–11.

"Old Order Mennonites"

    1955 *Mennonite Encyclopedia* 4:47–49.

    1990 *Mennonite Encyclopedia* 5:654–55.

Olshan, Marc A.

    1993 "The National Amish Steering Committee." In *The Amish and the State,* ed. Donald B. Kraybill. Baltimore: Johns Hopkins University Press.

    1994 "Amish Cottage Industries as Trojan Horse." In *The Amish Struggle with Modernity*, ed. Donald B. Kraybill and Marc A. Olshan. Hanover, N.H.: University Press of New England.

Olshan, Marc A., and Kimberly D. Schmidt

1994 "Amish Women and the Feminist Conundrum." In *The Amish Struggle with Modernity*, ed. Donald B. Kraybill and Marc A. Olshan. Hanover, N.H.: University Press of New England.

Packull, Werner O.

1995 *Hutterite Beginnings: Communitarian Experiments During the Reformation.* Baltimore: Johns Hopkins University Press.

Peter, Karl A.

1987 *The Dynamics of Hutterian Society.* Edmonton, Alta: University of Alberta Press.

Peter, Karl A., Edward D. Boldt, Ian Whitaker, and Lance W. Roberts

1982 "The Dynamics of Religious Defection Among Hutterites." *Journal for the Scientific Study of Religion* 21(4): 327–37.

Peters, John F.

1987 "Socialization Among the Old Order Mennonites." *International Journal of Comparative Sociology* 28(3–4): 211–23.

1994 "Old Order Mennonite Economics." In *Anabaptist/Mennonite Faith and Economics*, ed. Calvin Redekop, Victor A. Krahn, and Samuel J. Steiner. Lanham, Md.: University Press of America.

2000 "The Old Order Mennonites: Application of Family Life Cycle Stages." In *Maintaining Our Differences: Minority Families Within Multicultural Societies*, ed. C Harvey. London: Ashgate Publishing.

Peters, Victor

1965 *All Things Common.* New York: Harper and Row.

Pickering, W. S. F.

1982 *The Hutterites.* London: Ward Lock Educational.

Plain Communities Business Exchange

1993— Lampeter, Pa.: Moses B. Glick.

Putnam, Robert

1995 "Bowling Alone: America's Declining Social Capital." *Journal of Democracy* 6:65–78.

2000 *Bowling Alone: The Collapse and Revival of American Community.* New York: Simon and Schuster.

Raber, Ben J.

1970— Comp. *The New American Almanac.* Published annually by Ben J. Raber, Baltic, Ohio. Gordonville, Pa.: Gordonville Print Shop. The earlier almanac, in German, *De Neue Amerikanische Kalender*, dates back to 1930.

Remnick, David
　　1998 "Bad Seeds." *New Yorker,* 20 July, 28–33.
Riedemann, Peter
　　1970 *Confession of Faith: Account of Our Religion, Doctrine and Faith.*
　　　　Rifton, N.Y.: Plough Publishing House.
　　1993 *Love Is Like Fire.* Rifton, N.Y.: Plough Publishing House.
Roth, John D.
　　1993 Ed. and trans. *Letters of the Amish Division: A Sourcebook.* Goshen,
　　　　Ind.: Mennonite Historical Society.
Rubinstein, Ruth P.
　　1995 *Dress Codes.* Boulder, Colo.: Westview Press.
Ryan, John
　　1977 *The Agricultural Economy of Manitoba Hutterite Colonies.* Toronto:
　　　　McClelland and Stewart.
Satterlee, James
　　n.d. *The Hutterites: A Study in Cultural Diversity.* South Dakota State
　　　　University Agricultural Experiment Station.
Schlabach, Theron F.
　　1977 "Reveille for *Die Stillen im Lande*: A Stir Among Mennonites in the
　　　　Late Nineteenth Century." *Mennonite Quarterly Review* 51 (July):
　　　　213–26.
　　1988 *Peace, Faith, Nation.* Vol. 2 of *The Mennonite Experience in America.*
　　　　Scottdale, Pa.: Herald Press.
"School Directory: 1995–1996"
　　1995 In *Blackboard Bulletin* (November): 9–28.
"School Directory 1999–2000"
　　1999 In *Blackboard Bulletin* (November): 7–22.
Scott, Stephen
　　1981 *Plain Buggies: Amish, Mennonite and Brethren Horse-Drawn Trans-
　　　　portation.* Intercourse, Pa.: Good Books.
　　1986 *Why Do They Dress That Way?* Intercourse, Pa.: Good Books.
　　1988 *The Amish Wedding and Other Special Occasions of the Old Order
　　　　Communities.* Intercourse, Pa.: Good Books.
　　1996 *An Introduction to Old Order and Conservative Mennonite Groups.*
　　　　Intercourse, Pa.: Good Books.
Shirk, John B.
　　1998 *History of the Groffdale Conference in Missouri, 1970–1998.*
　　　　Morgantown, Pa.: Masthof Press.
Snyder, C. Arnold
　　1995 *Anabaptist History and Theology: An Introduction.* Kitchener, Ont.:
　　　　Pandora Press.

Stephenson, Peter H.

1991 *The Hutterian People.* Lanham, Md.: University Press of America.

Stevick, Richard

2000 *Amish Youth: The Critical Years.* Unpublished manuscript.

Stoffer, Dale R.

1989 *Background and Development of Brethren Doctrines, 1650–1987.* Philadelphia: Brethren Encyclopedia, Inc.

Stoltzfus, Louise

1994 *Amish Women: Lives and Stories.* Intercourse, Pa.: Good Books.

1998 *Traces of Wisdom: Amish Women and the Pursuit of Life's Simple Treasures.* N.Y.: Hyperion.

Swartz, David

1997 *Culture and Power: The Sociology of Pierre Bourdieu.* Chicago: University of Chicago Press.

Umble, Diane Zimmerman

1996 *Holding the Line: The Telephone in Old Order Mennonite and Amish Life.* Baltimore: Johns Hopkins University Press.

Waldner, Tony

1990 *History of Forest River Community.* Fordville, N.Dak.: Forest River Community.

Weaver, J. Denny

1987 *Becoming Anabaptist: The Origin and Significance of Sixteenth-Century Anabaptism.* Scottdale, Pa.: Herald Press.

Weaver-Zercher, David

1997 "Homespun American Saints: The Discovery and Domestication of the Old Order Amish." Ph.D. diss., University of North Carolina, Chapel Hill.

1999 "Putting the Amish to Work: Mennonites and the Amish Culture Market, 1950–1975." *Church History* 68(1): 87–117.

2001 *The Amish in the American Imagination.* Baltimore: Johns Hopkins University Press.

Weiler, Lloyd M.

1993 "An Introduction to Old Order Mennonite Origins in Lancaster County, Pennsylvania: 1893–1993." *Pennsylvania Mennonite Heritage* 16 (October): 2–13.

1995 "Historical Overview of Weaverland Conference Origins." In *Directory of the Weaverland Conference Mennonite Churches,* 3rd ed. Womelsdrof, Pa.: Ruth Ann Wise.

Wenger, J. C.

1985 *The Yellow Creek Mennonites.* Goshen, Ind.: Yellow Creek Mennonite Church.

Willoughby, William G.

    1999 *The Beliefs of the Early Brethren, 1706–1735.* Philadelphia: Brethren Encyclopedia.

Yearbook of American and Canadian Churches.

    2000 Nashville, Tenn.: Abingdon Press.

Yoder, John Howard

    1973 Ed. and trans. *The Legacy of Michael Sattler.* Scottdale, Pa.: Herald Press.

Yoder, Paton

    1991 *Tradition and Transition: Amish Mennonites and Old Order Amish, 1800–1900.* Scottdale, Pa.: Herald Press.

    1993 "The Amish View of the State." In *The Amish and the State,* ed. Donald B. Kraybill. Baltimore: Johns Hopkins University Press.

Index

agricultural technology. *See* technology, agricultural

agriculture. *See* occupations, farming

alcohol, 36, 194

alms offering, 109

Amish: church districts, 110–11; distinctives, 104–6, 135; history, 6, 101–3, 128, 294n. 3; identity, 130, 132–33, 135–36; migration, 102–3; *Ordnung*, 106–7, 109, 131; origins, 101–3, 239

Amish affiliations: Beachy Amish, 297n. 39; Elkhart-Lagrange Amish settlement, 108, 123; Nebraska, 239; New Order, 294n. 3, 297n. 37; Old Order, 103, 105, 297n. 37; Swartzentruber, 231, 239

Ammann, Jakob, 6, 102

Anabaptist(s): definition of, 1; history of, 1–19

Annual Meeting, Brethren, 161–74, 176–78, 180, 204, 210, 223, 252, 300nn. 24 & 25

appearance, 67, 144–45, 173–75, 179, 182, 185, 195–96, 225, 256. *See also* dress

Arnold, Eberhard, 283n. 3

athletics, 119, 195

auctions, 117, 190, 192

Ausbund, 108

avoidance. *See* shunning

ban. *See* shunning

bandanna. *See* prayer cap

baptism, 1,7, 25, 35, 45, 40, 44–45, 81, 85–88, 91, 109, 180, 185, 201, 207–8, 225, 243, 264, 292n. 42, 299n. 9, 302n. 1

bartering, 25

beards, 174–75

beliefs. *See* Amish; Brethren; Hutterite colonies; Mennonite; Old Order

birth control, 50–51, 133–34, 187

birthday celebrations. *See* social gatherings

birth rate, 48–51

bishop, 71, 96, 90, 92–93, 111, 210, 224, 233. *See also* ordained officials

Blackboard bulletin, 84

Blackbumpers. *See* Mennonite Conferences (Old Order), Weaverland

Botschaft, Die, 70

Bourdieu, Pierre, 245, 305n. 2

Brethren: baptism, 137; branches of, 7–8; distinctives, 145, 175; history, 7, 137–39; location of, 8; origins, 238
Brethren beliefs: inner transformation, 146–47; love, 147–48; unity, 147–48, 301n. 30
Brethren practices: baptism, 148–51; extending liberty, 156–57
Brethren's Reasons, The, 302n. 41
Bruderhof. *See* Society of Brothers
buggies. *See* horse and carriage
business involvements, 112–13, 118, 123–25, 169–71, 190–92, 194, 197, 221, 230, 232–33, 303n. 7

cameras. *See* technology, cameras
Canadian pension plan, 80
careers. *See* occupations
cars. *See* technology, motor vehicles
casting of lots. *See* lot, use of
CB radios. *See* technology, CB radios
children: punishment of, 28, 59, 184–88; rearing of, 81–85, 88, 106, 133–34, 149, 180, 183, 187–89, 206–7, 231; socialization of, 41–43, 55–56
Christmas. *See* holidays, Christmas
Chronicle, 29–30, 283n. 1. *See also* persecution, Hutterite
church districts. *See* Amish
church services. *See* worship services
civic organizations, 192–93
clergy. *See* ordained officials
communal authority, 40–41
communal property, 24–28, 223, 226, 262–64
communal society, 181, 185, 193, 277–78
communion, 15, 90, 92–93, 102, 108–9, 145–46, 180, 192, 200–1, 207, 299n. 15
community, 210

community of goods, 26–27, 237
comodification of group images, 275, 276, 306n. 10
computers. *See* technology, computers
conference organizations, 90–92, 229–31
confession, 109, 176
conscientious objection, 182–83
counsel meetings, 38–39, 90–91, 145
curriculum. *See* education

deacons, 72, 92–93. *See also* ordained officials
defection, 66–67, 297n. 39
defenselessness. *See* nonresistance, definition of
deviance, 26, 74–75
dialect. *See* Hutterisch; Pennsylvania German
discipline, church, 40, 51–54, 285n. 17, 144–46, 175–78, 183, 188, 206–7. *See also* children, rearing of
disfellowshipped. *See* excommunication
distinctive characteristics, 146, 240–57
divorce, 62, 87, 121, 145, 179, 186–87, 299n. 6
domestic life, 129–30, 143
Dordrecht Confession of Faith, 79, 85, 109, 226, 231, 290n. 19, 292n. 30
dress, 12, 26, 36, 58, 78, 85, 104–7, 121, 135, 144–45, 150, 173–75, 177, 179–80, 185, 189, 192, 195–96, 199–200, 210–11, 224–25, 227–29, 233, 243, 245, 246, 255, 291nn. 23 & 24, 294n. 1, 302n. 41
drugs, ix
Dunkers. *See* Brethren
dwellings, 218

Easter. *See* holidays
economics. *See* finances

education: Amish, 106, 113–17, 128–29,
135, 226, 297n. 35; Brethren, 144–45,
194; curriculum, 267; general, 11, 32,
35, 187–89, 209, 220, 228, 234, 261,
278; higher, 61; Hutterites, 32, 40–44,
48, 55–56, 253, 286n. 37, 40, 41;
Mennonites, 60, 62–63, 66, 72, 81,
83–84, 226, 292n. 37, 39; private
schools, 83, 145, 149, 188–89,
285n. 28; teachers, 114–15
elderly, 48, 205
elders. See also ordained officials
electricity. See technology, electricity
English language, use of, 84, 87–88,
114, 219–20
Enlightenment, Age of, 189, 258–59,
266
entertainment, 33, 168–69. See also
technology, entertainment
evangelicals, 207–8, 211
excommunication, 12, 64–65, 75, 77, 93,
110, 121, 176, 180, 182–83, 192, 206–
7, 263, 302n. 2. See also shunning
exclusion. See shunning

family, 186–87, 194; extended, 48; immediate, 41, 63, 181; size, 46–47, 49–
51, 67, 110, 133, 227–28
farming. See occupations, farming
finances, 122, 204. See also Hutterite
colonies; finances
food, 121, 200, 303n. 15
footwashing, 15, 102, 200, 225, 299n.
15. See also communion
free-time. See leisure activities

Gelassenheit, 26–27, 188, 194, 195–96,
201, 264; definition of, 54, 181,
302n. 3; ethos of, 181; principles of,
181–83; submission, 181. See also
humility

gender roles, 38, 46–47, 113, 174–75,
180, 187; female, 39–40, 62–63, 78,
87–88, 92, 106, 114, 174–75, 183,
185, 204, 300n. 29; male, 174–75,
178, 185
gentleness. See Gelassenheit
German Baptist Brethren. See Brethren
Gibb, Donald, 284n. 3
Gibbs group. See Hutterite branches
Giddens, 245
Gideons international, 171–73, 176
government, relations with, 32, 112–14,
126–29. See also political involvement
government aid, 80, 110, 127–28,
296n. 30
Groffdale Mennonite Conference. See
Mennonite Conferences (Old Order)

habitus, 245, 305n. 2
head coverings. See prayer cap
high school. See education
holidays, 117–20, 199; Christmas, 119–
20; Easter, 119–20
holy kiss, 15, 150–53, 192, 200–201,
225, 286n. 42. See also communion
homosexual relations, 62
honeymoon. See weddings
horse, 241–42
Horse-and-buggy Mennonites. See
Mennonite Conferences (Old Order),
Groffdale
horse and carriage, 65–66, 185, 200,
211, 221–22, 243–44
Horst, Isaac R., 288n. 2
humility, 52, 62–64, 76–78–81, 92,
112–13, 126, 181–83, 201, 208–9,
211. See also Gelassenheit
Hutter, Jakob, 20
Hutterian Brethren. See Hutterite
colonies

Hutterisch, 24, 284n. 7
Hutterite branches: Darisleut, 286n. 41;
    Gibbs group, 283n. 3; Kleinsasser
    group, 283n. 3, 287n. 49; Lehrleut,
    20–21, 286n. 41; Prairieleut, 283n. 2;
    Schmiedleut, 20–21, 47, 49, 283n. 3,
    285n. 31, 286n. 42, 287n. 49
Hutterites. See Hutterite colonies
Hutterites/Hutterite colonies: authority
    of, 20–21; colony manager, 26, 33, 38,
    40; conflicts with civil authorities, 31;
    defections from, 51–54; division of,
    20–21, 23, 283n. 3; expansion of, 31,
    48–51; field boss, 38–39, 287n. 53;
    finances, 25, 32, 56, 285n. 29; German
    teacher, 28, 35, 38–39, 42–43; history
    of, 20–22, 29; kitchens of, 24; living
    arrangements of, 20–21, 23, 25, 27,
    41; location of, 20–21; minister, 34–
    35, 38; size of, 23, 57; social roles in,
    44
hymns, 43

identity, 135–36, 199, 24, 236–37, 255–
    56
individualism, 181, 189, 262–64, 279–
    80
    rejection of, 58, 188, 264–65
industrialization, 9, 268, 270, 306n. 3.
    See also technology, rejection of
industry. See business involvements
inner transformation. See Brethren
    beliefs
insurance, 73, 80
Internet. See technology, Internet

jewelry. See taboos
jury duty, 81

labor unions, 171, 183

language. See English language; Hutter-
    isch; Pennsylvania German
Last Supper. See Love Feast
leadership. See ordained officials
legal involvements, 183
Lehrerleut. See Hutterite branches
leisure activities, 12, 111–12, 117–19,
    144, 180, 189, 191–93, 195, 211, 227,
    250
lifestyle, 278–79
Lord's Supper. See communion; Love
    Feast
lot, use of, 92, 204
love, 147–48, 182, 208
Love Feast, 153–61, 176, 201–2, 225,
    261–62, 299n. 14, 304n. 16

Mack, Alexander, 7, 299n. 8
makeup. See taboos
marketing Old Order identities and
    products, 275–77. See also comodifi-
    cation of group images
marriage: Amish, 113–14; Brethren,
    142, 145; Hutterite, 39–40, 45–46,
    57; Mennonite, 86–88, 290n. 18; with
    outsider, 142, 221
martyrs, 29, 181, 237, 303n. 7
Marx, Karl, 26
Matthew 18. See discipline, church
Media: Amish, 101; Brethren, 150–51;
    coverage, 295n. 15; Mennonite, 81;
    outside, 276; meetinghouses, 64, 67,
    145, 200–202, 225, 605n. 8
membership, 207–8; Amish, 135;
    Brethren, 298n. 4, 299n. 5; Hutterite,
    27–28, 35; Mennonite, 82, 85
membership growth: Amish, 103, 133–
    35, 231; Brethren, 138–42; Hutterite,
    48–51; Mennonite, 67–68. See also
    population, size and growth of

Mennonite: history, 4–5, 60–62, 288n. 3; *Ordnung*, 73–75, 77–78, 80–81, 85–86, 92–93, 99–100, 290n. 19

Mennonite Conferences (Old Order), 68; Groffdale, 61, 65–68, 73, 75, 78, 80–82, 85–86, 88, 93, 95–87, 99–100, 290n. 11; Ontario, 70, 78–82, 84–86, 93, 96–97; Virginia, 88; Weaverland, 96, 290n. 10

Mennonite Disaster Service, 190

Menno Simons, 5, 60, 102

military service, 30, 32, 62, 75, 81. *See also* conscientious objection

ministers, 71–72, 89–90, 100, 145, 203–5, 293n. 48. *See also* ordained officials

modernity, xiv, 258, 266, 267, 279; Old Order critique of, 259

modernization, 9, 143–44, 189, 258–80

moral order, 74–75, 179–80, 206–7, 252

Moravia, 20

motor vehicles. *See* technology, motor vehicles

music, 77, 117, 121–22, 145, 195, 198, 205, 231

mutual aid, 73, 112–13, 127–28, 278

myths about Old Orders. *See* stereotypes of Old Orders

National Steering Committee (Amish), 112, 128

nonconformity, 177, 185. *See also* separation from the world

nonresistance, definition of, 32, 80–81, 183–85, 196. *See also* conscientious objection

occupations, 66, 122–26, 143, 145, 169–71, 174–75, 189, 191, 193, 218–20, 222, 227–28, 296n. 24, 25; farming,

22, 24, 66, 117, 122–23, 191, 196, 230–31, 236, 241

Old German Baptist Brethren. *See* Brethren

Old Order: beliefs and practices, 33–36, 108–9, 127, 146–47, 183, 193, 223–26, 228, 229, 231–32, 234–35, 261–62, 264–65, 274, 277–78; definition of, 15–19, 260–66, 282nn. 2 & 5; distinctives of, 207–11, 260–61; faith of, 209–12; values, 18–19, 136, 279–80

Old Order Amish. *See* Amish; Amish affiliations

Old Order Mennonites. *See* Mennonite Conferences (Old Order)

one-room schools. *See* education

ordained officials, 71–74, 76–78, 85–86, 88–93, 100, 178, 183, 198, 203–5, 224, 229, 263–64

Order of the Brethren, 167, 173–74. *See also Ordnung*

ordination, 92–93, 97. *See also* lot, use of

Ordnung: definition of, 15, 179–80, 229; enforcement of, 204, 209; violations of, 75–76, 194, 206–7. *See also* Amish; Mennonite

outsiders, perceptions from, 213, 270, 277. *See* social relations with outsiders

pacifism. *See* nonresistance, definition of

parochial schools. *See* education

Pathway Publishers, 71

peace. *See* nonresistance, definition of

Pennsylvania German, 62, 66, 87–88, 106, 108, 114, 143, 201, 219–20, 225

persecution: Anabaptist, 181, 237; Hutterite, 29–30

photographs. *See* technology, cameras
Pietism, 7, 137, 299n. 14
political involvement, 80–81, 145, 150,
    183–84, 194, 220
population, size and growth of: Amish,
    101, 110, 294n. 6; Brethren, 139–43;
    Hutterite, 48–51; Mennonite, 67–68.
    See also membership
possessions, 194–95
post-modernity, 258, 265, 268–77
practices. *See* Old Order
Prairieleut. *See* Hutterite branches
prayer, kneeling for, 201
prayer cap, 180, 185, 243
pride. *See* individualism
privacy, 189–90
private property, 24, 26, 44, 56, 58–59,
    66, 194
private schools. *See* education
Protestant Reformation, xi, 1–2, 11
protracted meetings. *See* revival
    meetings
pulpits, 64, 289n. 8
punishment. *See* discipline, church

radio. *See* technology, radio
recreation. *See* leisure activities
repentance, 176
revival meetings, rejection of, 64
Rideman, Peter, 25
rituals. *See* worship services

sales. *See* auctions
salvation, understanding of, 81–82, 85,
    207–8
Schmiedleut. *See* Hutterite branches
school. *See* education
self, 27, 109, 181, 270; surrender of, 27–
    29. *See* Gelassenheit
self-esteem, 228, 234

self-examination. *See* communion
separation from the world: belief in, 200,
    207; geographic, 216, 227; practice,
    104–5, 119, 126, 211–12, 214–22,
    226–27, 237, 265–66, 267–68, 270
sermons, 34–35, 88–91, 108–9, 156–59
sex education, 114
shunning, 12, 39, 52–54, 56, 93, 100,
    110, 135, 176, 180, 206–7, 208, 225,
    233, 287n. 55, 57, 295n. 12
singing. *See* music
social change, 57, 62–64, 98–100, 129–
    33, 167, 247–57, 305nn. 4 & 5
social control, 28, 32, 46, 56, 226–29,
    233, 252, 255
social gatherings, 117–20; birthdays,
    120
socialization, 44, 46–47, 56–57, 144,
    188, 264
social organization, 214–16, 249
social relations, 186–93, 207–8; with
    outsiders, 22, 25, 32–33, 46, 56–57,
    62, 65, 116–17, 125, 146, 151–53,
    169–70, 172–74, 180, 185, 190–94,
    196–97, 211, 219–21, 232–33, 237,
    240, 272–72
social restrictions, 74, 77, 79, 82–83, 85
social security. *See* government aid
social services. *See* Mennonite Disaster
    Service
Society of Brothers, 283n. 3, 287n. 55
sports. *See* athletics
state. *See* government, relations with
stereotypes of Old Order, 9–15, 213
submission. *See* Gelassenheit
suffering, 29
Sunday school, 61, 62–64, 188, 205, 241
surnames, 142
Swartzentruber Amish. *See* Amish
    affiliations

symbols, 186, 201–2, 228, 240–45, 255–57, 275–76

taboos, 56, 74–75, 77–78, 80–81, 84, 94–99, 167–68, 180–81, 194–95, 197–98, 199
taxes, 32, 127
taxi service, 94–95, 199, 219
teachers. *See* education
Team Mennonites. *See* Mennonite Conferences (Old Order), Groffdale
technology, 9–12, 13, 24, 65, 94–100, 106–7, 129–33, 135–36, 143–45, 167–69, 180, 189, 193, 199, 233–34; acceptance of, 57, 223, 259; agricultural, 95–99, 122, 130–31, 198, 222, 227–29, 241; cameras, 182, 234, 272, 304n. 5; CB radios, 223, 250; communicative, 198–99; computers, 75, 106, 168, 200, 223, 250–15, 273, 284n. 8; consumptive, 197–98; control of, 227, 247–52; electricity, 66, 97, 106, 198, 222–23, 229, 230, 248–49, 305n. 8; entertainment, 180, 222–23; Internet, 11, 106, 213; motor vehicles, 10–11, 56, 65, 75, 94–95, 132–33, 135, 143–44, 180, 194, 197, 199, 211, 219, 221–22, 229, 236, 241, 242, 248–49, 253, 267, 273, 304n. 4; productive, 196–97; radio, 56, 135, 145, 250; rejection of, 56, 60, 179–80, 244–45, 259–61, 266–68, 272–74; selective use of, 33, 36, 43–44, 50, 177, 217, 254–55, 286n. 41; telephone, 56, 66, 97, 132, 198, 222, 229, 230, 248, 253–54, 267, 273–74, 303n.12; television, 11, 56, 75, 82–83, 106, 135, 145, 194, 240–41, 250; tractors, 66, 96, 200, 230, 241–42, 253–54; VCR, 250, 255
television. *See* technology, television

testimonies, 208, 211
tourism, 256, 270–71
tractors. *See* technology, tractors
tradition, 210–11, 243–48, 270
travel, 119, 144, 195, 211, 221
trucks. *See* technology, motor vehicles

U.S. Supreme Court rulings, 113–14, 297n. 35

vanity. *See* wordliness
Virginia Mennonite Conference. *See* Old Order Mennonites
visiting, 70, 144, 195, 206, 249
voting: non-political, 204, 300n. 29; political, 80, 127

Waldner, Michael, 20
Walter, Darius, 20–21
Weaverland Conference Mennonite Church. *See* Old Order Mennonites
Weaver-Zercher, David, 275, 306n. 7, 10
weddings, 87–88, 120–22, 145, 177, 187. *See also* marriage
welfare. *See* government aid
wills. *See* finances
Wipf, Jacob, 21
Wisconsin v. Yoder. *See* U.S. Supreme Court Rulings
witness. *See* evangelicals
women. *See* gender roles
work. *See* occupations
world: fear of, 29, 79, 265; separation from, 79–81. *See also* outsiders
worldliness, 168–69, 182, 185
world view, 55
World Wide Web. *See* technology, Internet
worship services: nature of, 34–35, 38, 46, 57–59, 61, 180, 195, 211; rituals

worship services (*continued*)
of, 40–41, 62–64, 86, 88–92, 108–9,
200–3, 205, 210, 225, 228, 231,
303n. 13, 15, 304n. 16; setting, 144–
42

yieldedness. *See Gelassenheit*
youth, 27, 35, 44–45, 85–87, 95, 135,
144, 205, 210, 264, 298n. 40

Zwingli, Urlich, 1

ABOUT THE AUTHORS

Donald B. Kraybill's books on Anabaptist groups include *The Upside-Down Kingdom* (1990), which received the national Religious Book Award; *The Riddle of Amish Culture* (2001), a standard reference for understanding social change among the Amish; and *The Amish Struggle with Modernity* (1994). He edited the award-winning *The Amish and the State* (1993) and coauthored *Old Order Amish: Their Enduring Way of Life* (1993); *Mennonite Peacemaking: From Quietism to Activism* (1994); and the award-winning *Amish Enterprise: From Plows to Profits* (1995). Kraybill is a professor of sociology and Anabaptist studies at Messiah College in Pennsylvania.

Carl F. Bowman is a professor of sociology at Bridgewater College in Virginia and since 1995 has been a research associate with the Institute for Advanced Studies in Culture at the University of Virginia, where he has directed national surveys on character, morality, and public culture in the United States. He is a coeditor of *The Brethren Encyclopedia*, Volume IV (forthcoming) and *Anabaptist Currents: History in Conversation with the Present* (1995), and author of *Brethren Society: The Cultural Transformation of a "Peculiar People"* (1995).

CENTER BOOKS IN ANABAPTIST STUDIES
published by Johns Hopkins

The Amish and the State
edited by Donald B. Kraybill

Amish Enterprise: From Plows to Profits
Donald B. Kraybill and Steven M. Nolt

The Amish on the Iowa Prairie, 1840 to 1910
Steven D. Reschly

Amish Roots: A Treasury of History, Wisdom, and Lore
edited by John A. Hostetler

Brethren Society: The Cultural Transformation of a "Peculiar People"
Carl F. Bowman

*Creation and the Environment: An Anabaptist Perspective on
a Sustainable World*
edited by Calvin W. Redekop

Holding the Line: The Telephone in Old Order Mennonite and Amish Life
Diane Zimmerman Umble

Hutterite Beginnings: Communitarian Experiments during the Reformation
Werner O. Packull

Mennonite Entrepreneurs
Calvin Redekop, Stephen C. Ainlay, and Robert Siemens

Old Order Amish: Their Enduring Way of Life
Lucian Niemeyer and Donald B. Kraybill

The Riddle of Amish Culture
Donald B. Kraybill

Two Kingdoms, Two Loyalties: Mennonite Pacifism in Modern America
Perry Bush